EO

D1261486

Conceived in Crisis:

A History of La Salle College

1863-1965

Thomas J. Donaghy, F. S. C.

LA SALLE COLLEGE

PHILADELPHIA

1966

Printed in the United States of America by
WALTHER PRINTING HOUSE, INC.
PHILADELPHIA, PA.

TO MY PARENTS:

ANNE HOUSTON DONAGHY

HARRY JOSEPH DONAGHY, SR.

CONTENTS

ILLUSTRATIONS

Introduction

SEVERAL YEARS AGO the British Museum staff news-
letter carried a series of articles entitled *Your
Station Has A History*. These essays explored the history of London
Underground and city rail stations used by staff members. Many
on the staff were surprised at the extent of history behind several
seemingly unimportant stations. To them the buildings had always
been there and were of minor importance other than their convenience as transportation hubs.

Too frequently, educational institutions are thought of by their
constituents in much the same way. Young men enter college, one
perhaps that was conveniently available. Where, when, or why it
began: such questions are rarely asked by the student. All seems
alive and current. The future means taking leave of the institution.
The past consists only of the short time spent at college or perhaps
a recollection of circumstances that enabled the student to become
acquainted with his future alma mater. The alumnus, looking
back, thinks only of his school in terms of his time, his former class-
mates, friends, and instructors. He vaguely remembers some passing
references to the past: professors recalling certain events, or he himself taking a casual glance at past files of college yearbooks and
newspapers. In general, however, the history of educational institu-

tions is rarely investigated by students, faculty, or alumni. As a result, the rich traditions and lessons of the past are lost to those who deserve them most. In an attempt to avoid this loss, *Conceived in Crisis* is intended as a reminder to the La Salle family, its friends and neighbors that this College has indeed a history.

Chartered during a national crisis in 1863, La Salle College seemed destined to rise and fall with the economic and diplomatic crises of the nation. Ten years after its founding, La Salle was a flourishing institution, academically and economically. By 1883, the College was facing one of its major problems, the lack of space. In transferring to a larger campus, administrative discord and fiscal strain nearly ruined the College. For many years the College experienced a period of deadening calm when leadership seemed to be a forgotten element. When at last a vigorous leader rejuvenated La Salle, World War I brought new obstructions. Postwar elation was followed in rapid succession by the valleys of the great depression of our century and World War II. In the decades following the uncertain peace, La Salle experienced its greatest expansion and prosperity, attendant with the usual problems of acceleration in growth. Today, the traditional problem faced by the College, space, remains a significant obstacle to further fulfillment. Despite the fluctuating fortunes of La Salle, an ideal of quality education and an unflagging élan provided a central theme in the College's history.

When one considers the checkered history of La Salle, it is not surprising to find that the character of the College changed as it grew. La Salle in the 19th century was a small college run and taught by the Christian Brothers. From time to time, an occasional layman appeared on the faculty. As the College moved into its expansion period, this picture changed. The layman became a permanent, significant part of the institution and, although the Brothers still control and share the College administration, there are over 100 laymen, eleven priests, and twenty-three Brothers on the faculty. Thus, in telling the story of La Salle, the writer has avoided, as far as possible, the history of the Brothers' community attached to the College. In some instances, during the early period, however, this was impossible because of the direct connection of community events with the organization and operation of the College. Further, every effort was made to avoid, where possible, the history of La Salle College High School and Benilde Academy, both of which were at one time under the direct supervision of the President of La Salle. Finally, the reader will note apparent gaps in the story and, at the same time, definite selection of material and choice of interpretations. Admittedly, there are gaps in the College documents. It is believed many important papers were destroyed in the fire of 1909, while other valuable documents were lost in the move from North Broad Street to the present campus. As for interpretations and selections, the author takes full responsibility.

Any work of this type could not be accomplished by one man. The writer has benefited from the kindnesses and cooperation of many persons, especially Brother Daniel Bernian, F.S.C., President of La Salle College, who made available many confidential College documents; Brother E. Joseph, F.S.C., Librarian, La Salle College; Brother Frederick John, F.S.C., Archivist, District of Baltimore; Brother Basil Leo, F.S.C., Archivist, District of New York; Kanardy Taylor, Librarian, Department of Health, Education and Welfare; Public Relations Area, La Salle College; John Moss, Photographer, City of Philadelphia; and Betty Maher, United Airlines. The author is deeply indebted to Brother F. Patrick, F.S.C., Director Honors Program, La Salle College; Dr. Robert Eugene Carlson, West Chester State College; and Brother Edward Patrick, F.S.C., editor, *Four Quarters,* for having read the manuscript. Finally, Brother M. Fidelian, F.S.C., Academic Vice-President, La Salle College, was more than generous in writing the Epilogue, reading the manuscript, and providing the necessary encouragement to see the project through to completion.

1. A Suggestion

WAR, THE MOTHER OF SURPRISES, seems unable in the course of civilization to halt the higher aspirations of men. The American Civil War was indeed in mid-passage when the dream of a new college nourished by a group of hardy and far-seeing educators became a reality in the city of Brotherly Love. Philadelphia in 1863 was, of course, distracted by quite other concerns.

As the Negro segment of the population rejoiced over emancipation and its implications, the City Treasurer gloomily reported expenditures of $367,000 for defense and $657,000 for relief of soldiers' families. Chestnut Hill was the site of a vast military hospital, while a few miles down the Delaware River, the Monitor *Lehigh* was launched. A flag presentation ceremony to the 90th Pennsylvania Volunteers took place at the "High School for Young Ladies." The social whirl included receptions for Majors-General B. F. Butler and George B. McClellan.

Philadelphians, however, were not one in their thinking about the war and its political implications. On January 29, 1863, the Philadelphia *Evening Journal* was suppressed for seditious publications. President Lincoln was bitterly attacked by the Young Men's Democratic Club, a group who forcefully supported "States Rights," and who were labeled "Copperheads" because of the liberty-head pennies which they displayed.

Spearheading the efforts to incorporate the College was a group of religious educators, the Brothers of the Christian Schools, who had been working in the city for some years previously. The Christian Brothers, as they are familiarly called in the United States, are a group of lay religious devoted to the common purpose of eternal salvation through the Christian education of youth. Although professing public vows of poverty, chastity, and obedience under the auspices of the Roman Catholic Church, the Brothers, under a rule of their founder, St. John Baptist de La Salle, do not enter the clerical state, so that their entire energies can be dedicated to the work of Christian education. In 1853, Philadelphia Catholics welcomed the Christian Brothers to Assumption and St. Peter's Schools. Although their work terminated after one year at Assumption School, the Brothers continued to labor zealously throughout the decade at St. Peter's. Five years after the opening of the first schools, a third school was opened in St. Michael's Parish, located today at 2nd and Jefferson Streets; here La Salle College was destined to begin. It was to the Director of St. Michael's School, Brother Teliow, that Bishop James Frederick Wood suggested the incorporation of a secondary department, which the Brothers had opened in 1862.

When Bishop Wood approached Brother Teliow about a Catholic college for young men, Roman Catholics constituted about one-sixth of the 674,000 Philadelphia residents, and despite the drain on the population made by the demands of the War, Philadelphia between 1860 and 1870 continued to grow, adding a total of nearly 150,000 people. Bishop Wood clearly saw the need for Catholic higher education, and he viewed that need in rather immediate terms since he had high hopes for a quick solution to the Civil War. The Bishop's concern for Catholic higher education was demonstrated in his deep disappointment when the Jesuit Fathers requested his permission to close St. Joseph's College, located at Juniper and Filbert Streets. When the first request in 1860 came to the Bishop, the Jesuits were told that the Bishop would not oppose the withdrawal, but it would not be done with his approval. In grave financial distress, the Fathers sent a second request to the Bishop, who in turn withdrew all opposition but determined to find other means to establish a college. Father Ward, S.J., President of St. Joseph's College, 1857-1860, was indeed also reluctant to see St. Joseph's close. He cited the spiritual good done at the College, along with its excellent central position, and the probability that once withdrawn the Jesuits might never again be allowed to open a college in the city. He regretfully pointed out that many "Catholics of Philadelphia complained of the lack of Catholic educational opportunities, while at the same time neglecting to support those already in existence."[1] Actually, grave financial distress closed St. Joseph's College, and in 1862 Catholic higher education ceased to exist in Philadelphia. It was at this juncture that Bishop Wood turned to Brother Teliow.

Brother Teliow, a native of Prussia, had come to America at the age of twenty-one. For a while he worked in Wisconsin and Iowa and then decided to join the Christian Brothers. From the outset his teaching career was marked with success. As too frequently happens in educational circles, successful teachers are given the burden of administration. In 1852, in any event, Brother Teliow was placed in charge of St. Mary's School in Detroit. Two years later he took charge of St. Peter's, Philadelphia. His excellent administrative ability was immediately recognized and was in part responsible for the invitation by Father Laughlin, Pastor of St. Michael's Parish, to open a school there. September, 1858, saw the new St. Michael's School a reality. Four years later a secondary department was opened. Bishop Wood was now convinced that he had found the nucleus for a new college and used all the persuasion at his command to have Brother Teliow agree to the Bishop's suggestion for incorporation of the high school.[2] Brother Teliow agreed to the proposition and, along with the Bishop and several laymen, sought a charter for a college.

La Salle College in the City of Philadelphia, the legal title con-

ferred by the Act of Incorporation, was described in the Act of
March 20, 1863 as a "College within the limits of the city of Philadelphia, in which are to be taught the elementary branches of education, together with the sciences, and modern and ancient languages." The College was not to have a yearly income of more
than ten thousand dollars, a rather conservative restriction in view
of the economics of higher education today. Although legality was
conferred on the College in March, the Corporators, James F.
Wood, Nicholas Cantwell, Thomas Kierans, Bernard Fackeldey,
Jeremiah Dugan, Bernard Maguire, William V. Keating, Hugh
O'Donnell, John Gegan, and William Morony, did not accept the
Act of Incorporation until May 18, 1863, when the first meeting of
the Corporators was held. At the same meeting a Committee of
Three, Bishop Wood, Father Kierans, and Brother Teliow, was
appointed to draft the constitution. One week later the Corporators
again met and completed the College Constitution. Of grave significance to the infant College and of tremendous importance throughout the history of La Salle, the Constitution specified that the
Roman Catholic Bishop of Philadelphia would be ex-officio Honorary President of the Board of Managers. Under the devoted and
sensitive care of Bishop Wood, this provision proved a great boon
to the College; as the College matured, however, this provision was
dropped. The Constitution likewise stated that the Director of the
Christian Brothers "shall be the ex-officio President of the Board
of Managers." What seemed to be the logical thing to do in 1863
sometimes proved to be a matter of concern in the later history of
the College. The complexities of a dual role, a superior of a
religious community and college president, have sometimes proven
too much for even highly talented and robust individuals. Add to
this the uncertainty of tenure of all religious, and the problems
involved can be difficult but, of course, not insurmountable. The
ironic fact is, however, that Brother Teliow, founder and first ex-
officio President of the Board, was called to other duties of very
serious responsibility just nine months after the College was incor-
porated. A talented man, Brother Teliow's services had been sought

by the Society for the Protection of Destitute Roman Catholic Children, whose President, L. Silliman Ives, appealed directly to the Superior General of the Christian Brothers in order to have Brother Teliow assigned. Ives's request was granted on December 1, 1863 and La Salle College lost a co-founder and its first president.[3]

Organizationally, the College was hardly off the ground. The first regular meeting of the Board of Managers was not held until May 20, 1869. In the absence of Brother Teliow, Brother Oliver had been appointed President. The Board elected Brother Romuald, Vice-President, Brother Alban, Secretary, and Brother John, Treasurer. For the time, then, administrative order was established and the academic development of the new College proceeded, though rather slowly.

Having acquired a legal title, which it did not at first use publicly, and having the power to confer degrees, the Brothers' School at St. Michael's in 1863 was not, of course, a college in the modern sense. Three classes begun in the basement of St. Michael's School, in fact constituted something more like a high school. Nonetheless, it appears that the school in its first year flourished under the experienced eye of Brother Teliow. An anonymous manuscript describing the closing exercises held in the spring of 1863 is our chief source of information. The writer refers to the school as the Christian Brothers' Academy. The closing exercises took place at 1421 Second Street, the parish hall for St. Michael's. Bishop Wood and several members of the clergy were on the platform, and the hall was quite crowded much to the discomfort of the anonymous writer who alleged that "acrobatic feats" were required to obtain a seat. Music was provided by the school orchestra under the direction of Mr. Baumann; and the exercises were garnished with German and English choruses, the former being a reflection of the national influence in the early schools of the Diocese.

Since the audience was invited to question the students, a fair estimate of the curriculum can be made. Rev. F. V. Sharkey asked questions in mensuration, natural philosophy, and geometry. Professor Hertzog posed questions in French, Brother Oliver emphasized English grammar, and the Bishop examined bookkeeping. Because of a lack of time and the excessive heat, questions in algebra, German, and Latin were omitted. The writer assures us that the students performed very well, "much to the credit of the Brothers."

The new school had actually stayed in St. Michael's basement for only three months. In November, 1862, a house at 1419 Second Street had been purchased and the high school moved there in November, 1862. The Brothers continued to teach at St. Michael's (parish school) while running their own academy.[4] But even after the purchase of the new building, it was quite obvious that the school would have to be moved again. The great enthusiasm for the school, along with the granting of the charter, encouraged many interested parties to pledge their economic support to the Brothers and Bishop Wood. In fact, one group of men banded together and offered to pay the rent for any building needed to expand the school. Their enthusiasm seemed to know no bounds and, by public statements, put the Brothers in a very difficult position. For example, this group alleged that the Brothers "can teach well, and every parent whose means will not allow him to send his children to expensive colleges, will do well not to forget that there is a college as good as them all, a college whose rates of tuition are within the limits of his purse — La Salle College, or the Christian Brothers High School."[5] No doubt the sentiments in favor of the Brothers were well deserved, but the supply of Brothers was not plentiful at this time, and the war conditions did not easily allow for the communication and transportation necessary to bring more Brothers to Philadelphia. Accordingly, the Academy was to maintain operations at 1419 Second Street for about four years.

Apparently the Catholics of Philadelphia took the advice given them by the men supporting the school and continued to send their sons to the Brothers in ever-increasing numbers. We know little of the school between 1863 and 1867 except for the fact that the Academy was filled to overflowing, a condition that was, to say the least, gratifying to Bishop Wood and the Brothers, but, likewise, a condition not conducive to the best education. It become obvious the Brothers would have to move from North Second Street, and the hunt for new quarters was on again.

The pleasant but responsible task of seeking a new location fell on the shoulders of Brother Oliver. He had succeeded Brother Teliow as Director of the Brothers' Community at St. Michael's and was, therefore, ex-officio President. (In many instances, Brother Oliver is inaccurately referred to as the first President of La Salle College, and the President today is numbered according to this thinking. Actually, Brother Oliver was the second president, succeeding Brother Teliow in January, 1864). Brother Oliver seemed well qualified to develop the new college. Known among his colleagues as a self-made man, he had the distinction of being an excellent teacher and competent administrator. He guided the high school on North Second Street along the difficult path of academic excellence. That he and his colleagues were successful in this venture is widely attested to both by those who came under the Brothers' care and by many professional and business houses where these well-trained students followed their careers. Meanwhile, however, the new President sought new property.

Brother Oliver did not have to look far. Bishop Wood told him of a sizeable building located in the center of the city at Filbert and Juniper Streets. Originally the building had been erected by the people of St. John's Parish for a school. However, once erected, funds were not available and the Jesuits of St. Joseph's College occupied the premises for a time. The building was three stories high with a full basement. It was forty-two feet wide and one hundred feet deep, fronting on Filbert Street with its one side facing Juniper Street. The property went back another twenty feet.[6] However, this small space proved to be inadequate for complete recreational purposes. Architecturally, the Filbert Street property looked very much like the prototype public school of the day. Even so, the Jesuits had found it quite difficult to provide convenience in the matter of classroom construction. But compared to conditions at 1419 North Second Street, the Filbert Street property appeared promising.

Title to the Filbert Street property had passed to Bishop Wood in 1860, when the Jesuits moved back to Willings Alley. For a short time, the building was occupied by Sisters of Notre Dame de Namur, who were awaiting the completion of their new academy on Rittenhouse Square. Understandably, the Bishop was anxious to have the building occupied. At first, the Brothers agreed to pay a yearly rental of $1,800. It seems this was unsatisfactory, but it is difficult to determine which party to the contract reneged. Finally, the Brothers agreed to buy the building outright for $30,000. The terms offered by the Bishop were very liberal, and there is little indication that the Brothers had any difficulty financing the property. In all fairness to Bishop Wood, it must be pointed out that in 1867, the Juniper and Filbert Streets location seemed an excellent one for a college, despite the economic disaster encountered by the Jesuits. Bishop Neumann, who first invited the Christian Brothers to Philadelphia, described the Filbert Street site in a letter to the Jesuit Provincial in 1857, saying, "Its healthy and central location, so near St. John's Church, convinced me that a more convenient place for a college could not be found in Philadelphia." Bishop Neumann went on to warn that "it will probably be several years more yet before the College will meet with that active approbation of the clergy and laity, when they will be convinced by the manly faith and piety of the gentlemen brought up there."[7] A decade after these words were written, some physical changes had taken place at Filbert Street, and now perhaps the clergy and laity were less skeptical about higher Catholic education. With faith in Divine Providence and a certain measure of boldness, the Brothers moved to Filbert Street in August, 1867. The school was now officially called the Christian Brothers' Academy. On that twentieth day of August the hopes and aspirations of the Brothers could not be smothered by the oppressive heat. The future was theirs for the taking, and who can say that these men of vision did not dream of a tree-shaded campus of wide lawns and many stately buildings. That they were more than dreamers, however, became obvious as they tackled the immediate task of readying the "new" school for instructional purposes. The very renovation of the Filbert Street property was a clear indication that an interesting college was in the offing.

2. Front and Center

JUST HOW MUCH FACT OR FICTION IS CONTAINED in the expression "in Philadelphia, nearly everybody reads the *Bulletin*" is difficult to determine. But, nearly everyone in Philadelphia believes that the huge figure of William Penn atop City Hall indicates the very center of urban Philadelphia. Visible on a clear night from all major arteries leading into the downtown, William Penn is presently the object of much solicitude by those who would save his statue from being obscured by a modern skyscraper or two. Philadelphia traditionalists want the heart of their city preserved and have given Penn the most hallowed spot.

Actually, this favorite "center" was not always considered the nucleus of Philadelphia. It was one of the many open areas William Penn decreed for his "greene countrie towne." However, as the city expanded westward, Center Square, as it was called, became more and more important. Actually the space was circular rather than square. The first building erected on the circle was the Philadelphia Water Works, completed in 1801, but closed in 1822. This rather ornate building was surrounded with an ornamental fence and was graced by a fountain. Philadelphians used to stroll around the building on leisurely Sundays. In 1822, the Philosophical Society occupied the building, but remained only a few years. The building was demolished in 1828 and, at the time, the land was divided into four large squares with Broad and Market Streets intersecting in the middle.

In 1867, the new La Salle College or Christian Brothers Academy occupied a building on the extreme northeast corner of the square. At the time, buildings of note fronting the square were few in number. Diagonally across the square stood the United States Mint, which had been built in 1833. Fronting on Chestnut Street, the Mint is celebrated as the spot where the first photograph in America was taken. Almost directly south on Juniper Street stood Philadelphia School for Boys. This was the predecessor of modern Central High School for Boys, which borders the Belfield campus. In 1867, Boys' High had the best-equipped observatory in the country under the direction of Otis E. Kendall. The proximity of such an installation to La Salle enhanced the Astronomy lessons at the College on more than one occasion. Immediately adjacent to the College front entrance was the remnants of what was at one time Tivoli or Columbia Park, reputed to have been quite beautiful in its day. Now, however, storage tracks of the Pennsylvania marred the scene. Farther south, the railroad had a rather large and ugly freight station.

Despite the presence of the railroad, there was enough wide, open space at Center Square to compensate for the railroad nuisance. Further, it was becoming the center of much activity beneficial to an educational institution. Thus, with bright prospects for the future, the Brothers began to set their house in order. Ironically enough, the future held still other and rather vast changes. In fact, the College might never have gotten away from 1419 North Second Street if the Brothers had known in 1867 that in less than a decade things on Center Square would so change as to force the school to seek a better situation.

In any event, the physical layout of the new Center Square building was not satisfactory for the needs of the academy and, accordingly, extensive alterations were planned. In the plans as recorded, we are able to see the intended use of the building. Provision was made for three divisions of the College: the Collegiate, academic or, in modern parlance, secondary, and commercial departments. Faculty quarters were also provided. That secondary and commercial classes were planned should not cause any undue difficulty for the modern. The ordinary meaning of the word (college) implied the three branches. Thus, the floor plan for the new college proved quite simple. A kitchen, dining room, and small rooms for Alumni activities were contained in the fore section of the basement. Both students and faculty shared the dining facilities. The remaining basement area was remodeled for gymnasium purposes. Space allotted for this project was thirty-two feet wide, one hundred twelve feet long, and seven feet high. Because of a lack of space behind the building, this conversion project received priority. The first floor contained four high school classrooms, a chemistry laboratory, and a toilet. The latter was the only one in the building but was supplemented by four in the back yard whose angle of construction discouraged laggards. Four "Collegiate" lecture halls were on the second floor. Further, a large community room, chapel, and sacristy served the needs of the Brothers. Naturally, the chapel was available to the students; and the community room contained the College library and, at the same time, provided an indoor area for general study. Finally, two commercial classrooms were on the third floor, along with sleeping quarters for the Brothers, which included a small bedroom for the stokers. Although the first classes were held at the new College in September, 1867, the alterations continued through 1870 to the extent that Commencement Exercises had to be cancelled.[1]

Other than the building at 1419 North Second Street, which had just been vacated, the total college was housed at Filbert Street till 1882. No attempt was ever again made by the College to use the North Second Street property. It was at too great a distance from Filbert Street to be feasibly utilized. Therefore, in 1873, the Board decided to sell it. Completed in April, 1873, the sale brought $4,750.[2] It is difficult to say why the Board hesitated so long in taking this appropriate action; probably there was little, if any, demand for the home, since St. Michael's Parish finally purchased it. Likewise, one must bear in mind that College administration and corporate action was a new venture for the Brother involved. It seems unfortunate that the organizational structure placed all responsibility on one man, the President.

In most corporations, the position, duties, obligations, and responsibilities of the president are clearly stated, the same being true for subordinate administrators. This recognized procedure provides for a well-coordinated operation with the least amount of friction. La Salle College in its early days was quite precisely organized, the Constitution and By-Laws being perfectly clear and simple. As with most Catholic colleges sponsored by religious, however, administrators are subject not only to the traditional occupational hazards of corporate operations, but also to the possibility of removal from office for motives which frequently have nothing to do with college administration. In the second matter, it is difficult to estimate in the history of La Salle College just what effect this sword of Damocles has had. Admittedly, it has not always hurt the College; but, in the case of Brother Oliver, President from 1863 to 1872, hasty action seemed to deprive the young College of experienced, intelligent leadership.

As successor to Brother Teliow, Brother Oliver was aware of all the implications of college operations. Securing a new location and developing a Collegiate department were due in great measure to his genius. As will be seen, it was Brother Oliver who carried on important experiments with the original college curriculum.

Once established at Filbert Street, Brother Oliver decided to change the name of the institution from Christian Brothers Academy to La Salle College; although not officially legal, this title the College bears today. In August of 1868, the official public announcement effecting the changed name was made. *The Catholic Standard* noted the change enthusiastically and praised the retention of Brother Oliver as President. It was confidently stated that he would, through his careful and able guidance, immediately gain public favor for La Salle in view of the work already accomplished.[3] True to his public, Brother Oliver did expand the College and was responsible for the development of a truly professional spirit in all segments, but especially in the Collegiate department. During his short tenure at Filbert Street, he saw the student body rise to 205 young men. He was the first to point out, in 1871, that the building was already overcrowded. Collegiate courses were established and a well-balanced curriculum carried the first college graduates to many places of prominence throughout the city. However, Brother Oliver was to see only one graduating class at the College.

For some time, there seemed to be friction between Brother Oliver and Brother Patrick, Provincial. The latter, of course, had the power of assigning teachers to the College. Apparently, Brother Oliver, in his zeal to develop La Salle into a respectable college, constantly harassed the Provincial for more Brothers. From Brother Oliver's view, some of the teachers were not qualified, and he felt it the Provincial's obligation to find and assign Brothers who were qualified. On the other hand, an old notebook of Brother Patrick's reveals his dismay at some of the community customs at Filbert Street. He writes of the Brothers' smoking cigars and visiting the seashore, both of which he interpreted as being contrary to the Brothers' Rule. Likewise, he mentioned that many Brothers, including the Director, Brother Oliver, were sometimes skipping attendance at Chapel in the mornings. Just how much these irregularties had to do with the decision to transfer Brother Oliver is difficult to say. In viewing the whole situation, one must remember that Manhattan College was under Brother Patrick's control and requests for qualified men came from Manhattan also. Although no one ever actually said so, the underlying feeling among the La Salle College Brothers in 1872 seemed to be that Brother Patrick favored Manhattan over La Salle. Whatever the complete story was, the fact is that Brother Oliver was removed from La Salle in March, 1872, and Brother Romuald became acting President. Brother Oliver was sent to San Francisco, and the community historian predicted the progress of the College would end.[4] This was a mild sentiment compared to the almost open rebellion on the part of the Brothers when they learned that Brother Paulian, President of Manhattan, was eventually to replace Brother Oliver. He was accompanied by a Brother Noah, who was assigned as sub-superior. In view of the conditions Brother Paulian found at La Salle, a compromise settlement was made after rather painful nego-tiations. Brother Paulian went back to New York, taking with him the distinction of having been President of La Salle for only a few hours, while Brother Noah remained and became President. At twenty-six years of age, he was to be the youngest man ever to hold the office.

Before leaving for San Francisco, Brother Oliver sought to assure the public that the recent changes were no cause for the consterna-tion displayed at the original announcement. He was quoted in *The Catholic Standard* for March 30, 1872, as being pleased that his successor at the college would be Brother Noah. "Under his able direction this young institution will continue to flourish and hold its name among that of the best colleges in the country, and thus our Catholic young men of Philadelphia may drink with safety and success at the fountain of its moral, intellectual, and religious spring . . ." Brother Oliver then left La Salle in the hands of Brother Noah with high hopes for its future.

Brother Oliver's prophecy proved true. Brother Noah, having stepped into a very delicate situation, soon won the admiration, affection, and praise of faculty and students and citizenry alike. Although hampered by poor health, he turned out to be one of the most brilliant and effective presidents in the College's history. In just a few years the accomplishments of Brother Noah were widely noted in public. *The Catholic Standard* stated: "To the business enterprise and unflagging energy, as well as the scholarship of this esteemable gentleman, is due in great measure the signal success of La Salle College during the past few years." With the return of Brother Noah's good health, it was hoped that greater accomplish-ments lay ahead.

As President of La Salle College, Brother Noah had many responsibilities apart from the College. He was the religious superior for twenty-three Brothers, many of whom taught in several different parish schools whose students numbered over 1,400. Dealing with the parents of these children was a task in itself. Further, he taught English on the senior collegiate level, authored a series of readers for Catholic schools, and edited a volume of English literature for college use. His pronouncements on education gained him a very favorable national reputation as a leader among educators. Despite these auxiliary obligations, Brother Noah's administration of La Salle College met with great success. Commenting on the 1873 Commencement Exercises, a Philadelphia editor wrote, "Brother Noah has . . . by his untiring zeal and ceaseless labors raised this institution with such marvelous rapidity, that it is now considered one of the first in the country. This was clearly proved by the knowledge displayed last evening by the pupils."[5] Perhaps the writer was carried away, but there is little room for doubt that La Salle College was a good college in 1873.[6] This was, in great measure, due to its able President. Unfortunately, Brother Noah's health failed again, now quite seriously, and he was taken from the College in November, 1875. Despite grave distress from an un-willing body, Brother Noah continued his zealous labors in England until an early death released him from constant pain.

At the time of Brother Noah's removal, La Salle College was in excellent condition. But then, in less than a decade, three Presi-dents followed Brother Noah and one another in quick succession, and they presided over rather fluctuating fortunes in the College. During the administration of the first, Brother Joachim, the College was, it must be admitted, nearly destroyed in less than one year. Brother Joachim, at the time of his appointment, was the oldest Brother in seniority in the United States. He was a very able teacher and had had vast experience, but by the time he was President, he was quite eccentric. At the same time, the nation's economy was rapidly falling into a very depressed state. In these circumstances Brother Joachim's subordinates considered him totally unfit to administer the College. During the first several months of his administration, sixty-five students withdrew from the College; this was a severe blow which nearly put the College out of existence. Finally $10,000 had to be borrowed to pay off the creditors. Much to the relief of the College community, Brother Joachim was removed as President by the Brother Provincial and replaced by Brother Stephen.[7]

La Salle Institute in New York City had been put in a flourishing condition by Brother Stephen, and his experience at St. Mary's College, New Orleans, where he served as President for seven years, made him quite capable of taking over the administration of La Salle College. Brother Stephen plunged into the crisis at hand and, with much patience and understanding, began to win back the confidence of many students who had withdrawn from the College. Likewise, he began to chip away at the rather burdensome debt the College carried, but this was not an easy matter to solve. To bring La Salle back to fiscal responsibility, Brother Stephen lacked nothing but time. Unfortunately, his tenure of office ran just two years, until 1878.

In that year, a general reorganization of the Christian Brothers in the United States took place. The Province of New York was split, and the new Province of Baltimore was formed. La Salle College was within the territorial limits of the latter. In the ensuing change of personnel usually necessitated by newly-organized provinces, Brother Stephen was changed to San Francisco, much to the disappointment of faculty, students, and parents at La Salle. In a very short time, they had grown to love this kind, gentle leader and educator. He had saved the College in time of crisis, and the College constituents respected him deeply for this.

Their sorrow was soon relieved, however, when they discovered that Brother Romuald, formerly executive Vice-President of La Salle and popular teacher, was to return as President. In the early days of the College at 1419 North Second Street and at Filbert Street, Brother Romuald impressed his colleagues, students, and their parents with his distinguished teaching. Moreover, Brother

Romuald had been President pro-tem between the time Brother Oliver was removed in March, 1872, and Brother Noah arrived in August. He had been transferred from La Salle to become Provincial Superior of the St. Louis District, a good indication of his leadership ability. A very intelligent man, Brother Romuald was fluent in Latin, Greek, German, and French. In the College, he taught mathematics and science.[8] On many occasions, Philadelphians were inspired by this great orator. Brother Romuald continued the fine work started by Brother Stephen, and it was during Brother Romuald's administration that La Salle College acquired a new campus. With Brothers Stephen and Romuald, La Salle returned to course, and its reputation was retained, if not enhanced.

To appreciate more fully the basis of that reputation, one has to examine the academic program itself. Prior to 1872, the College records contain little more than generalizations concerning the curriculum. However, it would appear that a collegiate curriculum was in effect as early as 1867. Brother Oliver established a series of experimental courses of college calibre the first year the College opened at Filbert Street. Immediate success followed his efforts and a decision was made to put a full college curriculum into effect in 1868. For reasons unknown, Brother Oliver's plans went awry, but in May, 1869, the Board of Managers voted studies at La Salle to "be of a more strictly collegiate grade."[9] With this mandate, a full college program was then established in September, 1869. Some few students who had participated successfully in the earlier experiments in 1867 were thus able to graduate in 1871 with the Bachelor of Arts degree. In the winter quarter of 1870, study of Latin Classics was made obligatory in the entire collegiate department. At the same time, a commercial department was established with emphasis on English and Business Education. This department, however, was entirely separate from the college section. The school year was divided into four quarters, beginning on the first Monday in September and ending the first week in July. Classes were held from 8:45 a.m. till 2:30 p.m. with all students free at a specific hour for lunch. No doubt this scheduling was due to the fact that primary, secondary, and commercial classes were all held in the same building. Apparently, the college students had little sophistication, since no mention is made of their displeasure at mixing with the younger students.

By 1872, the college curriculum seemed firm; the first La Salle College *Bulletin* appeared in 1872 with the curriculum clearly stated. It seems some questions had been raised prior to this by the parents relative to the promotion of their sons. With no printed schedule of courses, the parents seemed to jockey for unwarranted favors. Since students were allowed to attend any quarter period they chose, some conveniently forgot they had skipped a quarter or two. The *Bulletin* precluded this type of maneuver.[10]

Since the *Bulletin* was ready by March, 1872, Brother Oliver is credited with the establishment of the curriculum. Under the new system, students in the first-year college program were expected to take the following courses: Christian Doctrine; ancient and modern history; English essays, English grammar and rhetoric; bookkeeping; penmanship, geometry, mensuration; Latin, French; natural philosophy; algebra, written and mental arithmetic. This seems a formidable array of courses just from a scheduling point of view. However, some courses met only twice a week and others ran for only one or two quarters. Second-year men took advanced courses in Christian Doctrine, rhetoric, geometry, algebra, French, and Latin. In addition, they were introduced to advanced English composition; philosophy; astronomy; trigonometry and chemistry; and Greek. As college juniors, they pursued advanced courses in Christian Doctrine, English composition, chemistry, algebra, trigonometry, astronomy, Latin, Greek, and French. In addition, they had available studies in conic sections and surveying. In their final year, seniors followed additional studies in English essays, chemistry, algebra, astronomy, Latin, Greek, and French. They were likewise introduced to logic; English literature; analytical geometry, and calculus. As for electives, freshmen could choose German or music; sophomores, juniors, and seniors could elect German, music, or drawing.[11] In general, the emphasis of the curriculum seemed to be on three areas, namely, the Classics, English composition and literature, and mathematics, in that order. In the case of English and mathematics, the overall program would not measure up to modern standards. Contrariwise, the Classics program was ample. To the modern mind educated to specialization, the entire curriculum seems perhaps rather awkward but adequate.

All the courses indicated for each class had to be satisfactorily completed before "promotion" to the next class. Although the students were tested in class and were issued quarterly numerical grades — of which 60 was considered passing — they also had to submit to public examinations each quarter. Anyone was invited to come and question the students on a particular date, which fact was established well in advance. In addition, musical selections were added to these public examinations in order to encourage parents and others to attend. However, complete success in both the public examinations and private classroom testing did not assure promotions. A freshman who desired to pass to the sophomore level had to sit for "promotion examinations" at the opening of the school year in September. Having had a two-month period in which to read and prepare, the student was expected to perform well in the examination.

It would be a mistake to interpret these requirements as unnecessary obstacles for the students to hurdle. The Brothers felt the student would get a much broader education and understanding of the subject matter if he had time to read widely before sitting for the examinations. This is quite understandable in view of the practice in many colleges and universities today of making similar provision for periods of study and reading before semester exams, although the specified time is shorter than it was in 1872.[12]

Between 1872 and 1882, the curriculum of the College remained basically the same. When Brother Noah took control of La Salle, he put special emphasis on the study of English literature. As a great teacher of English, Brother Noah did much to augment the College's reputation in that field. Further, he built up the College library, making extensive purchases of literary and scientific works.

Putting first things first, Brother Noah explained that the first duty of the College was "to do justice to the students by affording them every reasonable facility for improvement." Thus, with clear conscience, he proceeded to purchase books with money originally earmarked for reducing the College debt.[13] Certainly this zealous Brother contributed more than just an expanded library; he enshrined a timeless ideal which administrators of La Salle College for all time cannot afford to ignore.

As the College continued to grow academically, more stringent requirements for admission were posted. To be admitted as a freshman to La Salle College in 1882, the student was required to have one year of Latin and German. In other studies such as English grammar, arithmetic, algebra, bookkeeping, history, and geography, a general average of seventy-five was required where the passing grade of 60 percent was in force.

In the same year, a few additions were made to the curriculum. In the area of theology, sacred history was added. Physics and navigation were added in the area of the sciences, and metaphysics was added in the area of philosophy. These were the last changes made in the curriculum until it was completely restudied when the College moved to new quarters in 1886.[14]

In great measure, the effectiveness of any curriculum depends on its implementation by the faculty. When La Salle College opened its doors on Center Square in 1867, the total faculty consisted of eight Brothers. Not all of these taught in the college program. During the scholastic year 1869, the first laymen on the faculty joined the Brothers. Dr. S. B. Howell was professor of chemistry and mineralogy. At the same time, he also served on the staff of the City Dental College and the Academy of Natural Science. The chair of geology was occupied the following year by Professor A. E. Rogerson, who held a graduate degree from Trinity College. Later in the year, Mr. William F. Harrity, one of the first graduates of La Salle, returned to teach mathematics and Latin. He remained only a few quarters and taught on a part-time basis. By 1873, nine Brothers and four laymen constituted the faculty. Rufus Adams lectured in education, while Henry Hollis, A.M. (Oxon.) taught languages. Instruction in music was handled by William A. Newland, and Professor Rogerson continued in the chair of geology.[15] Besides teaching duties, the following Brothers held administrative posts in the College; Brother Noah, President; Brother Romuald, Vice-President; Brother Paphylinus, Treasurer; and Brother Luke, Secretary.

From time to time, other staff changes were made, but those are difficult to trace since few detailed records have survived. In 1882, Professor E. F. McGonigle was added to the staff. He taught Latin, and *The Catholic Standard* felt he would be a tremendous asset to the College. In the same article, the editor noted the exceptional instruction in Greek given by Brother Isidore and saluted the "zeal and devotedness" of Brother Paphylinus. It was this type of public commendation for the College faculty which helped La Salle to retain its academic reputation. The high standards met by the teachers at La Salle and the gifted men who comprised its faculty proved too much of a temptation for higher religious superiors, however, who constantly resorted to the College faculty for able administrators. In 1885, Brother Clementian was sent to Europe as Provincial of England and Ireland. The transfer deeply affected the College.[16]

From the inception of the College, the number of students seemed plentiful. When it first opened at Filbert Street in 1867, the total student body numbered 200. The total remained at this level through 1886, save for the scholastic year 1875-1876, when Brother Joachim took control of the College in rather depressed times. However, the number of students in the College department itself was much smaller than 200 during this time. When the overall College averaged 200 students per year, there were generally between thirty-five and fifty students following college courses, the latter number being considered a "full college department." Compared to other schools, La Salle College, with thirty-five college students in 1871, was rather small. That same year, Columbia had

120 undergraduates, Fordham 80, Hobart 49, and Manhattan College 66.[17]

One of the difficulties in obtaining good students in 1873 was the familiar one that many talented young men just did not have any money. Brother Oliver had a committee of Brothers to study the problem, and in March, 1873, he was able to announce a plan for student aid which would be available the following term. As already noted, Brother Oliver was removed, but Brother Noah implemented the plan as announced. Whenever possible, gifted students would be given scholarship aid. Only the President and Treasurer knew the identity of such students. Obviously, it was impossible to admit a great many students on scholarship, but Brother Noah's principle was as follows: ". . . when Providence had destined a young lad, by his talent and mental ability, to take a high place in the world, it is judicious policy to gradually introduce him, by the associations of the College, into that class of society in which he will afterwards be called to move."[18]

Ever interested in the intellectual development of La Salle men, Brother Noah went to great pains to put an edge on the public examinations held quarterly. He invited the clergy of the city, parents of students, and professors of other local institutions of higher learning to these examinations. He urged them to bring their literary acquaintances "who were interested in education." He challenged all to study the methods of instruction used at the College and declare whether or not the system was a good one. Brother Noah was so convinced of the benefit of the public questionings that one time, in the presence of Bishop Wood, he chided the clergy who were noticeable by their absence from these scholarly endeavors. He felt the influence of the clergy on the students was great and went so far as to call the clergy the right hand of the diocese and the Brothers its left hand. Pardoning himself for interpreting Scripture, Brother Noah stated "while the 'left' hand is not desirous of knowing what 'the right hand doeth,' we are most anxious that the 'right' should see what the 'left' accomplishest."[19] The examinations put much responsibility on the students and many of them dropped from school rather than face the ordeal. Brother Noah took the dread of the examination as an indication of their thoroughness and felt no compunction for those "who, rather than have their indolence exposed, sought more congenial quarters." He was convinced, however, that the slight humiliation of the public test was much better than years of regret for not having completed one's education. With such sentiments as these from the President, it is difficult to conceive of anything but serious study being tolerated at La Salle College in its early decades.

Aside from academic requirements, there were comparatively few rules and regulations. The President seemed the sole enforcer of these requirements. Students, for example, were expected to start classes at the beginning of the term. No students were admitted once formal classes began. Likewise, the men were to be on time for lectures. With classes beginning at 8:45 a.m., this might have proved difficult for the men coming from places like Beverly, New Jersey; Phoenixville, Norristown, and Conshohocken. Other than these areas, all students came from the city. Finally, parents were asked to insist that their sons spend much of their time at home studying. As for the need for any strictly disciplinary regulations, it seemed to be nonexistent. With such a small student body in a rather confined area, little was left unobserved by the faculty.

The population of the College continued to hover around the thirty or forty mark through 1882. When it was decided to take the College to North Broad Street, College records indicate an immediate increase in population. However, this increase was in the academic or secondary department. After the other departments moved from Filbert Street, at the end of the scholastic year 1882-1883, there were seven juniors, eleven sophomores, and twelve freshmen in the College.[20]

Despite a small student body, limited campus, and a rather demanding academic schedule, the early students of La Salle College organized and participated in a number of activities that were not directly associated with lecture hall or laboratory. Although strictly speaking, not a student activity as we understand the term today, the Annual Commencement at La Salle College was, in its first decades, the major social event of each year. A population and student body not pampered by radio and television flocked to this annual event which honored not only the graduates but also many distinguished personalities. The programs were generally laced with musical selections and oratory, a display that was more than welcome by the graduates, the student body, their parents, and friends. It was a family affair; so extensive were the programs that every last member of the College was involved in some way. At the first official College graduation in 1871, two men received B.A.'s, six received B.S.'s, and four were granted commercial diplomas. Nonetheless, over 4,000 people crowded the Academy of Music to see Mayor Fox distribute the diplomas. The large stage was crowded with faculty, clergy, and distinguished members of the medical and legal professions. In 1876, the College had Dom Pedro II, Emperor of Brazil, preside at its commencement. This international figure drew a standing-room-only crowd to the Academy.

Although the students spent much free time preparing for the Annual Commencement, they found time to engage in other activities of a more personal nature. For example, in 1874, the La Salle College Literary Union was formed. Given substantial encouragement by the faculty, especially Brother Noah, the literary society became a very effective organization. The meetings were of the highest calibre and were usually held at the College on Friday evenings. A distinguished litterateur would lecture and discuss some phase of English literature. A social usually followed the meetings. However, since there were no young ladies present, the social consisted of further discussions over refreshments.

In 1878, the *La Salle Advance*, a news magazine devoted to "art, science, literature, and moral improvement" was started by Stephen Burke, Michael J. Ryan, and Hugh T. Henry. The magazine was intended for public consumption and contained newsworthy items from every Catholic school in the city. A subscription rate of fifty cents a year was established. In spite of this financing plus subsidies from the College, the magazine ceased publication after a few years. Its founders, however, went on to much more distinguished successes. Hugh Henry became a professor at The Catholic University of America, Ryan became a prominent Philadelphia lawyer and banker, and Burke became editor of the *Philadelphia Public Ledger*.

Activities that made La Salle well known in Philadelphia during the seventies and eighties were the plays and concerts given from time to time in the Academy of Music. The La Salle Glee Club and Orchestra, under the direction of Brother Luke of Mary, was noted for its performances, and it rarely appeared before anything less than a full house. The Dramatic Club, directed by Brother Paphylinus, included in its repertoire such rousing hits as *The Hidden Gem, The Bell in the Forest, Falsely Accused, Harvest Storm,* and *Maurice the Woodcutter. The Catholic Standard,* reporting on the last production, noted that "the group appeared to be well trained and, individually, the cast seemed to have no little talent." The troupe, so graciously complimented, took the show to Baltimore to perform for the benefit of Calvert Hall College. These plays not only contributed to the development of the students and the good name of La Salle, but were also financially helpful. A performance of *Abee de L' Epee* at the Academy in 1879, netted the College $1,100, a rather tidy sum for that period.

Another important student activity was the La Salle Debating Society, founded in January, 1885. This was to be one of the most active, well-organized, sophisticated groups on the La Salle campus. On one occasion, they had the temerity to refuse membership to a rather prominent member of the faculty who taught English. Interestingly enough, the first topic of debate assigned by the society in 1885 was "Is Warfare by Dynamite Justifiable?" One might wonder if our debaters today are really so far removed from 1885. After several months of successful operation, the debaters organized a newspaper. They decided to resurrect *The Advance* as the name of the paper. Committees were appointed to various jobs, the most important of which seemed to be the securing of advertisements for the paper. Finally, on November 13, 1885, the first issue of the

new paper, *The Advance,* appeared. Only members of the debate
society were entitled to free copies. Other copies had to be purchased. Like its predecessor, *The Advance* collapsed after one
edition, despite tremendous efforts to get out a second edition,
"efforts which nearly distintegrated the society."[21]

Finally, there is no record of organized sports activities. Since
a very small room in the basement at Filbert Street served as a
gymnasium, no doubt some sports or gymnastic activities took place.
It is not until 1886, after the move from Filbert Street, that public
mention is made of organized athletic activity. The La Salle *Bulletin*
for 1886 states: "The students are given every opportunity for developing healthful physiques. The play grounds are sufficiently large.
There are a well-equipped gymnasium, ball-alleys, and well-lighted
recreation rooms." It would seem, then, that athletic activity did
play some part in rounding out the social, intellectual, physical, and
spiritual opportunities found at La Salle in its first nineteen years.

La Salle College, in its early growth and development as an
institution of higher learning, had come full circle with the first
alumni meeting held June 28, 1871. The first graduates had gathered to honor Brother Oliver, President. He was presented with
a montage of the entire class, which he graciously accepted and
ordered that it be preserved in the College archives. In a spontaneous reply to the alumni, he urged them to preserve happiness,
"a jewel beyond price" by keeping good conscience. He also remarked, with what today seems to have been a gift of prophecy that
"from the progress achieved by this institution and the capacity for
development manifested by it, it is not too much to predict for it
an extension out of all proportion with its present dimensions. In the
not-so-distant future, the alumni of La Salle College, respected and
honored throughout the length and breadth of this wide land, when
recalling fondly the place of their intellectual birth, will retain
amongst their most pleasing memories, the features of the graduating class of old Alma Mater . . ."[22] Within the decade of his remarks, La Salle graduated such prominent men as William F. Harrity, lawyer, politician, statesman, and campaign manager for Grover

Cleveland; Bishops McCort and McDevitt; Maurice Francis Egan, and John McEvoy. Just nine years after the first alumni meeting, further efforts were made by the La Salle Alumni in 1880 to aid Christian education by promoting the interests of their Alma Mater. In order to formalize their proceedings, officers were elected. The first President was the Reverend Joseph O'Keefe; Brother Romuald was Honorary President. Thus, with a functioning, vibrant alumni organization, La Salle, by 1880, was a complete entity as an institution of higher learning. But this hardy result was not accomplished without a serious struggle and with a host of difficulties, many of which were plainly financial.

From its very inception, the College seemed to carry a sizeable debt. The Filbert Street campus had cost $30,000. Initially, the Brothers rented the property from the Bishop at $1,800 a year. In 1869, when the Board authorized the purchase of the property, the $3,600 already paid in rent was deducted from the total sale price of $30,000. However, a mortgage was made in favor of Bishop Wood at six percent for $30,000, payable semi-annually. If the College made partial payments at different times, the same rate of interest was allowed.[23] Since the maximum gross income of the College was limited to $16,000 annually, it was quite difficult to carry the debt. This was especially true since at no time during the first nineteen years of operation did the gross income even approach $16,000. In August, 1872, Brother Oliver was, through astute management, able to pay $2,500 on the debt. His successor, Brother Noah, appealed directly to the Catholics of Philadelphia, asking them to support a "Grand Union Concert" which was given at the Academy of Music. The concert was a success, and an additional $3,750 was paid on the debt by March, 1873. The debt was further reduced by September, 1873, to $18,000. More concerts were planned at the Academy, but as the national economy began to dip downward, little financial help was available.

Then financial disaster struck during Brother Joachim's term. By December, 1875, the College had to take an additional mortgage of $10,000 on the property at Filbert Street. Once again, Bishop

Wood held the mortgage. Things continued to go from bad to worse. Brother Stephen was unable to bring any fiscal balance to the college, and when Brother Romuald took office in September, 1878, a debt of over $32,000 burdened the College. Any money saved during the fiscal year was consumed by a six-percent interest on the debt. By September, 1879, Brother Romuald announced the College was able to more than pay its debt service. This was partially due to an increase in students. The following year a large fair was held and, as a result, the College paid off $15,702 on the debt.[24] This put the College back on a more firm fiscal basis with a debt of only $13,000, which it could very easily carry.

Both social pressure and financial need encouraged the Board as early as 1875 to approve a plan to sell the Filbert Street property and move to a new location. The building at Filbert Street did not lend itself to expansion. Further, the area around Center Square was becoming more and more noisy. As early as 1872, constructtion on City Hall had begun. The freight yards opposite the College had much business. During the scholastic year 1875-1876, a great evangelistic crusade took place in the freight depot opposite the College. Meetings were held every day for about three months, with as many as 13,000 people attending. Over one million people had attended during the three-month period. The day the meetings closed, it was announced that John Wanamaker had purchased the freight depot. Immediately, the old building was demolished and a vast store named Wanamaker's Grand Depot was opened with much ballyhoo on May 6, 1876.[25] All this activity tended to distract the students, and on warm spring days professors had difficulty communicating above all the noise. It was not, however, until the College debt was substantially reduced in 1880 that the first real steps were taken to secure a new property. Brother Romuald found a place at 18th and Race Streets, formerly occupied by the Diocesan Seminary. However, the Board turned this site down in hopes of finding a better location. A change was becoming imperative. With construction of the Masonic Temple on the opposite corner of Juniper Street, most of the natural light was lost to

the College. Two new noisy horse-car lines now passed in front of
the College. Since many public buildings were under construction,
it was felt it would be easy to sell Filbert Street. As a result, when
it was discovered that the Bouvier Estate at 1240 North Broad
Street was available, the Board approved the purchase on December
14, 1882. At the same time, the President was given the power to
take a $30,000 mortgage on Filbert Street. He was then to pay
off all debts and use the remainder of the money for the purchase
and improvement of the Bouvier estate.[26]

Michel Bouvier (1792-1874), great-great-grandfather of Jac-
queline Bouvier Kennedy, was a successful cabinet maker in Philadelphia. He invested heavily in realty, holding over sixty acres of
land in Philadelphia and 800,000 acres in Virginia. He was a
member of the Bourse and held a seat on the New York Stock
Exchange. In 1853, Bouvier felt he was in a position to build a
mansion on North Broad Street with other wealthy Philadelphia
families such as the Elkinses and Wideners. The house was completed in the fall of 1854, and Michel Bouvier took possession on
All Saints' Day, 1854. The house was of brownstone construction,
fifty feet wide and sixty feet deep. It stood in a beautiful garden,
with greenhouse, stables, and coach house in the rear, and the
interior was elegant. It was to this house that Michel's son, John
Vernou Bouvier, wounded a second time at the second battle of
Bull Run, was brought home — to recuperate — the same year, in
fact, that La Salle College was chartered. After Michel's death in
1874, the estate passed to his heirs, who decided to sell the property
to the Brothers in 1882.

Announcement of the purchase of the Bouvier estate was greeted
with much enthusiasm on the part of the students, parents, alumni,
and friends of the College. *The Catholic Standard* of December 9,
1882, stated: "The site of the new College is a most desirable one,
holding an elevated position and situated in a fashionable neighborhood. The lot has a frontage of 134 feet along Broad Street and
an extension of 160 feet along Stiles Street all the way back to Carlisle Street. . . . On it, facing Broad Street, stands an old-fashioned

brownstone mansion . . . This house is entered by high brownstone steps and a marble portico, while it is guarded from the street by a massive brownstone fence. Within the house there is a great quantity of stained glass, and its staircase in one of the finest in the city." Despite the great display of public approval, a crisis which nearly destroyed the College was developing behind the scenes.

In order to purchase the Bouvier estate for $67,500, the President was empowered by the Board to sell the college campus at Filbert Street for $100,000. He was to pay the Bouvier estate $17,500 in cash and secure a five-year mortgage of $50,000. However, as time wore on, prospective buyers for Filbert Street disappeared. Men who looked at the building felt the price too high in view of the many repairs necessary to make it fit for offices. The Brothers then decided to ask the superiors at Paris for permission to keep and operate both buildings. The Superior General sent Brother Patrick, Assistant General, to study the situation firsthand. This was the same Brother Patrick who, as Provincial, had clashed with Brother Oliver and the La Salle Brothers once before. Brother Patrick met with the Rev. M. A. Walsh, Administrator of the Archdiocese of Philadelphia. Father Walsh did not approve of the new high school at 1240 because of its proximity to the Jesuits' school at 17th and Stiles Streets and the projected Cahill High School at Broad and Vine Streets. Brother Patrick then suggested that La Salle College close its doors permanently so that the Brothers could be used in several parish schools. It is difficult to determine whether Brother Patrick was speaking his own sentiments or those of the Superior General, who, it would appear, did not too enthusiastically accept the idea of Brothers being engaged in higher education. However, Father Walsh's rather forceful reply, "Dear Brother Patrick, La Salle College is an absolute necessity to the people of Philadelphia," seemed to remove all doubt of the continued existence of La Salle. Brother Patrick, fresh from his meeting with Father Walsh and fully aware of the position of the Archdiocese relative to the future of the College, met with the administrators of the College and decided that the college classes would stay at Filbert Street, while the high school moved to 1240 North Broad.

With one crisis solved, another appeared almost immediately. Fiscal liabilities for the Bouvier estate were now overdue, and the Filbert Street property had not been sold. It was decided to quietly dispose of the plan to move the high school and try to find a buyer for the Bouvier estate. Caution was urged in seeking a purchaser so as not to discourage so many friends of the College who saw, in the purchase of the Bouvier Mansion, a new era of prosperity for the College. However, parties originally interested in the mansion wanted nothing to do with it eventually. The Administration was now desperate and had to sell the Filbert Street property or lose everything. Accordingly, a public sale for $75,000 was planned. Still the property did not sell. During the scholastic year 1884-1885, the Brothers expected to lose everything. Money was needed to pay off the mortgage on the Bouvier estate, and even if the Filbert Street property was sold at a loss, no money was available for construction of new facilities at 1240 to house the college department. Finally, in the fall of 1885, a ray of hope broke through the gloom of fiscal despair. La Salle College received $42,000 from the estate of Francis Drexel. This bequest, in a very real sense, actually saved the College. A short time later, there was more good news in the form of an offer to buy the Filbert Street property for $75,000. The offer, however, was soon withdrawn. In the general interest of the College, therefore, Pierce Archer, Esq., a member of the Board at La Salle, resigned his position, and, in partnership with Charles Gross, purchased the Filbert Street property for $75,000. He paid $60,000 in cash and secured the balance by bond and mortgage. The transactions were completed in December, 1885, but the College was allowed to remain on the premises until July 15, 1886.[27] In just a few short months, the College realized $102,000 in cash through the Drexel Estate and the sale of the Filbert Street property. This put an end to the crisis and assured the possibility of a greatly expanded La Salle at 1240.

As La Salle dipped into its period of grave crisis in 1883, Brother

Romuald, President, was replaced by Brother Clementian. Brother Clementian remained just two years as President, and, in view of the turbulent times for the College, he was probably glad to see his term end. He was a scholarly man, well versed in languages and music. During his short stay, his genial manners, superb teaching, and saintly character gained him the highest respect of both faculty and students. Brother Clementian, who had been recruited for the Brothers by Bishop John Neumann, was taken from La Salle to become Provincial of England and Ireland. He remained in this post for five years and then became Provincial of New York. In 1890, he was elected Assistant General and served in that capacity for twenty years. La Salle had indeed been fortunate to have Brother Clementian as President, if only for a short time. Its fiscal problems solved for the time, Brother Clementian left La Salle College in a mood for expansion.

3. Old "1240"

TEN YEARS AFTER THE DISPUTED ELECTION OF 1876, which threatened to rip open the nation's scars from the Civil War, the United States found itself in relatively prosperous conditions. Agriculture was advancing rapidly through technological innovations. Industry thrived on both domestic and foreign markets. Private enterprises in shipping, storage, transportation, and mining fared well. It was the last industry, in fact, that supplied much of the income for Michel Bouvier to maintain his grand home amid the opulence of Philadelphia's North Broad Street. Long after Michel Bouvier's death and the sale of his home to La Salle College, the North Broad Street area was one of desirable elegance, quiet, and attractiveness. Therefore, the Brothers and students of La Salle were quite enthusiastic about their new campus and saw a bright and prosperous future for the College. Once the difficulty over selling the Filbert Street property and Brother Patrick's threat to close the College had passed, old plans were again readied for action. All persons concerned agreed that, physically, the College must grow. This growth, in turn, would attract a larger and more qualified student body.

As early as 1882, plans for the new College at 1240 were revealed. *The Catholic Standard,* on December 9, 1882, reported that La Salle College would construct a five-story building along Carlisle Street. The entrance would be on Stiles Street. The building was to be fifty-five feet wide and 130 feet long. The basement would be set aside for the gymnasium with classrooms on the second and third floors, and one large hall would constitute the fourth and fifth floors. This desirable brick and brown-stone structure never became a reality because of the financial crisis created by the inability to sell the Filbert Street campus. Instead, between 1882 and 1886, primary and secondary classes were conducted in the Bouvier Mansion and coach house, while collegiate classes were taught at Filbert Street.

With the sale of Filbert Street, the building plans were of necessity reactivated. The College had to move out of Filbert Street by July, 1886, and increased accommodations had to be built at 1240. Fortunately, the Drexel money and the cash from the sale of Filbert Street were available. As a result, there was little delay in getting started. However, building plans proposed in 1882 were changed. A new building was to connect with the Mansion by an enclosed walkway on the south side and run thirty-four feet toward Stiles Street. It then ran east to west about seventy-five feet. A high basement was topped by three stories. The chemistry lab occupied the basement, and the remainder of the buildings were classrooms. Unfortunately, construction did not begin soon enough to be finished for the opening of the scholastic year. Naturally, the College had to improvise for space, a problem that plagued the Administration often in later years. In the Mansion, the Brothers' quarters were moved to the attic, and ten classrooms were jammed into the vacated area. Some classrooms were used as Brothers' bedrooms at night. Additional classes were held in the stable, and many regrets were uttered over the hasty destruction of the greenhouses. This almost untenable situation lasted until February, 1887, when the new building was finally completed. The new wing was joyfully opened and apparently filled the needs of all departments, since "all expressed themselves as highly pleased with the airy, lightsome classrooms; the capacious yard and healthy play-hall."[1] The total college expansion cost approximately $22,000, of which $17,000 was paid immediately, and the residue was mortgaged.

Just a few months after work was completed on the new building, it became obvious that a separate building would be needed for physical education facilities. The College administration was hesitant about expending additional funds for a new gymnasium. Instead, a subscription campaign among alumni and friends of La Salle was initiated. Also, several entertainments were given to secure additional funds. Both enterprises proved successful and, in 1887, Carlisle Hall was completed. It stood at the extreme northwest corner of the campus and fronted on Carlisle Street. It was generally conceded to be the largest gym and basketball court in Philadelphia at the time. Actually, it was only one-tenth the size of Wister Hall gym today. This new facility brought much publicity to the College and was frequently used as a drawing card in College advertisements.[2]

Essentially, La Salle College, between 1886 and 1930, consisted of three buildings. The Bouvier Mansion, South Wing, as the new addition was called, and Carlisle Hall. The latter was devoted entirely to physical education under the direction of Professor Frank, and to recreational purposes, the only exception being its annual conversion into a student chapel for the student retreat. The Mansion contained a chapel, music room, and parlors on the first floor; senior classrooms, a library, and reading rooms on the second floor; with the third floor housing the Brothers. South Wing housed nine classrooms, chemistry and physics laboratories, and a student lounge.

These facilities proved adequate only for a decade, and, in 1896, additions were required. There was very little ground space available for construction, so the only solution was to add to the existing buildings. At a cost of $14,906, a story and a half were added to the Bouvier Mansion and a full story to South Wing. All went well until the contractor ran out of money. By that time, he had removed the roof of the Mansion. The Brothers had to fix the roof to the best of their ability and, despite their best efforts, they suffered from the elements through the winter of 1896. The contractor was forced to assign his contract to Brother Isidore, President, who in turn sublet the contracts, and the work was completed by the spring of 1897. "The work was well done and, though very troublesome, completed without interfering with our school."[3]

In March, 1909, the Brothers were exposed to nature's most devastating menace — fire. Starting about one o'clock in the morning, the fire nearly engulfed the top two stories of the Bouvier Mansion. A passerby noticed the fire and awakened the Brothers who were sleeping on the top floor. Many of them, partially overcome by smoke and heat, barely escaped from the building. All inside stairs were cut off, and the only way out was over the Mansion roof to the roof of South Wing. It was miraculous that all reached the street safely. The top two stories of the house were destroyed and the lower floors deluged by water. Again, the Brothers went back to sleeping in the classrooms until repairs were made. School remained open and the $30,000 loss was completely covered by insurance.[4]

In 1889, an additional realty obligation was taken on by the College. The Brothers of the Baltimore Province had secured a property in Ocean City, New Jersey, from the Wanamaker Estate. The premises were to be used for college courses for Brothers teaching in the Province. To adapt the building to college needs, a large sum of money was needed. Further, the property had a rather sizeable, fast-maturing mortgage which had to be met. It was with an obvious lack of enthusiasm that Brother Isidore, President, announced that, in the name of the Board of Managers, he had accepted the "Deeds of La Salle Summer School, 'Ocean Rest.' "[5] Although summer courses were given at Ocean Rest, this institution, which is still in existence, never became an integral part of La Salle College.

Despite the rather severe crises of administration during the purchase of 1240 and the sale of Filbert Street, the educational process continued without interruption and, seemingly, without damage to the established academic standards. In October, 1885, the President spoke at length to the Board of Managers of the excel-

lence of La Salle graduates as indicated by their records in professional schools and in positions they had attained throughout the
city. Further, he spoke of the proficiency of the college students "in
the specialties taught," namely, languages, mathematics, and metaphysics.[6] As the College transferred to its new home, however, it
was soon evident that the Brothers had not become complacent or
satisfied with the college courses of study despite the evident success
of its graduates. The College *Bulletin* for 1886 announced sweeping
changes in the curriculum and academic requirements.

Prefacing the new college program was a restatement of the
aims and objectives of the College which read in part, "The Brothers
have, in consequence, reduced teaching to a science. Christian
Educators, it is their great aim, not merely to instruct the intellect,
but chiefly to cultivate the heart and mold the Christian gentleman." Nonetheless, the intellect was a major concern as was evidenced by the new curriculum. One major course of studies, called
"regular classical course," was available to the college students
under the new regulation. A Bachelor of Arts degree was the only
degree conferred, while the commercial diploma was still maintained. Students seeking the B.A. degree had to pass successfully
all the prescribed courses in addition to "Senior" or comprehensive
examinations. On paper, the prescribed courses seem rather
formidable.

In establishing the new curriculum, the College was divided into
areas of study such as physical science, mathematics, English, classics,
philosophy, and linear drawing. The latter area seemed to float
throughout the curriculum, and its evaluation is difficult to determine. Modern languages, which were required both for the classical
course and the commercial course, appeared to be placed in an
exclusive category without being an integral part of the regular
curriculum.

Offerings in the various areas of study are interesting in view
of curriculum structure at La Salle College today. In the area of
physical sciences, physics and physical geography were offered to
first-year students; inorganic chemistry in the sophomore year, and

organic chemistry and astronomy in the third year. In mathematics, algebra, geometry, mensuration of solids, and plane trigonometry occupied freshmen. Sophomores were given series, spherical trigonometry, surveying, and navigation. Higher equations, analytical geometry, differentials, and integral calculus were fare for juniors. The English department required rhetoric, English literature, and modern history of the freshmen. Criticism, English literature, essays, and the history of England challenged the sophomores, while Shakespearean studies, early and middle English grammar, old English literature, and ancient history interested third-year men. It would seem the area of English included theology, since Christian Doctrine was prescribed for the frosh and sophs, while the juniors were obliged to study "evidences of Christianity." For some unknown reason, all were listed within the area of English. A rather heavy classics program was indicated, divided between Latin and Greek. Latin grammar, Sallust-*Cataline,* Ovid-*Metamorphoses,* and Virgil's *Aeneid* were taught to freshmen. In the second year, students were exposed to prose composition, Cicero, Livy, and Horace. Cicero's *De Senectute* and *De Amicitia; Ars Poetica* of Horace, Tactitus' *Germania* and *Agricola,* and Roman antiquities were offered in the third year. Senior scholars studied Plautus' *Captives,* the *Satirae* of Juvenal, Roman literature, and Latin composition. Freshman Greek studies consisted of grammar, Xenophon, and *Anabasis.* Homer's *Iliad,* Herodotus, and Grecian antiquities were covered by sophomores. Third-year men entertained Demosthenes, Euripides' *Alcestis,* Greek literature, and Grecian antiquities. *Oedipus Tyrannus* of Sophocles, Plato's *Gorgias,* and Greek literature completed classical studies for fourth-year men. The area of philosophy offered the least number of courses. Logic was taught to third-year men, while metaphysics, philosophy of history, and philosophy of literature were offered to seniors. Again we find "evidences of Christianity" being taught to seniors, but, in this case, the course is listed under philosophy. No doubt this latter requirement, along with the three "religion" requirements in the area of English, provided at least one basic course in theology during each year of study, a requirement which related closely to the Christian aims and objectives of the College.

The area of linear drawing was designed to fill a specific need for the men graduating from the College in an age when Philadelphia was in a period of tremendous building activity. In all areas of business and professions, an understanding of blueprints, plans, drawings, etc. was almost a necessity. As a result, all freshmen were taught lettering and the use of instruments. Available to second-year men were courses in descriptive geometry, development, construction of solids, tinting and grading and shades and shadows. Fourth-year students could follow lectures in linear and isometrical perspectives, stereotomy, stone-cutting; arches, vaults, groins, and their construction; joinery, carpentry, and construction of joints; and topographical drawing. These offerings should not be misconstrued as an effort on the part of the College to introduce a full-blown course in engineering at this time. This simply was not the case, although engineering was introduced after the turn of the century. The linear drawing department was strictly a service department.

In the area of modern languages, French and German were taught. B.A. aspirants had to take four years of French and two years of German. To obtain a commercial diploma, one had to study two years of German.[7] This curriculum just described was in effect through the remainder of the 19th century. It is interesting to observe the reactions to the course of studies both from faculty and students. A description of the philosophy program reads thus: "It has been our constant effort to go beyond the mere abstractions and definitions of metaphysics and apply the truths and principles therein grasped to literature and history . . . Historical theories are discussed; methods of research are laid down; principles of criticism and discrimination are applied in such a way as to enable the student to distinguish the mythical from the historical elements in history."[8] If these efforts were successful, and there is no reason to doubt that they were, it would seem that although exposed to fewer class hours in philosophy than the modern Catholic college student, the 19th-century student received a quite substantial training.

Again, as always, much depends on student response to the proper type of training. From the student's view, one thing lacking in the curriculum of 1886 was electives, as is pointed out in a letter by Frank T. Matthews, '97. Mr. Matthews, likewise, stated that required courses in Greek, Latin, French, and German proved to be a burden throughout his collegiate career. Joseph J. Shields, '99, described the College as a "pre-professional school for law, medicine, dentistry, and, of course, theological seminaries." He felt La Salle superior to colleges in its own class and "equal to the best." Commenting further on the curriculum, Mr. Shields stated that "the College and the curriculum were on a grade with small colleges throughout the country at that time; and in conversation with other schools' graduates, I got the impression that the education I received at La Salle was superior." Unfortunately, the favorable situation described by Mr. Shields was to be disrupted by the so-called Latin Question.

The Christian Brothers were directly affected by the Latin Question; La Salle College was indirectly affected, especially in the area of the curriculum. In essence, the problem centered on the question of teaching Latin in schools conducted by the Brothers. Such practice was actually forbidden by the Community Rule, common to the Brothers throughout the entire world, local customs to the contrary notwithstanding. The wisdom of the stricture inserted by St. John Baptist de La Salle, founder of the Christian Brothers, need not be discussed here. It was obvious that St. La Salle had no idea he was starting a worldwide organization. Thus, there was little inclination among European Brothers to think in terms of the development of the Order in places where customs differed. In America, however, one of the first needs the Brothers attempted to meet was that for general academic or liberal arts training, the curriculum for which throughout the nineteenth and early twentieth centuries remained essentially classical. The Brothers were also frequently called upon to assist dioceses in training young men to enter seminaries. Latin was first taught by the Brothers in the United States in St. Louis in 1854. Letters from the hierarchy of St. Louis, New Orleans, Baltimore, and New York requested the Brothers' General Chapter of 1854 to allow Latin studies in colleges in the United States. Approval was given, and all seemed settled until 1858. Battersby, in his *19th Century History of the Institute,* alleges "vested interests" outside the Institute raised the question again. He does not identify the "vested interests"; neither does he document the allegation. Nonetheless, the Holy See asked Francis P. Kenrick, Archbishop of Baltimore, to investigate. His favorable report quieted the matter for a while. At the Second Plenary Council of Baltimore and at the General Chapters of the Christian Brothers held in 1873, 1882, 1884, and 1894, the question was again discussed apparently to the satisfaction of all concerned. Actually, the Chapters of 1882, 1884, and 1894 passed decrees "more or less precise" with the intent of arresting the "extension of the dangerous system in the States." But these decretals were never published. Latin had been taught at La Salle College from the school's very inception. In 1881, the Superior General left the Latin situation to the discretion of Archbishop Wood, who readily encouraged the Brothers to continue teaching the classics, since many young men had already gone to the seminary upon graduation. However, the final break came at the Chapter of 1897. Latin was ruled out of all schools in the Institute, even those in the United States. Immediately, members of the American hierarchy and Brothers in the United States planned an appeal. Archbishop Riordan of San Francisco and Bishop Byrne of Nashville represented the American hierarchy in Rome. The appeal was based on the need of the Brothers' colleges as substitutes for junior seminaries. Despite the fact that the Bishops felt the Superiors of the Institute lacked realism in their decision on Latin, the Chapter was sustained by the Holy See. Superiors of schools in the United States wherein Latin was taught were told to phase out the Latin program within one calendar year.

To many of the Brothers involved in these schools, the order proved a severe sanction. At first, dismayed by a seeming lack of understanding of local conditions on the part of the Superior General, many Brothers began to give way to chauvinistic anger. Added to this, the Superiors, allegedly wishing to avoid friction, ordered leading Brothers in the United States into exile abroad. Not only did this affect the morale of the Brothers in the United States, but it also brought the entire Latin Question into public focus. Many students and parents, along with the Brothers, openly protested against the distasteful exile. Eventually, the American press took up the story. *The Chicago Sunday Times Herald* of January 22, 1899, headlined the events and cast them as a struggle between the "two greatest Catholic educational bodies, the Jesuits and the Christian Brothers." It was claimed that only a few members of the hierarchy supported the Jesuits, while the majority favored the Brothers. The paper further stated that since the Brothers began to teach Latin in the United States, the Jesuits had difficulty in surviving and, as a result, "the Jesuits have succeeded in having the Superior General of the Christian Brothers in Paris revoke the permission granted his order to teach classics in the United States." *The Times Herald* further suggested that Archbishop Ireland wanted an independent Superior General for Brothers in the United States if the Latin Question was not settled favorably.

When the exiled Brothers, all of whom displayed heroic submission and obedience, departed for their foreign assignments, they were accompanied to the ship by many Brothers, friends, and students. On February 21, 1899, a dockside interview of an unidentified Brother from La Salle College appeared in *The Philadelphia Inquirer*. He stated that the Brothers in the United States were really attaining the aims for which the Institute was founded, but he felt "the superiors, in France, are too much cribbed, cabined, and confined by tradition and European prejudice to comprehend the situation." Further, Brother said the Arts course at La Salle corresponds to that at the University of Pennsylvania. The College, he stated, was a legitimate outgrowth of elementary education and prepared young men for duties of life. "Without these Colleges, the Christian Brothers would have no real reason for existence here." Obviously, the Brother was not alone in his feelings. On August 4, 1899, *The Catholic Standard* alleged that the Brothers "rather than submit to what they regard as the unjust demands of the superior of the order, steps will be taken which will, if necessary, lead to a united and open revolt." Although this step was probably considered, *The Standard* admittedly was on thin ice in describing the situation.

La Salle College and the Latin Question is our immediate concern. Thus, the entire situation must be kept in proper perspective. On the one hand, the faculty of the College was certainly dismayed, disappointed, and dejected, if not angry, as a result of the Latin decision. These feelings, fed by chauvinistic complexes, did not pass swiftly; rather they remained for a long period in the College faculty. Why did the Latin Question occur? Who pushed the question? Recently discovered correspondence of Brother Maurelian, one of the principals in the Latin Question, indicates Battersby's suggestion of "vested interests" was not without foundation, although the French superiors seem to have been responsible for a majority of the agitation. If it is difficult to establish precise reasons and causes for these events, it is clear the curriculum at La Salle College suffered a direct hit. The extent of damages and consequences are germane to our story.

The author of the Community history of the Brothers at La Salle in 1899-1900 asserted that the College received a "severe setback" because of the Latin Question. He claimed at least one-third of the normal student body went to other institutions and, as a result, the College began deficit operations. Four laymen were hired to teach the Latin and Greek programs while they were being phased out. However, when the writer indicated one-third of the student body left, he failed to indicate the majority of these were from the preparatory or high school department, while less than six students left the collegiate department during the first year of restriction.

The college curriculum was quickly altered to meet the proscription on Latin. A new emphasis was put on the development of "literary culture" by extensive study of English and modern languages. Scientific and mathematical studies were not changed, and training in commercial subjects was still available. In general, the classics were replaced by modern languages. Other than that, the curriculum remained unchanged.[9] When the first group of students graduated from La Salle College without training in the classics in 1904, there were some misgivings among the College administration as to the effectiveness of their degree. These doubts were dispelled when William Draper Lewis, Dean, School of Law, University of Pennsylvania wrote "I therefore reply that a student who has had no Latin or Greek may enter the University as a graduate student and proceed to the degree of M.A. or Ph.D." Again, in 1909, the State Board of New Jersey approved the course of study at La Salle, making it possible for graduates to obtain certificates to practice law or medicine there, this in spite of the lack of Latin in the program.[10] Evidently the immediate effects of the Latin Question on the collegiate department were not overpowering. In his annual reports, however, the President continued to mention the loss of students due to the problem; but one must remember he spoke collectively of all departments. Nonetheless, the resentment, anger, and disillusionment caused by the Latin Question remained for a long time. Still, it did not discourage the College from expanding its curriculum.

In the scholastic year 1902-1903, a new grading system was introduced. Reports were issued quarterly and were based on written examinations. A grade between 90 and 100 was considered "excellent"; 75 to 90 was "very good"; 60 to 75 labeled "satisfactory"; while grades below sixty were deficient. Further, the B.Sc. and M.A. programs were introduced. Those who successfully completed the course in chemistry and electricity earned the B.Sc. degree. Graduates of the College could earn the M.A. by matriculating in a "learned profession," or by following graduate courses at the College, or by giving evidence of achievement in some branch of "letters or science." In all cases, the degree candidate had to complete a thesis on a given topic. In the same year, a new course in Civil Engineering was introduced. The *Bulletin* listed an almost unbelievable number of engineering courses. Arrangements were made to take a majority of the courses listed off campus. La Salle College was not equipped at the time to provide such instruction.[11] Further, very few men availed themselves of the engineering course. The establishment of the program was an unsuccessful attempt to win back students lost by the dropping of classics. Since that scheme did not work, in 1906 the College made special arrangements for those who wished to study Latin: "a kind of bridging over in hopes of a return to the old time conditions." In spite of the difficult times the College was passing through, academic standards were maintained. No one was graduated from the Collegiate department in 1908 "because we insisted on the Catalogue requirements."[12] The College was maturing.

La Salle College was fortunate in having presidents of high calibre during its period of maturation. Between 1885 and 1911, La Salle had six presidents, one of whom served two non-consecutive terms. Brothers Isidore and Abdas served during twenty years of the twenty-six year period. The former was president of the College longer than any president to date. In 1885, while La Salle was still in a period of great flux, Brother Fabrician was appointed President. He remained president for only two years. This noted philosophy teacher was once publicly praised by Cardinal Hayes, a former pupil. W. Howard Haynes, a Protestant acquaintance, wrote in *The Baltimore Sun* of Brother Fabrician: "Love of America was one of Fabrician's outstanding qualities. The Cardinal Gibbons tradition of great patriotism and great comradeship toward all men was the very cornerstone of his attitude toward life."

Brother Fabrician's successor as president was Brother Isidore, who served his first term between 1887 and 1889. In 1890 he was again appointed President and served for a decade in that capacity until his retirement in 1900. His long term brought a long-sought-for stability to the College. Unfortunately, the provisions of lengthy terms for the presidents of the College was not maintained. Brother

Isidore had charge of the physics and chemistry departments when the College was at Filbert Street. During Brother Romuald's presidency, Brother Isidore had also served as Treasurer. When appointed President in 1887, he continued as professor of science. He had great influence on educational work in Philadelphia and frequently worked hand in hand for the cause of higher education with his intimate friend, Dr. Russell Conwell, founder of Temple University.[13]

Between Brother Isidore's two terms, Brother Abraham served for one year as president. For forty years he had taught at Rock Hill College and was President there for several years. This very able teacher of mathematics, physics, chemistry, and philosophy had to resign his office as President of La Salle after one year because of poor health. Brother Isidore returned for ten years and was followed into office by Brother Wolfred for a three-year term.

A member of the Canadian Province, Brother Wolfred first came to La Salle for two years in 1886. Returning in 1890, he taught English for a decade and then became President. While in office, he took his Ph.D. at Harvard University. Today it would be considered rather strange to have a Canadian Brother as President. One likewise wonders just how much administration was accomplished while the President attended Harvard. Perhaps this partially explains a relative period of calm in the College history.

Following Brother Wolfred, Brother Abdas served a seven-year, uneventful term as president. This president had a tremendous knowledge of history and literature and had been a very successful teacher at Calvert Hall, St. John's, and Rock Hill College. His affable and humorous nature won him many friends. If there were any major changes during his administration, he was quite successful in concealing them from posterity. Further, in the case of both Brothers Wolfred and Abdas, it is unfortunate that contemporary accounts of their administration are not extant. Considering the times, it is understandable that nothing sensational happened at the College. On the other hand, the fact that the College survived is evidence enough of competence on the part of these two men.

Some important changes in the organizational structure of the College corporation were made in 1897. A constitutional change making "the Director of the Community of the Brothers of the Christian Schools" the Chairman of the Board of Managers was approved. Due to a change in the By-Laws, the College President could be elected Treasurer of the Corporation. This latter change helped to facilitate fiscal operations and remains in effect today.[14]

Generally speaking, despite the Latin Question the student body of the College during these years averaged around fifty. In overall numbers, 289 students in 1887 proved to be the highest number of students to that date in La Salle, but these figures represent three departments of the College and likewise reflect the increase of space available in the new building. June, 1896, saw the largest number of college graduates to that date — ten. These figures do not vary much throughout the first decade of the 20th century. In 1905, four B.A.'s and one commercial diploma were granted, while two years later there were only two degrees granted, one in engineering. Six M.A.'s, two B.A.'s, and five commercial diplomas were awarded in 1910. Students at the College received what was tantamount to individual instruction at this time and, as a result, indications are of high academic achievement. Students in 1892 who transferred to local universities were admitted to higher grades. Two years later, the President publicly asserted that "none but industrious students are retained." In 1902, it was noted that with registration up twenty percent over the previous year, a much larger proportion of students were drawn from professional classes "and from those whose parents appreciate better the advantages of higher education." All indications are that the College worked to keep an intellectually elite student body.

Correspondingly, the faculty, though small, was top-notch. In 1889, the College faculty consisted of five Brothers. Strangely enough, Brother Julian held the M.D. degree. By 1894, there were twelve Brothers and three laymen on the staff. A. M. Brillon taught

French, while Professor Sprissler taught music, and Professor Funk handled physical education. One of the most brilliant men on the faculty at this time was Brother Firminian Joseph. A graduate of La Salle, he was professor of science and mathematics. His sudden death in the fall of 1902 caused the administration grave anxiety. None of the Brothers was academically qualified to replace him, and two laymen were hired in his place.

When Brother Abdas took over as President in 1903, the faculty was reorganized. It took on a form more comparable to the modern College. Brother Orion, Vice-President, taught philosophy and English; Brother John Evangelist, Dean of Faculty, was manager of athletics; Brother Isidore, past president, was appointed chairman of the science department. The chair of mathematics was filled by Brother Eliphus; and Brother Patrick, formerly Vice-President of St. Thomas College, Scranton, was professor of political economy. Concerning the faculty, the College *Bulletin* for 1902-03 stated: "Their aim is to educate under the most approved modern methods in an environment which insures the safeguards of religion. Their methods of teaching have been successful in all parts of the civilized world." Obviously this was a blurb and referred specifically to the Brothers. For actually, no layman served on the faculty from 1903 through 1905. A sentiment, wholly unacceptable today and questionable even in 1903, voiced by the President to the Board of Managers explained the absence of laymen. "No secular help is employed — this adds to the efficiency of the work and is economical and more satisfactory." Given the long and sustained history of lay and religious cooperation in the history of the College, both before and after this three-year period, Brother Abdas's remark is rather incredible.

A minor, though important, aspect of education at La Salle developed through student activities. Much time and attention was devoted to developing the artistic talents of the students. In 1888, the College held an exhibition of the students' work. *The Catholic Standard* called it one of the best exhibitions in the city. The Dramatics and Literary Association, under the direction of Brother

F. Francis, had over fifty members. They gave several entertainments and dramatic performances throughout the city in such places as the Park Theatre, the South Broad Street Theatre, Chestnut Street Opera House, and the Academy of Music. These players enjoyed a highly creditable reputation and kept the College in the public eye.[15]

With the construction and opening of Carlisle Hall gymnasium, athletic activity increased at the College. However, it was kept under rigid control and, for the most part, consisted of gymnastics under careful supervision. The physical development of the individual student was the main concern, and intercollegiate activities were frowned upon. Such was the case when the first La Salle football team was organized in 1893. St. Joseph's College students challenged La Salle students to a football game. Brother Isidore, President, refused to approve the notion and said he would expel anyone who dared break his orders. Nevertheless, the challenge was accepted, the game played in November, 1893, and La Salle won 7-0. The next day half the participants stayed out of school, fearing Brother Isidore's threat. Actually, no one was expelled, and there seemed to have been general rejoicing among students and faculty, which leads one to believe Brother President was quite adept in the art of negative suggestion.

Still, school teams were not formed immediately. Frank Matthews, '97, writes that "a regular Athletic Director" had been appointed. Regular exercises plus instruction in various sports were given, but "we never had a football team and there were no competitive sports with other colleges." However, around 1896, an athletic organization was formed at La Salle which had over 200 members, including graduates. From this organized source came a good deal of pressure for an intercollegiate sports program. As a result, in 1899 the College officially sponsored an Athletic Association to represent the College in sports. It seems almost prophetical that the first intercollegiate sport organized at La Salle was basketball. Joseph McHugh was the (first) captain. In 1901 and 1902, La Salle College had championship teams. But for some unknown reasons, organized basketball disappeared from the College until 1930.

There is evidence also that the College fielded a baseball team from 1901 through 1903. Of this group, there is little information. Between 1910 and 1930, when the College again started intercollegiate basketball under captain Ted Praiss, Philadelphia newspapers carried notices of basketball and football teams at La Salle College. These teams actually represented the preparatory department. Even after La Salle College officially fielded a football team, many sports writers failed to distinguish between preparatory and college teams.

Gymnastics thus remained the order of the day at La Salle. In 1906, an exhibition, given during the annual elocution contest, included pole climbing, parallel bars, wand drills, foot calisthenics, and "chicken fight." With increased interest and participation in athletics, a noticeable concern was voiced in the annual reports to the Board of Managers. The general tone of these notices was that studies take precedence over athletics, which were not permitted to interfere with school work. "Championship athletics and championship studies can not go together in a day school."[16]

Alumni activities were also becoming more and more evident. In 1889, a series of organizational meetings were held to set up a formal Alumni Society. All men who attended professional school without receiving a La Salle degree were invited to join. In all, former students numbered about two thousand, the greater majority having left the College before earning a degree. By January, 1890, the alumni was organized and officers were elected. In June, 1892, on graduation day, the alumni held their first annual banquet in the College gym with over 200 attending. It was nearly midnight before the speeches, of which there were several, began. In just a few years, the annual banquet was changed to a winter date. In 1894, at the suggestion of Brother Isidore, President of the College, a continuing education lecture series was inaugurated for the alumni. The lectures, given monthly on Friday nights during the winter months, were well attended and proved highly successful.

Other facilities were made available to the alumni. In 1901, lights were installed in the gymnasium "so that members of the alumni given to athletics could meet there several nights a week." In general, during the early decades of the 20th century, the alumni remained well organized and very close to the College. That the College appreciated their interest was evidenced at the Annual Commencement in 1909, when thirty-five alumni were given honorary Master of Arts degrees. Many of these men continued to sustain the interests of the College at the cost of great personal, fiscal sacrifice on their own.

A false sense of financial stability seemed to pervade the College shortly after the opening of 1240. In 1888, the President reported the College in "good financial condition" with a debt of $5,000 and $3,000 in taxes. The latter was eventually successfully contested in the courts, and this seemed to add to a sense of fiscal complacency. Again in 1891, the President reported a mortgage of $5,000 while, at the same time, indicating that attendance dropped slightly with "the opening of the High School and Free College of the Jesuit Fathers." This new college was located at 17th and Stiles Streets and practically adjacent to the La Salle campus. It was at this time that the administration demonstrated fiscal shortsightedness. Perfectly capable of carrying the $5,000 debt, every possible effort was made to erase the obligation. Instead of investing annual income, it went into the debt payments and never worked for interest to benefit the College. By October, 1893, the College was entirely out of debt, and it took only one short year for the administration to realize its mistake. Reporting to the Board of Managers in 1894, the President indicated that although the College was out of debt, the annual income was insufficient for operating and improvement expenses. The latter were constantly needed to keep the old Mansion in repair. As a result, nothing was done in repairs, and all surplus money saved. By 1895, the College announced savings of $5,000 and a treasury of $6,000 by 1896. But, by 1896, over $10,000 was needed for repairs. Now the College had to go back into debt for $10,000 at five percent interest.

In 1895, the College was offered $175,000 for the entire campus by their next-door neighbor. The Brothers expressed interest in the offer, especially if a new site were available. The prospective buyer, Robert Foederer, had a good piece of land at 13th and Thompson Streets. Since he refused the College's offer of $70,000 for the site, the College refused to sell 1240. From the outset of negotiations, the Brothers realized they were being offered a bargain and played Foederer's game. Subsequent events proved that La Salle College at 13th and Thompson Streets would have faced eventual obliteration.[17]

The College, already burdened with a $10,000 mortgage, saw its fiscal problems increase. In 1898, with the mortgage due in one year, the College had no funds. Many students had defaulted on their tuition payments. The mortgage had to be renegotiated and money remained scarce at the College. Some relief was had in 1902, when, for the first time in its history, the College raised its tuition from $80 per year to $100 per year. Things improved slightly.

In 1905, Archbishop Ryan suggested that a yearly statement of "Resources and Liabilities" be made available to the Board in order to acquaint the members with the actual fiscal status of the College. It was obvious the Archbishop was embarrassed by the financial condition of the College, and he realized that, in the long run, fiscal responsibility of the corporation was the obligation of the Board. Therefore, since 1906, yearly financial statements have been presented to the Board and a more orderly picture of corporate finance developed at La Salle. However, mere improvements in bookkeeping did not solve the College deficit. By 1908, revenue from the major source of income at the College, annual tuition, increased notably due to an increased enrollment. Annual total income in 1908 proved to be $11,226, an amount that would just about pay one professor's salary sixty years later. But the amount at the time was enough. The College would be saved from receivership proceedings. The corporation would get by. This seemed to be the prevailing attitude at the time.

It is difficult to say what the basis for this feeling was. Perhaps the Latin Question, admittedly a source of discouragement, was having its effect. True, because of the cutback in the curriculum, it proved more and more difficult to secure students each year. Again, the times in the United States were rather ordinary. Things economic, political, social, and religious just seemed to tread water throughout the nation. There seemed to be little enthusiasm or creativity among the people. That this spirit rubbed off on the College is not surprising. Every people is a product of its time. Just as the world and our nation were jolted to reality by the Moroccan crisis and the Balkan crisis, so too La Salle College needed a jolt to bring it around to a more creative and active life. It was not a series of circumstances that rocked La Salle back to reality. It was a man, Brother Denis Edward, appointed President in 1911.

4. *An Encounter with Reality*

As the second decade of the 20th century dawned, master plans were being implemented throughout the whole world, some sinister, others good and productive. Europe was tense and apprehensive, while the United States was determined to ignore Europe's fears. The creed of the American entrepreneur was business as usual with no involvement with world conflict. However, most men realized that the latter notions were impractical and that, in fact, the United States might well become involved. True, because of increased demands of European markets for heavy manufactured goods, American business improved, but all realized the risks were greater and the conflict inevitable. But to stand still would have been disastrous. Therefore, the American people planned for the future with one eye on the United States and the other on Europe.

In 1911, it seemed to the new College President, Brother Denis Edward, that La Salle had been standing still. With a look to the future, a future he was to know for an unusually long period of time, Brother Edward exploded into action with innumerable and grandiose plans for the College. Here was a man of talent, energy,

zeal, a deep love of God and his fellowmen. It was this latter sentiment that inspired his actions at La Salle. The College owed the
best possible education available to its students. Nothing short of
a high professional ideal was acceptable in Brother Edward's eyes.
He inspired others to self-development by his own professional attitude. Despite the many administrative posts he had been called to
fill as a young Christian Brother, he had never allowed these onerous
duties to distract him from his own intellectual development.
Brother Edward was fifty-seven years old when after many years
of parttime work and delays he earned his doctorate at Fordham
University. This, in itself, indicates the type of President he was.
His presidency will always remain as a challenge to all future presidents, while his professionalism, industry, and idealism provide
excellent goals for future administrators and faculty alike, both
religious and lay. Despite what seemed to be overwhelming odds,
his plans for La Salle's future were multiple, professional, visionary,
and ideal.

From the beginning of his term as President, Brother Edward
was dissatisfied with the physical conditions and equipment of the
College. Thus, in his first year, he undertook several programs of
renovation. The entire first floor of the College building was taken
over by the science department. A lecture room, physics laboratory,
and chemistry laboratory, the latter complemented with the best
equipment available, were installed. Projection-lantern apparatus
was secured as well as new blackboards, student chairs, and other
furnishings. Finally, a new drawing room was installed. The entire exterior and interior of the Mansion were renovated; improvements included new frescoes in the chapel, improved and enlarged
toilet facilities, modernization of the library and administrative
offices, and the installation of electricity in both the Mansion and
South Wing.[1]

Despite all the renovations, the College would have remained
relatively the same. However, this was not the mind of Brother
Edward. His vision was a modern college, capable of educating all
the worthy students who applied. La Salle had to expand. It was

not large enough. The matter was presented to the Board of Managers: ". . . if the College is to keep abreast of the times, it is necessary to have more buildings and modern equipment in order that it may attract students who might otherwise be led to non-Catholic institutions." After a rather heated discussion, the President was directed to submit his plans for expansion.

In one year, Brother Edward's plans were completed. It was an ambitious scheme which called for two new buildings, estimated to cost about $100,000. Part of the money was needed for additional land. The project was to purchase land in the immediate vicinity of Broad and Stiles Streets. However, the overall cost was astronomical and completely out of the question. Was the President really serious in submitting such plans? Yes, in the sense that he drew up parallel requirements for what he saw as the future of the College. Although the Board was unwilling even to consider the plans, a reaction Brother Edward expected, he was directed to submit a new set, one which would be more economically feasible. The second plans called for construction of a north wing along with the enlargement of South Wing. The new North Wing was to have a student chapel, a larger science department, and several lecture rooms. Still, the cost of such an addition was much more than the funds available to the College. Knowing this, Brother Edward submitted a fund-raising plan along with the building plan. The alumni would be asked to manage the campaign. Final approval of the venture was given by the Board of Managers. Brother Edward swung into action and the campaign was under way. In the 1915 *Annual Report,* published edition, he wrote, "It will be noticed that all of these documents insist on the inadequacy of the accommodations furnished by the building as it now stands. Therefore attention is urgently directed to the work . . . namely, that of collecting a fund for the erection of a new wing." In the meantime, as the campaign progressed, architects prepared blueprints. Unfortunately, these were never realized. A disappointing total of $4,532 was collected in the drive. This was hardly enough to pay architects' fees and, as a result, not one spade of earth was ever turned for North Wing.[2] This was a great disappointment to Brother Edward, but he continued to work energetically with what he had. New buildings were not absolutely necessary to develop the academic atmosphere, and this latter he worked on with a vengeance. However, only many decades later did he, as President Emeritus, see La Salle become a multimillion dollar, multicampus, academically respected institution.

Ever alert to the changing times in higher education, Brother Edward, in his first encounter with the Board of Managers, reminded them of the necessity of improving instruction in chemistry and physics at the College. He felt the Council of Universities and Colleges would require higher standards in the future and he wanted La Salle to be found up-to-date. It was through this same University and College Council that Brother Edward sought accreditation for La Salle College. La Salle was allowed to apply for recognition under a clause which required member colleges and universities to have had assets valued at $100,000 in 1895. This requirement La Salle readily fulfilled. However, during the negotiations, Brother Edward introduced the question whether or not students from St. Thomas College, Scranton, who did their college work at St. Thomas College, could have degrees conferred on them by La Salle College. Apparently, this had been done in June, 1911, and Brother Edward questioned the propriety of the action. He pointed out that St. Thomas College did not have the property qualification to obtain a charter, but that St. Thomas College, as La Salle College, adhered to the College Entrance Examination Board standards for admission. Unfortunately, during the negotiations for accreditation and the St. Thomas College question, Brother Edward misinterpreted a casual remark of a member of the University Council. Brother Edward understood Dr. Brumbaugh, Secretary of the University Council, to say that there was no objection to St. Thomas' students graduating from La Salle. When Brother Edward repeated this to another member of the Council, Doctor Brumbaugh became incensed and demanded a thorough investigation of La Salle. Mr. William F. Harrity, a graduate of La Salle and close friend of Dr. Brumbaugh, was able to explain the misunderstanding. What Dr. Brumbaugh originally implied was that St. Thomas' students could be graduated from La Salle, but only after a year's residence at La Salle. Finally, the air was cleared and, on April 18, 1912, the College, along with the preparatory department, was accredited by the University and College Council. All degrees given by La Salle were accepted by the Commonwealth of Pennsylvania.[3] During the spring and summer, a committee headed by Brother Edward revamped and extended the entire curriculum. Further, admission standards were updated. These changes appeared in the College *Bulletin* for 1912-13. Students who applied for admission to La Salle College were required to score favorably on the College Entrance Examination Board tests, or to pass examinations prepared by the College, or both. "Clear and idiomatic English is expected in all examination papers . . . however accurate in subject matter, no paper will be considered satisfactory if seriously defective in punctuation, spelling, or other essentials of good usage."

In explaining the curriculum, the *Bulletin,* for the first time, contained the traditional format found in College bulletins today. Since the Latin restriction was still in effect, what had been known as the classical course, leading to the B.A. degree, was now called the "Arts Department." At the same time, each area of study was developed into departments as we presently understand this term. A new branch of study was inaugurated with the creation of the "Civil Engineering Department." Students following this course had a prescribed program of study in each year; and, in contrast to courses formerly offered in engineering, all lectures took place on campus. In all departments of instruction, many new courses were offered. We mention only two departments as examples. In English, such courses as Anglo-Saxon literature, poetics, philosophy of literature, principles of literary criticism, and literature of the drama were introduced. In history, the philosophy of history, constitution making, constitutional history of the U. S., Europe in the 19th century, French history to 1789, and religious revolt in

16th century Germany were added. In both departments, the
new offerings provided a more-than-adequate undergraduate training when combined with courses already offered. Further, all courses
were now numbered.

Freshmen and sophomores matriculating in the "Arts Department" had to follow a rather rigid core curriculum. In the first
year, French, German, and English were given four hours a week.
History, physics, physics lab, chemistry, and christian doctrine each
consumed two hours a week, while mathematics and chemistry lab
were given three hours a week. With one hour of elocution rounding
out the program, the men were carrying thirty hours. Sophomores
were required to take five hours of English a week, four hours of
French and German, three hours of history and mathematics, two
hours of geology and christian doctrine with one hour of elocution.
This schedule of twenty-four hours, even though a bit heavy by
today's standard, seems a bit more realistic. With such a heavy
load of courses, one is not surprised to find few survivors at the end
of four years. However, things got worse in the junior year. Thirteen hours of English and modern languages were required, along
with two hours of christian doctrine. In addition, six hours of
physics, four of philosophy, two astronomy, and one oratory were
required for a total of twenty-eight hours. Electives in biology,
Church history, and American political institutions were available.
Twenty-five hours were required of seniors with electives in American history, biology, principles of government, sociology, public
finance, and representative government available. In view of the
rather formidable requirements each year, it would seem that the
notion of allowing students electives was not wholly acceptable at
that time.

In the "Department of Civil Engineering," entrance requirements were the same as those of the "Arts Department." Although
the prescribed curriculum required as heavy a class-hour schedule
as that in the "Arts Department," there was a wide variety of
courses. This was necessarily the case since the course comprised
surveying, road and railroad engineering, bridge engineering, hy-

draulics and water works, and reinforced concrete construction. Studies were of both a theoretical and practical nature, and much of the lecture work was supplemented by field work. One summer of study was required for a period of four weeks. Those men who successfully completed the course were granted the degree of Bachelor of Science in Civil Engineering.[4]

Further additions were made to the curriculum in 1914. The Bureau of Medical Education and Licensure of Pennsylvania laid down new requirements for admission to medical schools. In addition to a "standard four-year high school course," applicants for medical school had to have "not less than one year of College credits in chemistry, biology, physics, and a modern language other than the English language." Save for the biology requirement, La Salle students qualified after their first year. In order to fulfill the requirements satisfactorily, a new curriculum was established for premedical students which included biology. In addition, to be more than able to meet the state requirements, a biology department was established. Hence, the more industrious premed student could receive advanced training in biology.[5] Since there were premed students who wanted to study Spanish rather than French or German and since provisions for Spanish were lacking, Brother Edward, in 1914, obtained two Brothers from Mexico to teach Spanish. It might seem that the College more than extended itself to provide for students in the premedical course at that time. This is true, and in view of the Latin restriction and the new State requirements, the College found itself well adapted to the needs of this type of student and made every effort to have these men take at least one year's training at La Salle. Tuition was still the major source of income at the College and every new student helped sustain the corporation. Perhaps the sophisticated might consider such motives unworthy, but, in the long run, a tradition was started which enables La Salle College today to enjoy the reputation of one of the best undergraduate premedical departments in the country.

When the new State requirements were listed, some controversy developed over the concept of Christian education vis-à-vis preparation for medicine and other sciences. Not one to retreat from a good intellectual argument, Brother Edward defended the role of Christian education in the teaching of science. He publicly stated that Catholic colleges that are functioning as they should, would "do well to give youth the opportunity to study biology, chemistry, history, and philosophy, surrounded by Christian influences." In view of conditions in institutions of higher learning at the time, and from a Christian viewpoint, the arguments for Catholic institutions of higher learning were unaswerable in Brother Edward's mind. Further, he compared chemistry taught at La Salle College with chemistry taught elsewhere. He found two distinctions. The first was the individual attention given to each student because of the small classes. This hardly seemed germane to the argument, but he made his point. Secondly, he spoke of attitude. "The attitude assumed toward chemistry is Christian as well as scientific. This is extremely important in view of the fact that scientific materialism is notoriously prevalent in most of our higher educational institutions."[6]

Curriculum at La Salle College remained one of Brother Edward's major concerns. His influence is seen in the College *Bulletin* for 1917-18. Due to an "increasing demand for chemists and chemical engineers," a full four-year course was established in the Chemistry Department which led to the degrees of Bachelor of Science in Chemistry and Bachelor of Science in Chemical Engineering. At the same time, since most medical schools were now requiring two years of college training, the premedical program was expanded with relative ease. The foresight in establishing the Biology Department a few years earlier enabled the College to incorporate the new program with little change in personnel or equipment. Therefore, when Brother Edward stepped out of office in 1917, the curriculum was well established and equal to that of most equivalent institutions of higher learning. The classics were still missing, but every opportunity had been taken to make their absence felt less and less and to give La Salle College a curriculum capable of producing well-educated, highly-trained students in many academic areas.

When Brother Edward took over as President of La Salle, there were 145 students in the entire school. Only two Bachelor's degrees had been conferred in June of 1911. As a result, every possible means was taken to increase the student body in all areas of the College. Brother Edward inaugurated a group of fairly successful, high-pressure public relations men on the faculty who were known as the "Flying Squadron." Their objectives were to secure students for La Salle and make the College known. Further, in 1914, La Salle College founded six scholarships for graduates of Roman Catholic High School. The individual scholarship holder was entitled to the full four-year course in either Arts or Engineering. After the first six scholarships were awarded, a terse resolution of the Board of Managers put an end to the grants. No indication whatsoever was given as to the reason. However, the fact that three competitive scholarships, granted annually, were founded at the same meeting, would indicate that the administrators were not satisfied with the academic qualifications of the original scholarship holders. Despite valiant efforts, student population on the collegiate level did not improve. During Brother Edward's last year in office, the total school population was 227. Only eighteen of these followed college courses, while 114 studied in the high school, and thirty-seven attended primary classes. The "School of Commerce," formerly called the "Commercial Department," which did not operate on the college level, had fifty-eight students.[7]

Numerically, the faculty remained quite small. This did not prevent Brother Edward from upgrading the faculty. He sent many of the Brothers to study at the University of Pennsylvania. Dr. Henry Strecker, Rev. Edward J. Curran, and Francis Shields were added to the faculty in 1912. Dr. Strecker taught physiology; Father Curran lectured in logic and metaphysics, while Mr. Shields taught business law. In 1914, the Reverend Dr. Corrigan lectured weekly in sociology. In developing extension courses, Brother Edward was concerned with the scholastic training of Brothers teaching in the parochial schools of Philadelphia. He provided professors to give them courses on week-day afternoons, evenings, and Saturdays. By 1917, there were fourteen Brothers and six laymen on the faculty. One of the latter was an ex-Army officer who conducted military drill, another innovation by Brother Edward. Actually, by this time there was a virtual balance between Brothers and laymen teaching in the college department, since eight Brothers were teaching in the secondary and primary areas.[8] This ratio was something new to La Salle.

Several other innovations were implemented during Brother Edward's administration. An active athletic association was organized and represented the College in basketball and track, producing championships in basketball in 1916-1917. Since graduates were actively involved in these events, they cannot strictly be classified as intercollegiate athletics. The alumni became fairly active in its financial support of the school. The Committee of Fifteen, composed of ten alumni and five prominent Philadelphians, was organized to raise funds for the College. Shortly thereafter, the money market began to falter and the Committee hesitated to take action. Unfortunately, little came of this enterprise. In 1916, upon the urging of Brother Edward, the Alumni Association applied for and received a charter for the organization. The charter, recorded on September 5, 1916, stated the purposes of the organization to be these: cultivation of brotherhood among matriculants and graduates of La Salle, fostering the general welfare of the College, and advancing the cause of higher education. In 1917, the first alumni magazine, entitled *The Budget,* appeared. This four-page monthly reported college activities and the whereabouts and interests of the graduates.

Several religious activities were initiated by Brother Edward. He organized the League of the Sacred Heart, introduced First Friday devotions, established Lenten devotions, and restructured the annual student retreat. His filial devotion to St. La Salle, patron of the College, led Brother to lecture extensively throughout the city on the work of St. La Salle in education. He even made arrangements to speak to students in the Education Department of the University of Pennsylvania, a task not for the timid when one considers the times.

In the spring of 1913, La Salle College paused shortly to celebrate the Golden Jubilee year of the granting of its charter. Archbishop Edmond F. Prendergast, Honorary Chairman of the Board of Managers, urged the College to commemorate fifty years of higher education with all the splendor and magnificence possible. On April 10, the celebrations were fittingly opened with a solemn pontifical Mass celebrated by the Archbishop in the Cathedral of SS. Peter and Paul. The historic old edifice was filled to overflowing by students, alumni, friends, and well-wishers. Present in the sanctuary were many members of the clergy who were graduates of La Salle. Many of these held important positions in the diocese of Philadelphia, such as Auxiliary Bishop of Philadelphia, Vicar General of the diocese, a Vicar Forane, and the Rector of the diocesan seminary. A masterly sermon, outlining the educational contributions of St. de La Salle and referring to the activities of La Salle College over fifty years, was given by the Rt. Rev. Monsignor Philip R. McDevitt, Superintendent of Schools. In his closing remarks, he established a high ideal for La Salle College in its next fifty years: "May this school today . . . take up with renewed strength and enthusiasm the noble mission to which it is dedicated." Further, he prayed that the future years would witness La Salle College taking its place among the foremost colleges in the United States.

That same evening, a banquet was held in the Bellevue-Stratford Hotel. Over three hundred guests dined amidst the splendor of the main ballroom, tastefully decorated with American flags, topped with a large sign in electric lights, reading "La Salle 1863-1913." The Archbishop occupied the place of honor at the head table. Over his place the Papal flag was hung with the Irish flag on the opposite wall. At the end of the meal, Brother Edward was asked to speak. In his opening remarks, he thanked the Archbishop for the encouragement he had given him as President. He then stated he knew few details about the early history of the College. For those who wanted to know what the College had accomplished throughout its history, he bade them look over the assembly where they would find hundreds of men prominent in both the Church and State who were trained at the "old" La Salle. As for the "new" La Salle, Brother Edward reminded the audience of Monsignor McDevitt's ideal, given in the sermon that morning and stated that "every Christian Brother who is true to his cloth should endeavor to attain that ideal."

The final commemorative gathering took place on Thursday evening, April 11, at the Metropolitan Opera House. The program consisted of speeches and a concert. The main speakers for the evening were the Honorable Joseph E. Ransdall, Senator from Louisiana, one of the great intellects in Congress at the time; Dr. James J. Walsh, outstanding research scientist; and the Rev. Hugh T. Henry, professor at The Catholic University of America and alumnus of the College. In his concluding remarks, Dr. Henry spoke of La Salle's past efficiency and present progressiveness and predicted the College "is surely destined to attain broader horizons of beneficent work in the future." Again, Brother Edward was called upon by the master of ceremonies, Joseph P. Gaffney, President of the Alumni, to conclude the festivities. In a very few words, Brother Edward thanked all who had contributed to make the celebration a success. But his remarks seemed to have a sense of urgency about them; something still had to be accomplished. All present felt Brother Edward was preoccupied with future plans, and all were confident a greater La Salle would celebrate one hundred years of Christian education.

In a short time, Brother Edward accomplished much. Yet, he did not have great fiscal resources with which to work. By 1915, necessary improvements took the College into $3,000 debt. The nation's economy at the time was halting. Investors were eyeing conditions in Europe. Money was scarce. Despite the willing efforts of the alumni, the building fund was a failure. Expenses continued high and income low. Money had to be borrowed from the Provincial treasury of the Brothers. By 1917, the liability of the College grew to $45,000 of which $10,000 represented a mortgage. Fortunately, the remainder was indebtedness to the Christian Brothers. That same year the net income was only $15,406, while disbursements were $7,866 plus $3,200 salaries for lay professors. It was not a bright picture when Brother Edward left office in September 1917. But, debt or not, La Salle College was now worthy of the name.

Now, however, the best-laid plans of Brother Edward were to be destroyed in the fruition of plans laid by his European contemporaries. World War I was on, and the United States became involved. Higher education suffered throughout the country, and La Salle College was no exception. As events in Europe moved to a climax in active hostilities, the United States, under the leadership of Woodrow Wilson, took the position of campaigners for peace. No doubt Wilson's efforts at peace were sincere, even though there were those of his house who worked to destroy his efforts. Yet, despite the prestige and efforts put forth, peace was not forthcoming. However, most people in the United States continued to hold with Wilson's ideal of "watchful waiting." In most cases, there was more waiting than watchfulness.

The entrance of the United States into the war found Americans in an unbelievable state of unpreparedness. But in a short time a massive effort was underway to put an American force in Europe as soon as possible. Naturally, the youth of the nation were to make up the bulk of this force; and educational institutions totally unprepared for the crisis found their student bodies decimated. Would that this had been the case at La Salle College; a mere decimation of students would have been welcomed. As things turned out, by the fall of 1918 the draft and volunteer enlistments practically closed the College. Most schools were spared the disintegration of their population by the formation of the Student Army Training Corps. The government asked the College to form such a unit, but the College had no housing or mess facilities. Therefore, during the war years, over 100 La Salle students enrolled in S.A.T.C. had to be sent to other institutions.[9]

Midway through the scholastic year 1917-18 conditions at La Salle reached the critical stage. During the Christmas recess 1917, the Brothers administrators of the College held a special meeting to decide how to solve the crisis. Brother Richard, President of La Salle for just four months, said several men had applied for engineering courses to warrant reopening these courses. Brother John felt the courses should not be given unless the financial returns would cover expenses involved. It was finally decided to reopen these college courses after the Christmas holidays even if the collegiate department had to operate at a deficit. The main reason given for this decision was the necessity of offering college courses in order to retain the charter.[10] This proved to be a wise decision; for just eight months later, the College was looking for more space because of an increased student body.

While the college classes were closed during the 1917-1918 scholastic year, the lay faculty along with the Brothers were absorbed into the primary, secondary, and the commercial departments, all of which managed to remain in operation. It was fortunate for the College, however, that the disruptive forces of the war did not last more than two years. With the close of hostilities in Europe, isolationist Americans demanded a return to normalcy. However, things are never normal after a world conflict. Thus, America was caught up in a great postwar boom.

At La Salle College, the effects of postwar rejuvenation of the economy were very definitely felt. By September, 1919, La Salle had the largest total number of students in its history, 320. But, the collegiate department numbered only twenty men, and reports of overcrowded conditions referred to the secondary department. After 1919, the student population of the College continued to increase steadily until the outbreak of World War II. Not once did the college population after 1919 drop below twenty students. By 1921, thirty-five men were following college courses, while thirty-two men were enrolled as special students in the area of education.

The school of commerce also showed an upward trend with a total of seventy-six students in 1921. Further increases in college students were recorded in 1926. By this time, the number of applications to the collegiate department was far too high, considering the space available. Many students seeking admission to the class of 1930 were turned away.[11] There was great significance in the development of student population after 1919. For an institution of higher learning which depended almost entirely on tuition income, student population was a serious concern. When La Salle College found itself in a position of having to turn qualified students away, new impetus was given to future plans.

The immediate problem of educating the increasing student body belonged to an ever-increasing faculty. By 1920, there were twelve fulltime professors in the College. Half of these were laymen, all of whom "had been secured from the University of Pennsylvania." The six Brothers on the faculty in 1920 all had advanced degrees. The President urged all faculty members to become active in educational and civic circles. Further, they were expected to exercise their leadership in the education world and to make contributions to the area of social service. All of this was considered to be part of their work as educators. At the same time, the faculty also made a favorable impression on their students. Francis J. Braceland, '26, one of the nation's outstanding psychiatrists, wrote that as he struggled to get an education on modest means, he was well taken care of at La Salle. "They did everything in their power to get me through. . . . Again I was impressed with the dedication and devotion of the Brothers and with the wisdom of my teachers. . . ." Between 1920 and 1928, the faculty remained fairly stable. When Brother Alfred was appointed President in 1928, the entire religious faculty with the exception of Brother Edward John, Secretary of the College, was changed. No reason or explanation is available for this sweeping change in personnel, obviously a dangerous and unreasonable way of directing a collegiate faculty. Under the new administration, Brother Felix was appointed Dean and Brother Timothy, Treasurer. Brother Gerardian Joseph was appointed Registrar, while at the same time teaching math and physics. He still holds the position of Registrar today (1966). Five other Brothers were added to the College faculty. The lay faculty consisted of Roland Holroyd and James Henry. Roland Holroyd, still actively teaching today, is the Dean of the College Faculty, which numbers over 150 full-time professors. The faculty likewise played an important role in the organization of the College by serving on such groups as the Committee on Admissions, the Committees on Degrees, and the Committee on College Activities, all of which had been formed in 1927. Early in 1929, Department Chairmen formed themselves into the "Faculty Senate." Brother Felix, Dean, served as President of the Senate, while Brother Gregory Auxilian acted as Secretary. Meetings were held monthly, and discussion usually centered on the development of the aims and objectives of the College and the best ways and means of putting them into practice.[12] In essence, then, the Faculty Senate, established in 1929, seems to have been more of a harbinger of the current Academic Affairs Committee rather than of the current local chapter of the A.A.U.P. Nonetheless, the organization was an indication of an active and interested faculty, a boon to any institution of higher learning. That the faculty was not dormant is witnessed also in the area of the curriculum.

The Civil Engineering program, established during the presidency of Brother Denis Edward, came to fruition at the June graduation in 1918. Four men received the B.S. degree in Civil Engineering. Two others received certificates upon completion of the premedical course. Great emphasis continued to be put on the engineering course. The Latin restrictions were still in effect, and engineering filled a very definite need in the early twenties.

But all was not calm beneath the organizational surface of the College. There was a divided sentiment over the prospects of La Salle's becoming an engineering school. Many men wanted to return to the tradition of the classics and hoped that repeal of the classics ban would soon be forthcoming. Others felt that such would never be the case, and if La Salle were to survive, it must pursue the engineering line. In 1920, two events weakened the latter argument. First, the number of students making application for the engineering course began to fall off. On the other hand, the President reported to the Board of Managers a movement in educational circles for the standardization of all institutions of higher education. Lists were to be prepared of those colleges and universities which met the requirements. Briefly, the standards for accreditation were as follows: all buildings and grounds must be worth $500,000; a minimum endowment of $500,000; approved courses of instruction, including Latin; a minimum of eight professors with advanced academic degrees; standard entrance requirements; and a minimum of 100 students. It was obvious that La Salle College in 1920 did not measure up to the standards, and the President warned the Board that unless the College improved academically, La Salle graduates would not be accepted in graduate and professional schools. "I venture to notify you that unless we secure recognition from the various accrediting associations we may as well give up our charter."[13]

The upshot of the President's warning was a decision to apply for accreditation and see just where the College stood. In the minds of some faculty and administrators, a twofold reply would be had. First, if things were as bad as some feared, then a decision about the charter would have to be faced. Others, hoping to see the engineering curriculum rapped, also favored the test. Everyone was surprised with the results. By the fall of 1921 the College had been refused accreditation, not because of equipment or curricula, but for lack of numbers. The immediate reaction of all concerned was that the numbers problem could be solved easily. But after further consideration, stable minds realized that the proscription of Latin still slowed the progress of the College. Further, engineering was just not the drawing card its backers had expected it to be. Also, to fulfill the minimum number requirement of 100 students, more space would be needed. Therefore, in December, 1921, the Board decided to gradually eliminate the primary grades from the College.

In a very short time, moreover, good news reached La Salle from Europe.

Early in 1923, Brother Philip, Provincial of the New York Province, sent a letter to the Brothers announcing the end of the Latin Question. Although a General Chapter was scheduled for 1923, long before it convened, the Vatican informed the Superior General that it was the personal wish of the Pope that the Brothers in the United States be allowed to teach Latin. The Pope felt the Brothers' schools could make a greater contribution to the Church by teaching young men the classics and thus preparing them for the seminary. No General Chapter would refuse a Pope's request, since it had always been the mind of St. La Salle to have his Institute in complete accord with the wishes of the Holy See. In the words of the Superior General, Brother Allais Charles, "Latin will be voted by the Chapter, and this, thank God, will be the end of the Latin Question. It is settled right now."[14] Immediate preparations were made to place Latin and Greek back in the College curriculum. Books that had been banned for over two decades suddenly appeared in surprising multiplicity. Brothers who had not studied the classics for the same length of time had an amazing burst of recall. It was difficult to realize after the restriction was lifted that such a gap of time had intervened. It certainly was not evident in the faculty or library. By December, 1923, the President reported that since the resumption of teaching of the classics at La Salle, "many who went elsewhere are seeking admission, but we have no room."

The same year that the Latin Question was settled, the predental course was formulated. Applicants for predental study were required to have one year of secondary school physics and trigonometry. The predental course included English composition, American literature, history of English literature, French or German or Latin, physics or social science, mathematics, chemistry, biology, public speaking, and theology. A predental certificate could be secured after one full scholastic year of study.

By 1925, engineering had disappeared from the La Salle scene. Also gone from La Salle College were the primary grades, but the junior and senior high school remained along with a two-year business course. On the collegiate level, the Arts and Sciences course led to the B.A. degree; those following premed and predent programs received certificates after three and one years, respectively. At the same time, a sweeping change took place in entrance requirements. According to the College *Bulletin,* dated 1925-1926, more stringent regulations were in effect governing admissions. A total of fifteen units in college preparatory courses was needed. Of the fifteen, nine were required: three in English, one in algebra, which had to include quadratics, one in history, one in plane geometry, and three in modern language. Likewise, all applicants had to fulfill the requirements of the National Conference on Uniform Entrance Requirements in English.

In 1927, several new degree programs were listed in the College *Bulletin.* The Ph.B. was granted for successful completion of the Arts courses, while the A.B. was awarded upon completion of the Arts and Science course. The B.S. degree in Business Administration was initiated, while a student could earn a B.S. in Education by following a new curriculum in Education. Former students who completed the first year of medical school curricula were likewise awarded a B.S. upon proper application and with a recommendation of the Dean of their respective school. In nearly every department save theology and philosophy, graduate courses were listed and numbered accordingly. Upon completion of fourteen units of graduate work and acceptance of a thesis by the faculty, the A.M. or M.Sc. candidate for the graduate degree could be called upon to defend his thesis or read his thesis at the graduation exercises. Further, it would seem that graduate study and degrees offered were open only to undergraduates from La Salle.[15] There is little indication of how many men availed themselves of graduate opportunity. Judging the times and circumstances of the College, we must conclude very few elected graduate study at La Salle. Further, there is question of how valid a graduate degree issued by La Salle was. No evidence exists to demonstrate that any formal application was made to the State for permission to grant graduate degrees. However, the fact can not be ignored that the concept of graduate study was entertained at the time, even though carelessly. The problem was presented but not solved. In view of the *Wallis* theory on the future condition of the small college, La Salle College today must again examine the question of graduate study, but perhaps in a more circumspect and tidy manner than that employed in 1927.

As the twenties drew to a close, both faculty and administration studied the curriculum in terms of a "new" La Salle. As the new campus was about to become a reality, a point described in greater detail below, Brother Denis Edward, President Emeritus, proposed an entirely revised curriculum for La Salle, the main purpose of which was to develop an intense college life. Copies of the proposed curriculum were submitted to the departments of education at The Catholic University and New York University and to many individual educators. It was highly praised and suggested that every effort be made to put it into operation. If this were done, one authority stated, the "scheme would place La Salle in a unique position among the colleges in America."[16] However, this plan would evolve in the thirties; some further developments of the twenties should be described.

One of the pleasures of postwar La Salle was an excellent spirit evidenced among the students, which displayed itself in an atmosphere of intellectual and social activity. Aside from the class lectures, La Salle, in the twenties, seemed to be a hotbed of student discussions. Oratorical and elocution contests were the order of the day. Visits to industrial plants and museums became more frequent. All of this activity of the mind led to an increased use of the library. Socially, the students engaged in a variety of athletic contests, class banquets, and class picnics. All of these affairs seemed to remain stag occasions; there was little evidence of female activity on campus or at College activities. Religious activities continued apace on campus, highlighted each year by the annual student retreat held during Holy Week, an activity which the students looked forward to with great anticipation.

The Alumni Association remained strong and loyal during the twenties. Perhaps the man elected President of the Alumni several times in the twenties exemplifies the spirit of the Alumni at the time. J. Burrwood Daly, '90, lawyer, statesman, and ardent devotee of La Salle College, is indicative of the Alumni loyalty to La Salle. Not only did Mr. Daly handle hundreds of legal items for the College, as will be seen below, but he likewise took an active interest in every activity at La Salle, even to the extent of purchasing out of his own pocket monogrammed sweaters for one of the successful athletic teams. Mr. Daly's work for and relations with La Salle College is a story in itself. In view of his tremendous efforts on the part of La Salle, one might justifiably wonder whether or not the College would have been sustained without his help. With alumni such as J. Burrwood Daly it is understandable that the College administration undertook the establishment of a new campus with little or no financial wealth, but with faith in God.

At the conclusion of the War, despite the increase in student population, the financial picture of the College was never too bright. In 1918, the total liability was $47,144, of which $37,000 was owed to the Province with no interest charged. Salary for the laymen was only $720 per year. The $10,000 mortgage continued to haunt the President until 1919, when $3,000 was paid on it. However, the total receipts climbed to $17,824, the highest in College history and by the following year had jumped to $25,900. As a result, the mortgage was completely paid off, but the indebtedness to the Brothers was still $37,500. This same year, because of the decision to apply for accreditation as mentioned below, the total resources of the College were examined and estimated to be $558,000. The breakdown was as follows: ground, $300,000; buildings, $200,000; equipment, $50,000; and building fund, $8,000. This latter was in the form of nonnegotiable bonds. Later, these estimates proved to be overly generous. In 1923, the financial condition improved somewhat when the College tuition was raised to $200 per year

and special fees charged for the first time: $20, lab fee for science
students; $10, Athletic Association fee; and $20, graduation fee.[17]
In 1925, the College was informed of a further bequest from the
estate of Francis A. Drexel. Cardinal Dougherty suggested that
Daniel C. Donoghue, Archdiocesan attorney, represent La Salle as
well as all other Catholic institutions involved. There was nothing
the President could do but agree to the arrangement. In view of
this bequest and in view of the prosperous condition of the economy,
hopes for a new campus seemed to get brighter. For several years,
the space situation at La Salle had deteriorated to an intolerable
level.

Brother Richard, President 1917-1922, worked hard to carry on
the programs established by Brother Denis Edward. But at every
turn Brother Richard was confronted with the space problem. In
1920, he reported "our material equipment, library, classrooms,
assembly room and even laboratories are not up to the minimum."
Again, in 1922, he "deplored the lack of adequate classroom facilities, the crying need for a gymnasium and athletic field." Brother
Richard's successor, Brother Lucian, President 1922-25, reported
to the Board of Managers in 1923 that the lack of facilities was so
acute that "we are unable to develop our College Department."
Just what were the overcrowded conditions these men talked of?
An appraisal of the total campus made in 1923 gives a clear picture
of the space problem. The Administration Building, the Bouvier
Mansion, contained the President's Office, the School Office, reception room, and chapel on the first floor. The library, three bedrooms, and lavatory made up the second floor. On the third floor,
there were eight small classrooms and a lavatory. Two classrooms
were used as bedrooms at night. The basement housed pantry,
kitchen, dining room, school lunch room, bookstore, and help's
quarters. All four floors of South Wing housed a total of nine classrooms and two laboratory-lecture rooms. The basement contained
an additional laboratory, plus locker and storage rooms. Carlisle
Hall consisted of one large, open hall containing a variety of athletic
equipment.[18] It takes little imagination to see how crowded con-

ditions were and why expansion at 1240 was out of the question. Over and above the space problem, Brother Lucian stated that the noise from traffic on Broad Street was interfering with classroom procedure, while, at the same time, he felt the value of the property was increasing. In all probability, the real value of the property was increasing, but with the collapse of the money market when the College did want to unload 1240, its real value never benefited the College. Few disagreed with Brother Lucian that the College must move, but Brother Lucian's term ended before definite plans were formulated. Brother Lucian was succeeded by Brother Dorotheus Lewis, a famous teacher of English and President of La Salle College from 1925 to 1928. It was Brother Dorotheus who was destined to break ground for La Salle College at 20th Street and Olney Avenue, where the College still stands and grows today.

Shortly after Brother Dorotheus took office as President in 1925, Brother Allais Charles, Superior General of the Brothers, visited America. He did not like what he saw at La Salle College and let it be known that he was sorely disappointed to find such conditions in a Brothers' college in the United States. The Superior General's remarks gave the necessary impetus for the move everyone was convinced the College should make. Brother Dorotheus did not let Brother Charles forget the remarks he made and carried on a vigorous correspondence with the Superior General. In his first report to the Board of Managers, Brother Dorotheus elaborated on the position taken by Brother Charles when at the College. He laid before the Board the methods of procedure along with the Superior General's mandate. "I am anxious that you should start as soon as possible . . . we cannot authorize you to go ahead unless you have the approval of your Board, a definite proposition of place, locality, price, and means of purchase . . . send the particulars and we will do our part quickly and joyfully."[19] Both Board and President had their work cut out for them. There was no hesitating now. For the second time in less than fifty years, the hunt was on for a new campus.

5. *A Step Toward Destiny*

AS THE YEARS AFTER THE WAR FADED, people in the United States were caught up in an ever-expanding prosperity. Jobs were plentiful, money and food abundant, most Americans were content, and new fads of entertainment thrilled even the dullest imagination. Everything looked positive as the inflated ball of prosperity bounced higher and higher. How could anyone, even those whose fiscal resources were thin, hesitate to take the great plunge into investment, especially for expansion and improvement. Such was the prevailing attitude as La Salle College took its plunge toward destiny by seeking a new and larger campus.

All the friends of La Salle were asked to keep a lookout for a favorable campus. Two Brothers, taking a relaxing walk one Saturday afternoon near historic Germantown, came across a piece of property well guarded from sight by high hedges. Their curiosity whetted, they pushed through the hedge and saw what they felt would be a perfect site for a college. The land was part of a large estate called Belfield, and the Brothers wondered whether or not the owners would sell. There was one way to find out. Upon their return to La Salle, the Brothers reported their discovery, and legal assistance was sought to make the necessary contacts.

Negotiations for the purchase of the land on which the main campus is located today were opened in 1925. College administrators, under the leadership of Brother Dorotheus, were interested in a ten-acre plot fronting on Olney Avenue and extending southward to Ellicot Road. James Starr, one of the heirs of the Belfield estate, owned nine-tenths of an acre where the elbow of College Hall stands today. When first approached about the sale of his land, he was reluctant to sell. The remaining ten acres desired by the College belonged to five heirs of the Fox estate, also part of original Belfield, who also seemed unwilling to sell because of the large income tax which would be incurred. In view of these difficulties, the College was fortunate in having the legal services of J. Burrwood Daly. An astute negotiator, he had secured by April 20, 1926, a tentative agreement of sale with negligible restrictions. It was agreed that the property would be used only to carry on the operations of the College, and that any necessary "garage, boiler-house, powerhouse, and kitchen" would be located at least one hundred feet from all boundary lines. Three days after the tentative agreement was secured, the Board of Managers of La Salle College voted to purchase ten acres of the Fox estate for $200,000 and the remaining fraction from James Starr for $27,500. After further legal clarifications and understandings, title to ten and a fraction acres of Belfield was transferred to the College. On this historic land, the present campus was initiated.

In earliest colonial times, the land in question was part of a grant made by William Penn to one Samuel Richardson. The grant is not to be confused with that made to Daniel Pastorius and his followers, which eventually became Germantown. Richardson's grant was within the territorial limits of Bristol Township, County of Philadelphia. Some years later, in 1696, Richardson gave 500 acres to his son, Joseph; and it is believed that the original mansion on the Belfield property was built at that time. However, the house was much smaller than it is today. The estate remained in the Richardson family through 1726. Between that year and 1810, the land was possessed by the Keysers, Funks, Neaves, Ecksteins, Correys, Smiths, and McShanes, names traditional to the environs of Germantown. Finally, in 1810, Belfield reverted to Charles Willson Peale, famous American artist.

No, George Washington did not sleep here. Although Charles Willson Peale was commissioned by the Supreme Executive Council in 1799 to paint a portrait of Washington, it is obvious that Peale had not yet moved to Belfield, although he knew of the place from his visits to Washington's headquarters during the Battle of Germantown. No doubt the Washington portrait was painted in Peale's city residence. (The original portrait, incidentally, was destroyed by the British. Fortunately, Peale had made a mezzotint of the portrait and managed to preserve it for posterity.)

Actually, poor health and perhaps old age forced Peale to look for a country home. When he took over Belfield, it consisted of about 100 acres. He described it in a letter to his son Rembrandt, as follows:

> . . . the situation is exactly the equal between the Old York Turnpike and Germantown Turnpike, ½ mile distant each. Two streams run through it. . . . These streams at present make a fine meadow. The mansion is old fashioned, with 10 or 12 rooms, a stone barn with stable room for 5 horses, and a wagon house, chaise house, smoke house, hen house, a spring house with a fine stream, 2 stories high, the upper to making cheese, a tolerable good house for the tenant, and sundry conveniences in the house way, with an excellent garden with respect to situation, good paling, and some good fruit.[1]

He had paid $9,500 for this prize.

Peale pursued the task of putting the property in good order with great energy. Repairing and enlarging the mansion took most of his time in 1810. This man of many talents, who had made a set of false teeth for George Washington and was America's first taxidermist, proved quite capable as carpenter, glazier, house painter, and, in general, master-builder. With the mansion in satisfactory condition, Peale concentrated on beautifying his grounds and tilling the soil. For three years, his son Rubens helped lay out a beautiful and intricate garden planted with a variety of exotic shrubs, trees, and plants. Peale's garden became one of the beauty spots of nineteenth-century Philadelphia, and it attracted hundreds of people whenever it was opened for inspection.

Although the formal gardens took much of Peale's time, he did not neglect the farm. He corresponded frequently with Thomas Jefferson, seeking advice on his agricultural pursuits. It was Jefferson who taught Peale the secret of contour plowing, which was a boon to tilling the undulating hills of Belfield. Despite many arduous hours of planning and work, Peale did not make his farm a financial success. Robert Morris, a neighboring farmer, came to his aid. Planting currants for wine making, Morris felt, would end Peale's financial difficulties. At first Peale hesitated because of his personal antipathy to the habit of drinking. But he overcame his doubts through some friendly persuasion and eventually realized a profit on the wine making. As one chronicler remarked, "The heady sweet wine of Belfield became, as years passed, famous among the connoisseurs of Philadelphia."

Considering the difficulties involved in making the farm pay, Peale probably felt that the name he gave his estate upon his arrival was fitting: Farm Persevere. However, his many friends thought the name was too forbidding, and they prevailed upon him to change it. In the summer of 1812 he agreed, and the present name, Belfield, was chosen. He named it for Bellefield, the home of John Hesselius, on the Severn River in Maryland, where Peale had received his first lessons in painting.

Despite the work required at Belfield, Peale never gave up his painting. During his short stay there, he is believed to have produced over one hundred pieces. A few times the garden at Belfield became the scene of public exhibitions of his works. Such events were received with much enthusiasm among the high society of Philadelphia and Germantown. In 1817, after a storm damaged part of the mansion, a new extension was built, with a special "painting" room over the kitchen. Peale had been planning just such a room for a long time. Unfortunately, the room would be used only a few years. Shortly thereafter both Peale and his wife were struck with a serious illness, to which his wife finally succumbed in 1820.

A few months later, Peale moved back to the city and occupied himself with his first love, a private museum of natural history. Belfield was offered in exchange for a "suitable museum site" in the city, but there were no takers. In 1823, Belfield was put up for rent at a price that hardly paid the taxes. The following year the property was mortgaged. In the meantime, Linnaeus Peale moved to Belfield, but he did not have his father's energy; and the place "ran wild." Finally, in January, 1826, Belfield was sold to William Logan Fisher, whose Wakefield property adjoined Belfield. That same year, Fisher made a gift of it to his daughter, Sarah, upon her marriage to William Wister.

William Wister was a descendant of John Wister, a Philadelphia wine merchant, whose famous summer house, Grumblethorpe, still stands on Germantown Avenue. John Wister's brother, Caspar Wistar, father of the noted botanist, Dr. Caspar Wistar, dealt in glass and buttons. (The difference in spelling of surnames is attributed to the mistake of a naturalization clerk. Genealogically, the Wisters and the Wistars are the same).

Belfield, under the Wisters, continued to be a place of beauty and interest. William Wister, sometimes called "the father of American cricket," spent many hours at Belfield teaching the sport to his Germantown neighbors. In 1854, Belfield was used for the first home of the American Cricket Club, later called the Germantown Cricket Club. Waxing eloquent in 1910, George M. Newhall expressed the following sentiments about Belfield:

> The memories of those days are precious, and it would seem that Providence had preserved this lovely spot intact for the sentimental old cricketers, as the Magna Charta and the Liberty Bell are preserved for the Anglo-Saxon race. All

cricketers and lovers of good sport should prize this scene, where American cricket had its birth and spent its childhood.[2] However, these glories had in reality faded before the end of the century. Manheim, west of Germantown, became the home of the Germantown Cricket Club in 1889. It was composed of the merged members of the club founded at Belfield and the Young America Cricket Club founded in 1855. Part of the Belfield Country Club, which was located on the north side of Olney Avenue, remained in operation until 1920.

Another organization established at Belfield was The Civic Club of Philadelphia, founded on January 6, 1894, by Mrs. Cornelia Frothingham and Miss Mary Channing Wister. It became the parent organization of similar groups throughout the country.

With the passage of time, many new members of the Wister family came to share in the estate. Moreover, before his death in 1862, William Logan Fisher had sold several portions of Belfield. The remainder was willed to his daughters, Sarah Logan Wister and Mary Rodman Fox. Fisher stipulated that the portion of Belfield containing the mansion should go to Sarah L. Wister, since she had spent considerable money in repairing and rebuilding the house. Upon her death in 1891, Sarah L. Wister willed her portion of Belfield to her four sons, William Rotch, John, Jones, and Rodman Wister. It was from these heirs and their descendants that La Salle College purchased the original plot of its present main campus.

While the purchase of the Belfield parcel was still in the negotiable stage, another property, located on Roosevelt Boulevard at Ashdale and Bingham Streets, was offered to the College. The twelve and one-half acre plot was priced at $200,000. Its front portion was elevated and contained 40,000 cubic yards of sand which could have been sold for $28,000. The rear portion was below grade and would have required 60,000 cubic yards of fill. Still, the price was tempting; the College would get more land for $75,000 less. But the Belfield property with its rural characteristics had a much better location and was much more suitable for an institution of higher learning. In 1926, the La Salle acreage was surrounded on three sides by woods and fields. Few city noises were present at the time, and its elevated position provided almost constant fresh breezes. Today one can look with ease at downtown Philadelphia from most campus buildings. It is significant that the view of City Hall tower is unobstructed, a constant reminder of La Salle's early days at Juniper and Filbert Streets.

With great courage, the negotiations for Belfield were completed. Final settlement for the property was made on October 11, 1926, at the Land Title and Trust Company. When all fees and licenses had been paid, La Salle College secured title to 10.2048 acres at a cost of $241,844. Obviously, La Salle did not have a cash reserve to cover the purchase price, so a $250,000 mortgage at six percent interest was secured from the Board of City Trusts on the 1240 property. In ordinary times such an arrangement would not have been possible. The realty market was inflated and expanding with optimism, and the Board of Managers felt the 1240 property could be sold easily at a very good price. The firm of Albert M. Greenfield was selected by the Board to sell 1240, although it would appear that Greenfield was Cardinal Dougherty's choice.

Once the land had been purchased and arrangements made for sale of the 1240 campus, the development of plans for new buildings at 20th and Olney was started immediately. First, architects had to be selected. Cardinal Dougherty, Honorary President of the Board, let it be known that he favored the architectural firm of Hoffman and Henon. No one on the Board dared suggest otherwise. The Cardinal further suggested that the Brothers get permission from the Superior General to borrow money to build "and that the details be left to Mr. Greenfield."[3] It was obvious that the Cardinal was interested in seeing the project initiated. He wanted his own men to handle the financial and architectural aspects of the program. No doubt the Cardinal showed the same intense belief in the burgeoning American economy as many of his contemporaries. Otherwise, it would seem he recklessly pushed the College

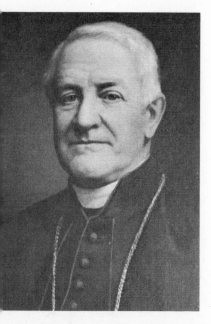

Archbishop James Frederick Wood
Co-founder of La Salle College

Brother Teliow, F.S.C.
Co-founder and First President
of La Salle College

St. Michael's Parish,
Philadelphia,
site of first College building.
Original college building
stood in the yard
shown to the left.

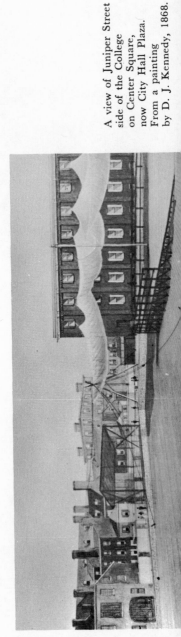

The First Public
Program Presented
by the Students
of La Salle College

A view of Juniper Street
side of the College
on Center Square,
now City Hall Plaza.
From a painting
by D. J. Kennedy, 1868.

PROGRAMME.

PART I.

(PART I.)

OVERTURE.	La Salle Band
WHEN BE YOUR FAME FORETOLD.	All the Pupils
ENGLAND'S MISRULE OF IRELAND.	J. H. Conlen
GREET.	F. Bartholomew
GERMAN MARCH.	String Band
DUE SISTERS' DUO.	John and Richard Watson
McLANE'S CHILD.	A. Martin
FAMILY'S DEDICATION.	All the Pupils
CASTING THE SAILOR'S BANNER.	F. A. Wilcome
PEOPLE WILL TALK.	Wm. F. Hewitt
DECANT INTEGRITY.	F. Murray
THE CONSTITUTION.	Brass Band
MORNING STAR WALTZ AND MOLLY DAWN.	Junior Department
I'LL BE A SOLDIER, solo and Chorus.	String Band
BASS AND GRUMBLES.	J. A. M'Coy
FREEDOM OF SPEECH.	Wm. H. Brogan
ORATION ON THE CRISIS.	Quartette
FANTASY FROM THAT FALLEN RIVER.	E. A. Whitely, J. H. Conlen, J. F. O'Keefe and F. Bartholomew
MY GRANDFATHER WAS A MOST WONDERFUL MAN.	Wm. E. Lees
SHUME'S CHINS.	F. F. M'Garigan
WHISPERING SUSPICION AND UNION POLKA.	Brass Band
LET THOSE FREEES (Piano).	Wm. H. Jones, C. Newland and J. A. Conlen
MARCH OF LA SOMBA (Piano).	F. Bartholomew and Wm. H. Jones
BOHEMIAN GIRL (Piano).	John and William Watson

PART II.

Dialogue.—Running for Congress.

Characters:

PEDRO SIMPES, Independent Candidate for Congress.	P. F. Whittington
MARK DONNELTLE, Popular Confidential Agent.	Wm. H. Brogan
MR. REAL, of the Free Trade League.	J. A. Tracey
MR. FOOT, an Advocate of Moral Suffrage.	J. A. M'Coy
MR. SELFISH, a Protective Tariff Man.	Thos. J. M'Veigh
MR. BIGELOW ME. Conservative.	A. J. O'Brien
MR. CREDENTEE, Washington's Union.	E. A. Whitely
MR. BALLOT, for Inflation of Currency.	F. Y. M'Cully
MR. BULLION, a Hard-money Man.	F. O'Keefe
MR. SEPT AFF, for Prohibitory Liquor Law	A. Martin
MR. POGY, Conservative.	Wm. F. Hewitt
GEN. COBDEN, Y. E.	J. M'Coy
HON. GAMBRINUS, a Free Lunchist.	F. Bartholomew
MR. STONEBOW, Female Suffrage Advocate.	J. Connor
Villains, &c.	
UNITY'S LIFE GUARD.	All the Pupils
FINAL.	Brass Band

LA SALLE BAND.

F. Bartholomew, 1 Bb. Cornet.	B. M'Laughlin, 1 Alto.	J. P. Murray, Baritone.
C. Finnegan, 1 Bb. Cornet.	Wm. H. Brogan, 2 Alto.	Thos. J. Tobin, Bass.
E. Eslin, Eb. Cornet.	George Schmid, 1 Bb.	G. Allman, Side Drum.
E. V. Clarke, 1 Bb. Cornet.	A. Bowery, 3 Alto.	O'Neill, Side Drum.
Gilroy, 1 Eb. Cornet.	A. J. Quigley, 1 Alto.	J. F. O'Keefe, Bass Drum.
F. J. Jackson, 1 Bb. Cornet.	J. A. M'Coy, 2 Alto.	Wm. E. Lees, Cymbal.
F. M'Govan, 1 Bb. Cornet.	Wm. F. Hewitt, 2 Tenor.	
C. J. Wirath, Eb. Cornet.		

P. S.—The first annual public examination of the pupils of the Christian Brothers' Academy will take place at the Academy, 1221 Filbert street, about the 20th proxo. The vacation commences this year on the 3rd July, and school will re-open on the first Monday in September next.

The grand Piano used on this occasion (fine 6 1/2 octave) is from the warerooms of J. E. GOULD, 923 Chestnut street.

First Annual
Exhibition and Concert
BY THE PUPILS
OF THE
Christian Brothers'
ACADEMY,
(1221 FILBERT STREET,)
AT THE
American Academy of Music,
1868.
Friday Evening, May 22,
1868.

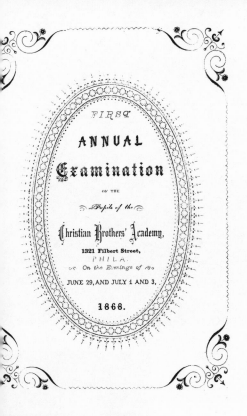

FIRST ANNUAL Examination

OF THE
Pupils of the
Christian Brothers' Academy,

1321 Filbert Street,
PHILA.

On the Evenings of

JUNE 29, AND JULY 1 AND 3,

1868.

Brother Noah, F.S.C.
President 1872-1875

Friday Evening, July 3, '68.

Rt. Rev. Bishop Wood, Presiding.

OVERTURE..*La Salle Brass Band.*
BLUEHT DER BLUMEN EINE (Trio)...*J. Michel, G. B. Kreine, F. Barthmaier.*
ENGLISH COMPOSITION AND RHETORIC.....*First Literary and Scientific Dept.*
DECLAMATION....................................*Wm. H. Bergan.*
GENTLY FLOW THOU FALLING RIVER................................(Quartet)
 E. J. McGinly, J. H. Comber, J. F. O'Keefe, and F. Barthmaier.
NATURAL PHILOSOPHY...........*First Literary and Scientific Department.*
DECLAMATION....................................*J. I. McAvoy.*
UNFURL THE GLORIOUS BANNER (Solo and Chorus)..............*The Pupils.*
LATIN (Cæsar)................................*First Class.*
DECLAMATION....................................*S. J. Martin.*
MY GRANDFATHER WAS A MOST WONDERFUL MAN..........*Wm. E. Loer.*
GEOMETRY, TRIGONOMETRY, CONIC SECTIONS.....*First Literary and Scientific Dept.*
DECLAMATION....................................*J. H. Comber.*
NEARING DEATH (Bass Solo)...............................*F. Barthmaier.*
ASTRONOMY.......................*First Literary and Scientific Department.*
DECLAMATION....................................*P. F. M'Gettigan.*
MEDLEY..*The Pupils.*
DISTRIBUTION OF REPORTS TO THE PUPILS, BY THE RT. REV. PRESIDENT.
FINALE..*Brass Band.*

LA SALLE BAND.

F. Barthmaier.	1 E♭. Cornet.	George Schimpf.	2 Alto.
C. Flanagan.	2 E♭. Cornet.	J. Henney.	3 Alto.
R. Tobin.	3 E♭. Cornet.	J. A. Quigley.	4 Alto.
E. V. Clark.	1 B♭. Cornet.	J. I. M'Evoy.	1 Tenor.
Gallen.	2 B♭. Cornet.	Wm. F. Harrity.	2 Tenor.
F. J. Gorman.	3 B♭. Cornet.	J. P. Murray.	Baritone.
M'Keone.	4 B♭. Cornet.	Thos. F. Tobin.	Bass.
C. J. M'Grath.	4 B♭. Cornet.	Moses Armstrong.	
H. M'Laughlin.	1 Alto.	D. O'Neill,	Side Drum.
Wm. H. Bergan.	2 Alto.	J. F. O'Keefe.	Bass Drum.
	J. H. Comber.		Cymbals.

Monday Eve'g, June 29, 1868.

Rt. Rev. Dr. O'Hara, Bishop Elect of Scranton, presiding.

OVERTURE..*La Salle Brass Band.*
COME, HOLY GHOST (Hymn).................*Pupils of the Primary Department.*
GEOGRAPHY (Western Hemisphere).......*Primary and Second Intermediate Depts.*
DECLAMATION....................................*John Shields.*
I'LL BE A SOLDIER (Solo and Chorus)................*Primary Department.*
ENGLISH GRAMMAR........*First Intermediate and Second Scientific Departments.*
KING OF THE AIR (Bass Solo)........................*Wm. P. Tracy.*
GALLOP..*String Band.*
ARITHMETIC.................*First Intermediate and Second Scientific Departments.*
DECLAMATION....................................*John Gallen.*
FAIREST OF MORTALS (Duet)................*J. P. Flood, G. B. Krein.*
GEOGRAPHY (Eastern Hemisphere)........*First Intermediate Department.*
MUSIC...*Brass Band.*
DECLAMATION....................................*J. J. Daly.*
BOOK-KEEPING (Double Entry).....*First and Second Literary and Scientific Depts.*
HANS AND GRETCHEN..............................*String Band.*
   ADDRESS BY RT. REV. PRESIDENT.
FINALE..*Brass Band.*
N.B. Exercises commence each evening at seven o'clock, and terminate at ten.

Wednesday Eve'g, July 1, 1868.

Rt. Rev. Dr. O'Hara, Bishop Elect of Scranton, presiding.

OVERTURE..*La Salle Brass Band.*
SWEET IS THE FACE OF NATURE (Solo and Chorus).....*Primary Department.*
ARITHMETIC...................................*Second Intermediate Department.*
DECLAMATION....................................*James P. Murray.*
MEETING OF THE WATERS........................*Francis M'Keone.*
ANCIENT HISTORY (Assyria, Persia, Greece, Rome) *First Intermediate Department.*
MUSIC...*Brass Band.*
EVER GREEN POLKA (Piano).................*J. B. Watson, W. J. Watson.*
LATIN (Grammar and Reader)................*Second and Third Classes.*
DECLAMATION....................................*A. J. O'Brien.*
IN THE STAR LIGHT (Duet)................*A. Felljar, J. I. M'Evoy.*
ALGEBRA.......................*First Literary and Scientific Department.*
MUSIC...*Brass Band.*
O'ER THE HILLS, O'ER THE DALE (Duet).....*H. M'Laughlin, F. M'Keone.*
ARITHMETIC.....................*First Literary and Scientific Department.*
MARCH...*String Band.*
FINALE..*Brass Band.*

Program for the First Public Examination of La Salle Students

The College in 1875 was dwarfed by the Masonic Temple; and construction on City Hall was progressing rapidly. These considerations led to the quest for a new location.

Medal awarded to Charles J. Halbeisen in 1878, oldest College award in existence.

College Faculty in 1873

Brother Romuald, F.S.C.
President 1878-1883

A group of College students pose with Brother
Paphylinus, F.S.C. Picture taken around 1880.

The Bouvier Mansion at 1240 N. Broad Street was acquired by the College in 1882.

Brother Clementian, F.S.C.
President 1883-1885

Brother Fabrician, F.S.C.
President 1885-1887

The Bouvier Mansion was enlarged and South Wing was added. College classes were moved there in 1886 and remained for over forty years.

taphysics (1) Philosophy of Style (2) thematics (3) eek (4)	Metaphysics (1) Shakespearian Criticism (2) Mathematics (3) Greek (4)	Metaphysics (1) History (2) English Literature (2) Mathematics (3) Greek (4)	Metaphysics (1) Shakespearian Criticism (2) Mathematics (3) Greek (4)	Philosophy of History (1) Essays, Literary Criticism (2) Mathematics (3) Book-Keeping (4)
tin Literature and Critical Reading of Latin Authors (1) gic (2) nglish Literature (3) athematics (4)	Latin Literature and Critical Reading of Latin Authors (1) Logic (2) English Authors Read Critically (3) Mathematics (4)	Latin Literature and Critical Reading of Latin Authors (1) Logic (2) English Literature (3) Mathematics (4)	Latin Literature and Critical Reading of Latin Authors (1) Mathematics (2) English Authors Read Critically (3) Mathematics (4)	Latin Literature and Critical Reading of Latin Authors (1) Mathematics (2) Essays and Criticism (3) Mathematics (4)
eparation of Lecture Notes and Theses, and Consulting of References (1) tin (2),(3) etoric (4)	Preparation of Lecture Notes and Theses, and Consulting of References (1) Latin (2),(3) Physics (4)	Preparation of Lecture Notes and Theses, and Consulting of References (1) Latin (2),(3) Rhetoric (4)	Preparation of Lecture Notes and Theses, and Consulting of References (1) Latin (2),(3) Physics (4)	Essays and Literary Criticism (1) Latin (2),(3) Rhetoric and Essays (4)
eek Literature and Critical Reading of Greek Authors (1) nch, German. cient History (2) story of England (3) dern History (4)	Greek Literature and Critical Reading of Greek Authors (1) French, German. Evidences of Religion (2) Church History and Christian Doctrine (3) Church History and Christian Doctrine (4)	Greek Literature and Critical Reading of Greek Authors (1) French, German. Astronomy (2) Physics (3) History (4)	Greek Literature and Critical Reading of Greek Authors (1) French, German. Evidences of Religion (2) Church History and Christian Doctrine (3),(4)	Philosophy of History French, German. Chemistry (2) Elocution (3),(4)
thematics (1) eek (2),(3) in (4) ustrial Drawing. ades, Shadows nd Perspective. reotomy and Topography.	Evidences of Religion (1) Greek (2),(3) Latin (4) Industrial Drawing. Shades, Shadows and Perspective. Stereotomy and Topography.	French Literature (1) Greek (2),(3) Latin (4) Industrial Drawing. Shades, Shadows and Perspective. Stereotomy and Topography.	Evidences of Religion (1) Greek (2),(3) Latin (4) Industrial Drawing. Shades, Shadows and Perspective. Stereotomy and Topography.	Elocution (1),(2) Latin (3) Book-keeping (4) Industrial Drawing. Shades, Shadows and Perspective. Stereotomy and Topography.

(1) Senior Class.   (3) Sophomore Class.
(2) Junior Class.   (4) Freshman Class.

re two or more subjects are entered together for the same class, it means that when one is dropped the other is taken up in the order mentioned.

College Roster, 1886

Three Distinguish
Nineteenth-Centur
Alumni of
La Salle College,
Bishop McDevitt,
Bishop McCloskey
and Bishop McCo

Interior view of
Carlisle Hall,
completed in 1887.
It stood on the extreme
northwest corner of
the 1240 campus.

The College Chap
on the first floor
of the Buovier Ma

Brother Abdas, F.S.C.
President 1903-1911

Brother Dennis Edward, F.S.C.
President 1911-1917

"Snake" Deal and his championship basketball team, 1903. After winning two successive ampionships, basketball disappeared from the La Salle scene for nearly thirty years.

Brother Richard, F.S.C.,
with an engineering class
in Fairmount Park.

Brother Richard, F.S.C.
President 1917-1922

The College wireless telegraph station, licensed
the United States Government, operated du
World War I.

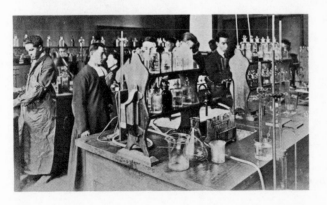

Brother Felician Peter, F.S
supervises chemistry labora

Brother Dorotheus, F.S.C.
President 1925-1928

Brother Lucian, F.S.C.
President 1922-1925

La Salle During Construction of Broad Street Subway, 1926-1927

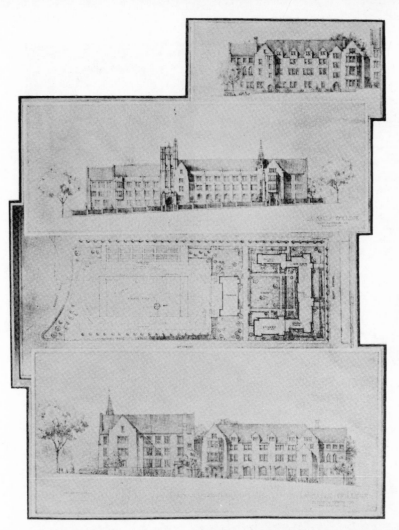

Architects' Conception of the New College, 1927

1928 — Brother Dorotheus, President, breaks ground at Belfield for the New Coll

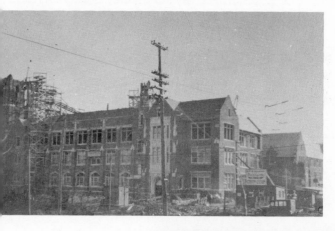

1928-1929
College Hall
under construction.

First Basketball Letter,
Awarded to
Ted Praiss, 1930

Brother Alfred, F.S.C.,
President 1928-1932,
signs Tom Conley
and Marty Brill
as first football coaches.
Brother Leonard, F.S.C.,
Athletic Director,
looks on.

Wister Hall
Gymnasium
1931

1933
First Football Field,
Paralleling the
Gymnaisium Building

Governor Earle Addresses Class of 1935

Debating was an outstanding activity during the thirties. The 1935 team poses with their moderator. Brother Alfred, F.S.C.

The College Library, 1935

The First Football Team To Represent La Salle

Sir John A. McCarthy, K.C.S.G.,
breaks ground for
McCarthy Stadium in 1936.
J. Burrwood Daly,
Brother Edward John, F.S.C.,
Mr. James Henry, and
Brother Anselm, F.S.C.,
President 1932-1941, look on.

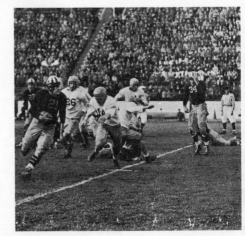

1941 — La Salle's
Bill Bynon sweeps end
against Canisius.

La Salle's Last Football Team

The Campus in 1940
showing the new McShain Hall.
The former
Charles Willson Peale mansion
is seen in the left foreground.

41 — Brother Alfred, F.S.C.,
·sident Emeritus and founder
of La Salle's Labor School,
·sents the De La Salle Medal
o Franklin Delano Roosevelt.
James P. McGranery,
Philip Convery,
John St. John look on.

Brother Emilian, F.S.C.,
President 1941-1945,
confers an honorary degree
on Judge Crumlish.

College student body on weekly hike as part of "Hale America" program during World War II.

The college cafeteria in 1946 after influx of veterans.

The 1942 College ice hockey team. Suspended during the war, ice hockey failed to make a come back.

Brother G. Joseph, F.S.C., ground instructor in the aeronautics course offered during the war, gives some spontaneous instruction at Wings Field.

Brother Gregorian Paul, F.S.C.,
President 1945-1952,
at dedication of Leonard Hall,
first post-war building constructed
at La Salle.

Dr. Joseph Sprissler, center,
founder of the Evening Division,
poses with his two successors
Brother Paul, F.S.C.,
and Brother Emery, F.S.C.

Bishop J. Carroll McCormick
accompanied by
Brother George Lewis, F.S.C., and
Brother Gregorian Paul, F.S.C.,
breaks ground for Benilde Hall.

Brother Gregorian Paul, F.S.C., President,
speaks at opening of Benilde Hall, September, 1948.

College Library opened October, 1952.

The students welcome
swimming ace Joe Verdeur
back from the 1948 Olympics.

Tom Gola, Everybody's All-American,
in action against Duquesne University.

1954 — La Salle's NCAA Champions
pose with the spoils of victory at
Philadelphia's International Airport.

Student Union Lounge
located in the basement
of the library, 1952-19..

1957
St. Bernard,
St. Cassian
and
St. Albert Halls.

1958 — Senator John F. Kennedy addresses an Honors Convocation. Seated on the Senator's
immediate right, Brother Stanislaus, F.S.C., President 1952-1958.

April, 1960 — Bishop Francis McSorley dedicates College Union Building as Brother Daniel Bernian, F.S.C., President, and Monsignor Charles B. McGinley look on.

October, 1960 — Dedication of the Science Center

Olympics participants Ira Davis and Al Cantello pose with Coach Wetzler.

Annual R.O.T.C. Review

Mark Van Doren autographs one of his volumes
for Student Council President Tom Lynch.

Governor Lawrence and Brother Daniel, F.S.C., open Centennial Year celebrations with flag raising ceremony.

Senator Eugene McCarthy lectures in the College Union Lounge.

Archbishop John Krol distributes Communion during Centennial
Mass at the Cathedral of SS. Peter and Paul.

March 1963 — Board of Managers: Dr. Joseph Sprissler, Brother F. James, F.S.C., John Kelly,
Brother E. James, F.S.C., John McShain, Brother Daniel, F.S.C., President, Brother D. John,
F.S.C., Chairman, Rt. Rev. Msgr. Thomas F. McNally, Brother Anselm, F.S.C., Joseph
Schmitz, Jr., Brother Paul, F.S.C., Brother Francis, F.S.C., and Joseph B. Quinn, Esq.

Baccalaureate
Services —
Immaculate Conception
Church

Commencement Exercises at Convention Hall

T. H. White
lectures in the
College Union
Theater.

Campus in 1964
as seen from
Science Center

La Salle after Dark

Katherine Anne Porter
lectures at Annual
Writer's Conference.

Marianne Moore
receives award
during Annual
Writer's Conference.

Laboratory scene during N.S.F. Summer Research
Program for talented High School students.

The crew glides swiftly up the Schuylkill.

The Soccer team in action against Temple University.

General Maxwell Taylor addresses a noonday gathering
of students in the College Union Lounge.

Student Chapel,
opened July, 1965,
occupies site of old
College Hall auditorium.

The College Faculty in 1965.

...her Charles Henry, F.S.C., now Superior ...eral of the Christian Brothers, speaks at the ...ng exercises of Summer Science Workshop for diocesan personnel.

H. Blake Hayman, M.D., newest member of the Board of Managers.

1965 — College Council: David Smith, Brother Emery, F.S.C., Brother Paul, F.S.C., Broth
Fidelian, F.S.C., Margaret Lennon, Brother Christopher, F.S.C., Brother Daniel, F.S.
Brother Robert, F.S.C., John McCloskey, Brother David, F.S.C., Dr. Joseph Sprissler, Broth
Lewis, F.S.C.

Brother Daniel, F.S.C., discusses the ten-year
projection with several College administrators.

to the brink of fiscal disaster. Events proved in the long run, however, that La Salle was better off in having its buildings erected and in operation when financial disaster struck the nation.

True to the Cardinal's wishes, Brother Dorotheus, President, sought and received permission from the Superior General to borrow money for new buildings. At a special meeting of the Board, called on April 27, 1927, the President was authorized to contract a loan for $700,000, "offering as collateral the new La Salle College site, and the new college buildings to be erected." However, the authorization given the President did not carry with it any suggestion or directions as to just where the money was to be borrowed. This was left up to the discretion of Brother Dorotheus. In his own quiet, pleasant, forceful way, this man of letters pursued his distasteful task remarkably. However, many other matters needed his attention in the meantime.

Brother Dorotheus, in several meetings with the architects, was deeply concerned over the housing of college and high school students in one building. Original plans and drawings called for the main building to be U-shaped, with the major base fronting on Olney Avenue. Connected to the west wing would be the faculty house, facing 20th Street. Brother Dorotheus wrote to the Department of Public Instruction at Harrisburg, seeking their ideas on a combination high school and college building. He was advised that "the fact that they may join with a partition between schools . . . will not interfere with the classification of the college." The department further stated that it was most important to see that the college was entirely under its own administration, management, and faculty, while the high school had its own organization, administration, and faculty. With that problem settled, the architects completed plans for what Hoffman and Henon labeled the "high school building" and the "faculty building." It must be understood, then, that from the very inception of plans for the Belfield campus, the administration planned to conduct college classes in the new buildings. Finally, for clarity, we will refer to the college buildings as they are known today.

The orginal plans for the construction of College Hall had to be set aside because of the prohibitive cost. The entire east wing was lopped off, together with about thirty-five feet of the main building along Olney Avenue. When the plans were finally approved in 1927, the bids went out. The lowest bid on College Hall was $333,000, while the lowest bid on the faculty house and connection was $141,000. Although the two buildings, as they stand today, are worth thousands more than the original price, the Board felt the bids a bit high. As a result, John McShain, a graduate of the preparatory department, was contacted. He had just finished building St. Joseph's College at 54th and City Line Avenue, and the Board agreed that it was an excellent job. McShain was asked if he would consider erecting the two buildings for $470,000, which total was $4,000 less than the combined lowest bids. He generously agreed to the proposition, and since then has not ceased to take a gracious and helpful interest in La Salle College. On February 8, 1928, J. Burrwood Daly, counsel for La Salle, formally announced the awarding of contracts for the "Faculty Building and the High School Building" to John McShain, Inc., for $470,000.[4] Work began almost immediately and was slated for completion in January, 1929. But a problem developed that continues to plague expansion plans today. The land was supported with a rather stubborn layer of rock. An additional $7,240 had to be expended for its removal and, whenever possible, excavation was avoided. The stories of exposed rock formations under the stage floor of College Hall auditorium proved true as demonstrated during recent alterations. Also, explanation for the elevation of the college quadrangle is found in the rock problem. Despite the rock, construction moved ahead at a rapid pace, and the new La Salle climbed toward the sky.

In the meantime, Brother Dorotheus had completed arrangements for financing the new buildings. The Market Street National Bank and the Corn Exchange National Bank both considered a loan to the College of $350,000 each. The money was to be used only for the erection of the new buildings, and the notes were to be issued for six months at 5½% interest. La Salle had to create a mortgage of $700,000 to cover both the property at 20th and Olney and the campus at 1240 North Broad, even though the latter already carried a mortgage of $250,000, held by the Board of City Trusts of the City of Philadelphia.

Midway in the negotiations, the banks reneged because of a clause in the deeds prohibiting the building of homes for fifty years. The creditors wanted further assurance of payment. As a result, Ocean Rest, Ocean City, N. J., The Ammendale Normal Institute, Calvert Hall College, Baltimore, and St. John's College in Washington, D. C., were all put up by the Brothers as assurance of payment. In short, everything owned by the Brothers of the Baltimore Province backed the new college. This, plus a first mortgage on the new school and a second mortgage on 1240, convinced the banks to continue negotiations. The Real Estate Trust Company acted as trustee for both banks at a charge of $100 per year, while at the same time, agreeing not to charge commission or bonus of "any nature or character." In addition, the College had to deliver to the Real Estate Trust Company a bond and warrant in the penal sum of $1,400,000 in order to secure payment of the principal sum of $700,000 at any time within three years from date of origin, with interest at the rate of 5½% per year. The bond and warrant included all buildings to be erected on campus.[5] Legally, La Salle College and the Christian Brothers put everything they had on the line. Times were good and the Board was looking forward to the successful sale of 1240 to give the College a reserve fund with which to pay it debts. On paper, if anything went amiss, the College and the Province stood to lose everything. This was a tremendous responsibility, one which Brother Dorotheus was happy to be released from when he terminated his presidency in the summer of 1928.

Brother Dorotheus was succeeded by Brother Alfred, President 1928-1932. This very energetic man was to push through the construction of the new La Salle despite the major difficulties accompanying the collapse of the money market. In his great drive and enthusiasm to build La Salle, Brother Alfred developed a knack of nettling those who worked closely with him. He worked hard and expected the same of others. Once in office, he initiated more extensive plans for La Salle than those already in progress. Diagonally across from the new college property on the northwest corner of 20th and Olney, stood the Belfield Country Club. Brother Alfred tried to secure a lease on the property, but the Club was in the process of being sold to one Mr. Johnson who was not willing to lease it for a full year, but only for periods of six and three months respectively. Brother Alfred accepted the conditions and the College was able to use the property to good advantage when the new buildings opened.

As the buildings neared completion, an amazing situation developed. In a letter dated November 28, 1928, John McShain, builder, notified Hoffman-Henon, architects, that no provisions had been made for heat in the new buildings. McShain was justifiably concerned about possible damage during the winter because of lack of heat. To the Brothers, this deficiency caused no surprise; they had planned it that way. When the original architects' plans had to be cut back due to costs, provisions were made to put the heating and electrical systems in a separate plant that could be conveniently topped with a gymnasium. Brother Alfred wrote a letter to the Assistant Superior General explaining the situation. This missive is a masterpiece of tongue-in-cheek. He informed the Assistant that the College expected to have a balance of $140,000 from the original loan of $700,000 when the buildings were complete. "The estimated cost of the gymnasium, in which unfortunately the heating plant is to be located, is $48,000 more than our unused balance." He went on to say the gym was not built first because the College did not want to put so much into a "mere" gymnasium. "But some kind of gymnasium we must have since the heating plant and electrifying have already been let." He reminded the Assistant of the urgency of the matter, "winter being now here and no heat in the buildings." He did not mention the buildings were unoccupied. In concluding his letter, Brother Alfred stated that the Provincial

Council had drawn up a plan which he was asking to have approved. First, with unused money, the Council suggested a gym and high school be included in one building. By borrowing an additional $75,000, this could be accomplished.[6] The high school building was to be built opposite College Hall, although originally some wanted it flush with the Faculty house along 20th Street. This was objected to because light and air would have been shut off from the faculty house. The plan worked and the Assistant's reply was prompt. By December 20, just eighteen days after Brother Alfred's letter had been written, the Board of Managers authorized the use of the $140,000 balance from the original loan plus an additional loan of $75,000 for construction of the high school building and gym and, of course, the heating plant. Ground was broken for the new building on May 15, 1929. Although estimated to cost $206,000, the final price tag on the high school building was $263,989. Total constructing costs incurred by the College in two years was $925,354. Today the three buildings thus acquired, College Hall, St. Joseph's Hall (faculty house), and Wister Hall, comprise the nucleus of the Belfield Campus.

In September, 1929, College Hall was occupied for the first time by the high school and Benilde Academy. The latter was the name given to the primary grades. College classes were held at 1240. Wister Hall construction had begun in May, 1929, and was scheduled for completion during the fall of 1929. However, this date proved optimistic, and the college students were not moved to 20th and Olney until Wednesday, February 5, 1930. On that date, there were over 700 students in all areas of the college. The high school students and Benilde Academy group were shunted to Wister Hall, and the College men were housed in College Hall. The great trek north proved to be a rather informal affair. All students who had cars or who could borrow them were asked to help with the move. Transportation was organized on a departmental level. Equipment, books, supplies, and the entire library were transferred in one vast operation. Once underway, the La Salle convoy up Broad Street created a mild sensation. People stood in awe as they watched the ungainly, automated academic procession. The biology students took special care to give the school skeleton a prominent spot in one of the cars. Where cars were insufficient, the overflow used the Broad Street Subway. Many riders, intent on observing their new transit system, were duly distracted by the human camel pack that boarded the trains at Girard Avenue and evacuated at Olney Avenue. Old man weather added to the scene by delivering a cold day spiked with a persistent drizzle which deepened the already mucilaginous mud that surrounded the new college. No casualties were reported, and few of the movers stopped along the way for refreshment; all were anxious to get into the new building, and with good reason.

One Paul Guischard wrote, on leaving 1240, that "it was sort of tough to leave the old brown stone building with its cracked windows and walls that needed painting and plastering." Even though the cement stairs were worn down to the wire foundations, Guischard felt the old campus seemed home-like. He averred he would miss the lunch hour freedom to eat in a variety of establishments that dotted the 1240 neighborhood. Another student, Marcel Sussman, found the new La Salle beyond his expectations. He was astounded that an unendowed school could erect such a campus. His impressions were as follows: "a new gymnasium which would do any university proud; new laboratories equipped with the latest word in apparatus; lecture halls with the most modern seating devices. A real college with a real atmosphere."[7] *The Collegian,* the new college weekly, editorialized on the unique environment of La Salle. The editor pointed out the rural setting in the middle of a large city, along with its convenience to "beautiful Wister Woods." He asserted the locality had not changed since Christopher Morley wrote: "It would be hard to find a more lovely spot in the flush of a summer sunset than Wister Woods. The quiet plateau stands in a serene hush, flooded with rich orange glow on a warm evening. . . ." Once settled at 20th and Olney, the students developed a deep sense of pride and loyalty to their alma mater, a lively vivacious spirit that would see the College through many difficult years.

With the opening of the third campus, a new element of life at La Salle developed — resident students. Accommodations for out-of-town students were out of the question at 1240. With a surplus of space in the new buildings, a policy of accepting boarders was initiated. The College had a very sad experience during World War I with the depletion of the student body due to a lack of residence and mess facilities. In order to avoid such a situation in the future, plans were made for a small resident student group. On September 24, 1929, John Brennan of Shenandoah, Pennsylvania, arrived with the distinction of being the first resident student at La Salle College. He lived in the Clubhouse of the Belfield Country Club with Brothers Eadbert of Mary and Francis Patrick, the latter two appointed to keep an eye on the buildings and, of course, on Brennan. The other Brothers who taught classes commuted each day from 1240. Meanwhile, Brennan commuted to 1240 for classes. Conditions in the Clubhouse were quite primitive, and during some winter nights, Brennan and the two Brothers slept between mattresses as well as blankets due to the intense cold. The Clubhouse was meant for summer use; above all, it was never intended for sleeping. On the night of December 31, 1929, New Year's Eve, Brother Felix, Vice-President, and Brother Edward John, Secretary of the Corporation, slept in the completed faculty house without heat, water, or electricity. By this "occupancy," the College was able to avoid taxes for the years 1929-30. Upon completion of Wister Hall with its vital heating plant, the Brothers occupied the faculty house, and Brennan moved in with them, occupying room 201, directly across from the President's suite, now within the confines of the Brothers' cloister. By 1931, twenty boarders were housed on the second floor of College Hall. Room 207 was used for athletes on scholarship, while other boarders used rooms 202 and 204. Naturally, as the college population increased, these accommodations made way for classrooms. However, financial conditions did not allow for construction of dormitory facilities, except in one minor instance as will be seen below, and resident facilities were at a minimum. Thus, the original plans for resident students were never completed, and a new policy was not implemented until 1951.

From the outset, serious problems developed at the new campus. Most of these, with the stock market crash and the ensuing national fiscal disaster, were financial. One of the most annoying problems centered on 1240. It just would not move on the realty market, and as a result the Board decided to leave the sale open to any broker. This proved to be of little help. In the meantime, as long as the 1240 property stood idle, it was liable to city taxes. There-fore, after some minor repairs were made in the spring of 1930, high school classes in biology and languages were moved to 1240. However, the inconvenience proved terribly disruptive to the high school. As a result, a commercial school was established, staffed by five Brothers. In the meantime, the Cardinal arranged to have first-year students from Roman Catholic High School take classes at 1240. This arrangement lasted from 1931 through 1939, at which time La Salle High School needed more space, and 1240 was utilized for this purpose. The name *1240* was dropped and replaced by La Salle Central High. In view of these circumstances, the city eventually dropped a $30,000 tax litigation against La Salle.[8]

When the city opened 20th Street, the College lost six-tenths of an acre, which damages were estimated to be $22,100. The city refused to pay damages and the College went to court and won a mandamus of $7,500 which was promptly appealed. Although the city lost the appeal, the mandamus was reduced to approximately $4,800. Obviously the city fathers were not convinced that the College had made much of a contribution to the cultural develop-ment of the community. Despite the $4,800 "gift" from the city fathers, the money situation at the College grew intensely critical. By December, 1930, the College was not able to make payments to the builder on time. A rather large sum of $15,000 was needed immediately. In desperation, a plan was devised whereby the Col-lege would sell bonds to raise enough money to pay its debts. How-ever, Archbishop Curley, of Baltimore, would not approve of the sale of the bonds in his diocese, so the plan was dropped. This proved fortunate, for as the College moved deeper and deeper into debt, it was able to deal directly and effectively with a few creditors rather than a large number of bondholders. Many members of the Board later reflected that if such a plan had been formalized, no doubt the College would have been lost through foreclosure.[9]

Nonetheless, the College was burdened with a tremendous responsibility. On December 29, 1930, Brother Alfred informed the Board of several disquieting situations. First, because of the depressed realty market, 1240 was still unsold. Secondly, La Salle College had only $1,805 on hand, and the $700,000 loan was due in just four months. The financial situation seemed practically hopeless. Some were of the opinion that La Salle College should be abandoned, while at the same time saving those schools in the Province which were mortgaged in favor of La Salle. But Brother Alfred would not hear of the closing of La Salle College. "God's will is being done," he stated. "It was He, through the Superior General's voice, that said a new La Salle should be erected. Therefore, He will never abandon this project, no matter how dark the night may be." Brother Alfred's mind was made up and the College would survive.

Although it was very difficult for his colleagues to see it that way, in view of the circumstances, Brother Alfred's faith paid off. The Board agreed to ask the bank for a three-year extension at a mutually agreeable percentage. Banking houses were having their own problems at the time and looked with reserve on the proposed extension. They finally agreed to a one-year extension of the loan at a rate of four percent, which proved to be one and one-half percent lower than the original charge.[10] La Salle would operate for at least one more year.

As the College waded through the tangled underbrush of financial depression, changes and improvements were being made in the curriculum. The College *Bulletin* for 1929 announced a revision of the type of degree program offered. The Bachelor of Arts degree would be conferred on students successfully completing the Arts, Arts and Sciences, and the Education program. The Bachelor of Science degree could now be earned only by those who completed the three-year premed course after they successfully completed their freshman year of medical school. Although the *Bulletin* made a distinction between Arts and Arts and Sciences programs, closer examination of the curriculum indicates that all students matriculated in the general Arts and Sciences, save for those who elected to follow the predental or premedical program. By selection of a major subject and electives, the general course was to prepare students for a variety of careers. To further help the students plan their program, each man was assigned a faculty advisor.[11]

In the spring of 1930, La Salle College was inspected by Dr. Chambers, Middle States Association of Colleges and Secondary Schools representative. In general, his reports were favorable, while recommending that an additional resident professor be secured, more reference works be added to the library, and cataloging the library holdings be completed. Dr. Chambers gave the President every reason to believe La Salle would be accredited. In December, 1930, the College and high school departments were admitted to the American Council of Education. In view of the financial condition of the College in 1930, the accreditations proved a welcome encouragement for faculty and administration alike. By December, 1931, Brother Alfred was able to report that La Salle College was approved by nine organizations, including the Association of American Colleges, American Medical Association, Regents of the State of New York, and the Pennsylvania State Board of Law Examiners.

Some few additions were made to the curriculum during the remainder of Brother Alfred's term. In 1930, courses in business administration, commerce, and finance were inaugurated. Further additions were made in the classics, modern languages, education, and pure sciences to the extent that these subjects could now be selected as majors. In 1931, the B.S. degree was offered in accounting. That same year, plans were drawn up for a school of music, a school of physical education, and a school of library science. It was alleged that special brochures were printed for these various schools, but none are extant today. The announcement of plans for these projects was probably made to elicit interest for the program. When this was not forthcoming, the plans were dropped.[12] An article in *The Collegian*, dated May 12, 1931, outlined plans for a graduate program in business administration leading to the M.B.A. degree. There is no evidence that this program was ever implemented. Again, the article seemed like a trial balloon to poll interest in the program. When there was no reaction, the plan was shelved. Finally, the premed program had to be rearranged in the winter of 1932. With very little advance notice, Jefferson Medical College required all applicants to have a college degree. This proved a shock to men in the third year of the premed program. Instead of going on to med school, they stayed on another year to secure their degrees, and the College adjusted the premed program accordingly.

With expanded facilities, the College was able to enroll many more students. When the new buildings were occupied in September, 1929, a total of ninety-four students was registered in the college department. Of these, forty-nine were first-year students. A total of eighty-five applied for admission as freshmen in 1929, but thirty-five were refused because of academic deficiency. Numbers gained steadily and rapidly during the first few years at 20th and Olney. During Brother Alfred's last year as President, 1931-1932, there were over 150 college men matriculating. It was noted that a change was taking place in the student body with a marked increase in non-Catholics. The majority of non-Catholics proved to be Jewish, while a small percentage were Protestants. In order to encourage outstanding scholars to apply to La Salle, ten scholarships commemorating the opening of the new La Salle and named "Cardinal Dougherty Scholarships" were founded. They provided full tuition. Room and board were included if the scholar lived outside Philadelphia. However, the open competition was limited to "Catholic graduates of private and public high schools." La Salle College completely supported the scholarships; and, if Brother Alfred, in seeking permission to name the scholarships after Cardinal

Dougherty, thought the Cardinal would help support them, the Cardinal did not take the hint but did allow his name to be used.

Naturally, the size of the college faculty kept pace with that of the student body. By 1929, there were twelve Brothers, eight laymen, and one priest on the college faculty. Among these men there were three Ph.D.'s, and one D.F.A.; the remainder had A.M. degrees. Full-time lay Professors Holroyd, Doernenburg, and Tolson taught biology, German, and English respectively. A number of laymen taught on a part-time basis. J. Vincent Taggart taught business law, James Henry taught economics, Doctors McElwee, Callaghan, and McGeary taught anatomy, osteology, and embryology respectively, while Mr. Valentine taught Spanish and Mr. Vaughan taught French. An anonymous essay found in the College archives that indicates the author was totally disenchanted with the concept of laymen teaching on the college staff gives an idea as to faculty salary in 1930. Professor Tolson, an Oxford graduate and a doctoral candidate at Penn, taught medieval and modern history, ethics, and first and second-year English. He likewise taught English at night to Brothers teaching at West Catholic. His total salary for his efforts was $2,000 a year. Apparently, the lay faculty were painfully aware of the financial crisis at the College. Despite the lugubrious picture drawn by our anonymous chronicler, it would seem the general faculty found favor with the students. J. P. Cummings wrote, "If a more sociable group of men than our beloved teachers can be found, I have yet to see them." From these sentiments, it is easy to conclude that despite the increase of numbers at La Salle, the Brothers and lay faculty carried on the enviable tradition of taking personal interest in their students, a tradition basically La Sallian.

Outside the lecture hall, activity continued apace at the new La Salle. Many facilities formerly unavailable at 1240 were put to good use on the new campus. Naturally, with the new gymnasium in the offing, interest in athletics increased. In November, 1929, Coach Vincent Taggart organized a freshman college basketball team. Practice was held in the auditorium of College Hall until the completion of the Wister Hall gym. In February, 1930, the gym was officially opened with a game between the college freshmen and the high school varsity. Brother Alfred made a short, official address and then tossed up the ball. In December of that same year, a student athletic association was organized, with Edward V. Stenton, Chairman, and Edward C. Coverdale, Secretary. At about the same time, the college administration decided to add intercollegiate football to the athletic activities at La Salle. It is important to note the date of this decision. Brother Alfred was still President when this decision was made; his successor, accused of wanting to make La Salle the Notre Dame of the East, is usually associated with this action. Following up this decision, the administration sought recommendations for coaches. It was Knute Rockne of Notre Dame who came up with the name of the future coach, Tom Conley. In the spring of 1932, another sport appeared on the La Salle scene: wrestling. The resident students opposed the day students in seven matches. The residents won by a score of 26 to 3, a favorable omen for the future of football at the College.

To complement the formal theology courses offered the students, Brother Alfred organized several religious activities. Special services were arranged for the first Friday of each month. In addition, chapters of the League of the Sacred Heart and the Sodality of the Most Blessed Virgin were formed. Provisions were made for the seniors to make their annual retreat at Malvern, Pennsylvania.

Other activities, disrupted by the campus transfer, took stock and reorganized. Under the direction of Brother Gregory, the Buskin and Bauble Society, the college dramatists, organized. Anthony Zenszer was elected first president. By May 9, 1930, the play *The Queen's Husbands* hit the boards in College Hall auditorium. La Salle men filled all roles, including those of the female characters. Although not as well organized as the thespians, the journalists at the College were busy. They had a fifty-year tradition of publication to uphold. In May, 1931, *The Collegian* appeared as the official weekly newspaper of the College. Its many predecessors included *The La Salle Advance,* the first college publication;

The Argosy; The Budget, an alumni publication; *The Go Getter,* published by the commercial department; *The Quadrangle;* and *The Acorn.* Despite depression, expansion, and controversy, *The Collegian* still thrives today.

As the spring term of 1932 lengthened, faculty and administration alike realized that Brother Alfred would not be able to continue as President. His health was visibly impaired by the great strain of fiscal and other responsibilities he carried. As religious superior of the Brothers, as chief negotiator with the builders and creditors, and as College President, Brother Alfred had pushed himself to the limits of his constitution. On May 15, 1932, Brother Alfred took advantage of the Founder's Day holiday and went to Baker Field to watch the Phillies. This was the first time he had taken relaxation outside the College in four years. And he slept through the entire game.

In a few months, Brother Alfred was succeeded as President by Brother Anselm. However, Brother Alfred was asked by his successor to continue handling negotiations with the builders. This he did during the first few months of the next administration. Brother Alfred stayed on the staff at La Salle College for twelve more years, retiring to Ammendale in 1944. He lived there until his death in 1957 at eighty-five years of age. During his last years at La Salle, he organized a Sunday Labor Management School. Men from labor, business, industry, government, and the police force met on Sunday mornings for lectures in leadership, psychology, labor problems, practical English, and public speaking. These lectures had a tremendous impact on labor and industry in Philadelphia. Local radio stations gave free time for evening lectures and for civic, social, and economic discussions. Forums were sponsored at outdoor rallies in the public parks. In January, 1941, Brother Alfred, representing the Labor School, gave Franklin Delano Roosevelt the "De La Salle Medal for Distinguished Service in the Cause of Peace and Social Security." Despite the popularity and success of the lectures and meetings, pressure in opposition to Brother Alfred's organization grew, until finally Cardinal Dougherty ordered the meetings discontinued. All that the Cardinal opposed in his order are taken as common ideas today in labor relations and social involvement. Brother Alfred was just about a quarter century too early in his thinking. The causes Brother Alfred fought for were to be realized in future events in American history, events which would have very direct effects on the College he set further on the road toward destiny.

6. Two Valleys: Two Men

As the summer of 1932 dragged on, despair crept across the United States. One of the few voices of optimism heard in the land was that of Herbert Hoover, acclaiming the upturn in the economy that summer. The people did not heed Hoover's claims, however, and Franklin Roosevelt was elected. Was Hoover right; had the economy really swung up only to be shattered by the misgivings of a new administration? Or was the 1932 summer increase only to be followed by deeper valleys in the economy? These are difficult questions to answer. But statistics indicate that the economy had plunged to depths never before experienced in the history of American finance. In 1929, 659 banks with total deposits of $250 million closed; 2,294 additional banks, worth $1.7 billion, closed in 1931; and in 1932, in spite of R.F.C., 1,456 banks closed their doors. Capital investments for production fell from $10 billion in 1929 to around $1 billion in 1932. Of all the nations in the world, the United States experienced the sharpest decline in its national income. As the national economy settled in the seemingly endless valley of fiscal depression, the populace turned in hope to a new leader. Thus it was in the nation when Brother Anselm, President 1932-1941, took charge of La Salle College in the summer of 1932.

Many believe that the times make the man. Nonetheless, before the man can be made by his times, something with which to build the man must have existed before the "times." Such was the case with Brother Anselm. This happy warrior of God would lead La Salle College through some of its darkest years in the great valley of national economic disaster. Destined to serve the second longest term of any president of La Salle to date, Brother Anselm brought to his task a lively and abiding spirit of faith in God, a wealth of common sense, an extensive and adhesive competence in fiscal matters, and a self-sacrificing sense of devotion to colleagues, students, and community alike. Despite the overwhelming odds against the survival of La Salle College during the Depression, Brother Anselm never gave way to the easy role of the defeatist. As he led the College out of the dark valley of depression, he found the College on the threshold of a still deeper valley: World War II. Even after his term as president expired, Brother Anselm still devoted much of his time and interest to La Salle, helping to see the College through the darkest war years. Today, he remains a living inspiration to administration and faculty alike. As a member of the Board of Managers, he generously gives of his experience and wisdom, when he might, in all justice, seek the peace and quiet of retirement.

When Brother Anselm assumed the presidency of La Salle College in 1932, the corporation's fiscal valley was hemmed in by nine mountainous debts. The Board of City Trusts claimed $250,000, while the Corn Exchange Bank and the Market Street National Bank claimed $349,549 each. La Salle owed $130,000 to the Metropolitan Bank of Baltimore and $60,000 to Calvert Hall College in the same city. The College was indebted to the Province for $162,000, while $9,000 was still owed to John McShain, the builder. In reviewing these obligations for the Board, Brother Anselm pointed out that the College had only $9,174.33 on hand to handle a debt service covering a total liability of $1,320,098. Furthermore, because of "bad times" and in spite of an increased enrollment, the College income was declining since many students were unable to pay their tuition. In fact, things were so bad that tuition payments came to

La Salle in the form of butter, eggs, chickens, paving blocks, shrubbery, fuel oil, and manual labor in a variety of forms.

There was, however, one ray of hope: the creditors had agreed
to carry the College until April 1, 1933, at four percent interest. In
other words, the College would remain open till the spring, for, in
truth, Brother Anselm knew, as did the Board, that the available
liquid assets of the College just would not pay even a four percent
interest rate.[1] Shortly after the Board had heard Brother Anselm's
report on November 29, 1932, a serious situation developed which
called for delicate negotiations. Brother Alfred, President Emeritus,
who was handling the contractual negotiations with the builder,
complained of some work poorly done. This brought the original
heat problem out into the open again. The builder reminded the
architects that he had willingly repaired the damages to College
Hall because of lack of heat, although he was not contractually
obliged to do so. He felt Brother Alfred's complaints were unjusti-
fied, especially in view of the fact that the builder had carried a
college note for construction work for over four years without charg-
ing interest. In view of the tense situation, Brother Anselm relieved
Brother Alfred of his duties towards the builder and assumed them
himself. Had the builder required the $9,000 immediately, as he
had every right to do, the College would have been at a complete
loss to make payment.[2]

April 1, 1933, came and went, and La Salle College was unable
to meet its obligations. Fortunately, it seems the banks looked the
other way. The College was open; a goodly number of students was
in attendance. Perhaps, thought the creditors, when the term is
ended, some attempt at payment will be made. Nothing happened
so far as the bankers were concerned. Brother Anselm, with the
storm clouds of fiscal disaster thundering through the valley, worked
feverishly to secure some fiscal resources for the College. An increase in the number of students taking science courses forced the
College to build more laboratories. To do this, Brother Anselm
sought aid for the College by the direct method: personal contact.
Many a Philadelphia businessman paled when he heard the familiar,

congenial laugh in his waiting room. Brother Anselm would leave, he knew for sure, more financially secure. By these visits, he was able to secure donations for the College totaling $9,975 and pledges totaling $10,275. The total cost of the improvements was $11,980. Considering the times, Brother Anselm's record was not too bad; his goal was missed by only $2,015. The money collected was spent immediately on the needed renovations.

In the meantime, the bank notes remained due. The College made no move. Finally, the banks held a joint meeting on October 24, 1933, in order to consider foreclosure on La Salle. After hearing the various arguments advanced in favor of La Salle, the bankers, in hopes that the nationwide depression would pass and in view of the increased enrollment at the College, adjusted the interest on La Salle's note. One percent was to be paid on February 1, 1934, and another one percent to be paid by April 30, 1934. After April 30, the bankers would meet again and determine the rates.[3] When the waiting period was up, the College was just about able to carry the interest rate. At this point, the banks asked the College to refinance the entire debt of $700,000 at two percent interest and three percent interest on the $250,000 mortgage. Cardinal Dougherty, when notified of the banks' decision, expressed serious doubt that such refinancing could be effected. Of course, the Cardinal's doubt proved true. Finally, the banks, feeling La Salle College would prove to be an enduring and profitable institution, agreed to carry the debt in the hope of some future return. The bankers had been advised that had they foreclosed on La Salle, they would have received a return of less than three to five cents per dollar invested. But while they carried La Salle's debt, the bankers insisted that the College take every means possible to increase revenue. There were some who felt that this mandate of the bankers could be met by increasing student enrollment and by "increased and sustained athletic activity in the major sports."[4] This, in part, explains a major expansion in intercollegiate athletics which took place in the thirties.

The alphabet agencies and the emergency legislation of the first hundred days in the New Deal provided a psychological shock absorber which helped the nation remain relatively calm. In electing Roosevelt to a second term in 1936, the people seemed unaware that the nation's economy was moving towards its lowest point. At La Salle, financial matters followed relatively the same pattern. Nonetheless, with total assets of $1,869,828 and total liabilities of $1,383,726 in 1935, the College struggled on, only to be met by another crisis in 1937. In that year, the Board of Education of the City of Philadelphia announced its intention of purchasing a tract of land immediately adjacent to La Salle's campus for the construction of Central High School, with plans for a future city college. Brother Anselm appeared before the Board of Education and tried to dissuade them from their plans, but to no avail. However, Add Anderson, a personal friend of Brother Anselm and Business Manager for the Board of Education, came forward with a solution which served La Salle's interests. He noted that it was the policy of the Board of Education never to stand in the way of progress of any educational institution; and, whenever it could, the Board would advance the cause of education in Philadelphia on any level. As a result, arrangements were made to cede the right of option through Anderson's office, clearing the way for the purchase of ten and a fraction acres on the east side of the college campus. In retrospect, the School Board's policy helped save La Salle; in return, La Salle has given the Philadelphia school system over 1,000 teachers, many of them now serving in both classroom and administrative capacity.

In June, 1937, La Salle purchased the option for the land in question at a cost of $1,500. James Starr, agent for the sixteen owners, handled the arrangements.

Once the option was attained, the College had to make purchase within the year. Naturally the major obstacle was to obtain the funds. It was absolutely out of the question to consider borrowing money from the banks; that was impossible. The only alternative was to appeal directly to the people of Philadelphia. The diamond jubilee of the opening of the College on Filbert Street occurred in

1938. Therefore, it was decided by the Board of Managers to carry on a city-wide campaign for funds to purchase the 10.1639 acre plot held in option. Cardinal Dougherty backed the campaign to the hilt. He sent a letter to every pastor in the archdiocese urging the people to support La Salle in its grave need. The entire situation was succinctly described, the Cardinal noting that if the College closed, the Christian Brothers stood to lose all their holdings. Further, in order that the purchase of the land might be concluded as soon as possible, the Cardinal advanced the College $70,000. In return, the College gave the Cardinal a bond, warrant, and mortgage on the new property. These would be returned to the College as soon as the campaign was over and the full purchase price of the land, $120,000, was paid. In planning the campaign, the Cardinal had suggested a goal of one million dollars. However, once the campaign committee was formed, they set a more realistic goal of $300,000. Again, when we consider the times, the campaign was rather successful. About $180,000 was pledged, and $149,000 in cash was actually collected, while the campaign expenses totaled $25,000.

Theoretically, any cash that came to the College belonged to the banks. Of course, the bankers realized that in order to get any return on their investment, La Salle College would have to survive. Therefore, they did not interfere with the purchase of the new land, realizing its necessity for La Salle. Nonetheless, the bankers pressured the College for a mortgage of $120,000 on the property. In view of the total situation, we must admire the courage of Brother Anselm when he maneuvered with the bankers for a bargaining position. The outcome was favorable to La Salle. On assurance by the banks that they would continue their interest rate of two percent "until the will of Francis Drexel vests," Brother Anselm agreed to give a mortgage of $120,000 on the new property. On the other hand, Brother Anselm, in the name of the College and in view of the living endowment in the person of the Brothers on the College faculty, agreed to reduce the $700,000 debt held by the banks by at least one percent per year after 1940.[5] With such an arrangement, Brother Anselm had placed the College on sound fiscal grounds.

The general impression in 1938 was that the economy was reviving. Under ordinary circumstances then and in view of the national situation, it was not too much to hope that the College would be able to hold out through 1940 and then handle the debt service of one percent with ease. Of course, future events ended in World War II and near disaster again.

In retrospect, it is obvious the College was moving out of the valley once the agreement with the bankers was formulated. But to Brother Anselm and his colleagues, money at La Salle was still tight. Two very bright fiscal landfalls in 1939 eased the burden just a trifle. Despite the fact the College was indebted to Ammendale Normal Institute for $38,807, the Province found itself in a position to advance $184,875 to the College. This noninterest-bearing loan was a great help to the College and enabled Brother Anselm to carry through several projects necessary to the ordinary management of any college. At the same time, the city suit against the College for taxes on 1240 for the year 1930-1931 came into court. The charges were approximately $24,000 and $6,000 in penalties. William T. Connor, Esq., loyal and devoted friend of the College, prepared the case, and it went into court, without a jury before Judge Kuhn. Mr. Connor filed a brilliant brief, and Judge Kuhn ruled in favor of the College, canceling the contested taxes and the penalties.[6] Since the banks had required La Salle to deposit $24,000 for tax purposes when they learned of the suit in 1933, the money with accrued interest went directly to the banks in partial payment of the $700,000 loan. This was the first substantial payment La Salle made on the loan since 1928. It would be quite some time before another was made.

Grave financial difficulties notwithstanding, Brother Anselm proved a vigorous administrator in other areas of presidential responsibility. As was noted above, when in 1933 the student demand for science and particularly premedicine curricula increased, Brother Anselm did not hesitate to implement plans for the completion of the third floor of College Hall. The third floor alterations seem miniscule in contrast to the new McCarthy Stadium project. Since the previous administration had agreed to inaugurate football, Brother Anselm felt it might be fiscally wise to construct a stadium at La Salle. There was enough space immediately behind Wister Hall. In fact, when the College first opened, a football field, running east to west, had been laid out right next to the rear of Wister Hall on a plateau barely wide enough for the field. Brother Anselm felt a larger area was needed. His first impulse was to dig down behind Wister Hall and meet the deep slope of the terrain to form a natural amphitheatre. However, the excavation soon hit solid rock, and the venture was abandoned. Brother Anselm then decided to fill the area. This project, which might be called "two men and a horse," took three years to complete, while consuming over 150,000 cubic yards of fill. The man in charge, Mr. Joseph Crowley, and another elderly man, along with a horse and hand-horse scoop shovel, completed the entire project. The high slope which resulted along 20th Street was held in place by layers of discarded chunks of asphalt from renovated city streets. The prophets of gloom predicted that eventually a wall would be needed. A glance down 20th Street today proves them wrong. Further, Mr. Crowley used only his eye and a line of string to lay out the field. Later, when the engineers made preliminary surveys before constructing McCarthy Stadium, they asked for the plans. When told how the field was constructed, they were astounded that such accuracy could be attained by seemingly primitive means.

The actual construction of McCarthy Stadium began in 1936. This project was made possible through a $10,000 gift by Sir John A. McCarthy, K.C.S.G. It was McCarthy also who was instrumental in getting the banks to hold the mortgages on La Salle and to continue the low interest rates as mentioned above. Obviously, without the latter agreement, stadium construction would have been impossible. Again, both the Board of Managers and the bankers felt that a stadium would contribute to the possibility of securing revenue through intercollegiate sports. The total cost of the stadium, including an eight-foot wire fence which circled the entire area, was $38,126. By December, 1936, $20,406 had been paid on the stadium. On November 1, 1936, McCarthy Stadium was officially opened and dedicated; the ceremonies concluded with Brother Anselm kicking the first ball. La Salle then played St. Mary's of Minnesota and, appropriately, won 47-12.

Other areas of the campus received attention during the stadium construction. During the first three years of Brother Anselm's administration, over 400 pieces of evergreen shrubbery and trees were placed on the College quadrangle and around the buildings. Many of these items substituted for payment of student tuition. In 1935, the library area was enlarged and stacks provided for 12,000 volumes. Then, by 1939, 1240 was in terrible condition, so extensive repairs, both inside and out, were undertaken. Again, much of the work on 1240 was done in complete or partial payment of student fees. It was fortunate the repairs had been made, since the number of students who applied to the high school could no longer be accommodated at the Belfield campus; and the overflow was sent to 1240.

As the thirties drew to a close, Brother Anselm, like his many predecessors, began to experience the happy but vexing problem of space. By 1939, every available corner in College and Wister Halls was utilized for instruction. Resident students were scattered about the neighborhood and housed in the most unlikely places on campus. The answer was simple: another building was needed. Again, the word went around the business houses: Brother Anselm was on tour. Among the friends and alumni of La Salle, Brother Anselm collected $10,000. Obviously, this was not enough. Yet John Mc-Shain agreed to construct a building for that modest amount. As a result, on September 30, 1940, the cornerstone of McShain Hall was laid by Denis Cardinal Dougherty. The building stands directly east of the faculty house at the opposite side of the quadrangle. The basement section constituted the college union building. Half was devoted to a lounge area, the remainder to recreational facilities. There were four classrooms and two offices on the first floor. The top floor contained eighteen private rooms, lavatory and shower facilities. Half of these were used by resident students, the remainder by religious faculty. Mr. McShain's outstanding generosity in a period of fiscal instability enabled La Salle to provide necessary conveniences for its students. The building today forms an integral part of the college quadrangle, symbolic of great generosity in difficult times of the College's history.[7]

In 1932, the academic structure of the College changed significantly. Departments of instruction were separated into two schools: the School of Arts and Sciences and the School of Business Administration. Each school had separate entrance requirements, the main distinction being in the area of required mathematics courses. In the School of Arts and Sciences, curricula were available in the classics, social sciences, philosophy, pure science, premedical studies, predental studies, and education. Premed and predental programs required four full years of study. The School of Business Administration offered a Bachelor of Science degree in accounting, prelaw studies, and a general course in business. The following year, a full course in journalism, leading to the B.A. degree, was offered. Students electing journalism followed the Arts and Sciences core curriculum for two years. The last two years were spent in studying the history, technique, and critique of newspapers, magazines, and books. Thomas P. O'Neil, a graduate of La Salle and city editor of the now defunct *Philadelphia Record,* headed this newly-formed department. The impact of this program is evident in the quality of college publications in the middle thirties, especially *The Collegian.*[8]

The College *Bulletin* for 1933-34 announced a new grading system for the College. Until this time, numerical grades were issued with word equivalents. Students scoring between 95-100 were classed as "Honors"; 80-94, "Excellent"; 70-79, "Satisfactory"; 60-69, "Condition"; and below 60, "Failure." In 1933, the quality point grading system was introduced. The first six letters of the alphabet served as grades and were evaluated according to a scale. An "A" grade earned three quality points for each credit hour, a

"B" grade earned two quality points and a "C" earned one point per credit hours. The remaining grades, "D," "E," and "F," received no quality points. In order to graduate, the student index or average quality point percentage had to be 1.0 or better. At the same time, all seniors had to present a thesis before graduation. Until 1934, the student was required to write one thesis of approximately three thousand words. In 1934, the student was permitted to write two theses on different subjects, but only about one thousand five hundred words in length. The student was also required to take an oral examination on his thesis. From the evidence available, it is difficult to determine whether or not these oral examinations included knowledge of several areas of study. *The Collegian* for April 16, 1937, gives the impression that a general examination was given but is not entirely clear on this matter. However, the *Student Handbook* for 1938 gives a more accurate picture. "Seniors who have a scholastic index of less than 2.8 as an average for their first seven semesters will be required to take an oral examination in their major subject, besides their final written examinations." The Committee on Degrees appointed a three-man panel from each department to hear the oral examinations.

In discussing the curriculum of La Salle during Brother Anselm's administration and those of his predecessors, it is interesting to note that most decisions on curriculum were reached by a faculty group known as the Community Council. Community here refers to the group of Brothers who composed the majority of the faculty throughout the first seventy-five years of the College history. Further, members of the Community Council were appointed by the Provincial Superior for the purpose of serving in an advisory capacity to the local superior, in this case, the president of the college. In studying the curriculum during this period, it is often difficult to discover motives for action. Frequently, the minutes of the Community Council were poorly kept and went into little detail. For example, minutes for a meeting of the Council held on February 16, 1938, indicate that Brother Anselm suggested the addition of Italian to the curriculum. "After discussion of details, the majority of opinion was found to be favorable. . . ." The next thing we find of Italian instruction is an announcement in the *Bulletin* for 1939. In view of these circumstances, it is difficult to evaluate the role played by graduate schools, faculty, administration, and students in the development of the curriculum through the early forties. Of course, one guideline is available, the aims and objectives of the College.

In the 1939 *Bulletin,* the aims and objectives of the College were restated. The threefold objectives were to combine the moral, intellectual, and physical development of the students; to foster "intellectual excellence" under the aegis of Christian philosophy; and to stress Christian morality in the development of character and "sound citizenship." As stated, the aims and objectives embody the Anselm image, what he felt to be best for La Salle men and that which his own life exemplified.

The following year, the last major curriculum change under Brother Anselm was announced. All students in B.A. and B.S. programs had to select a major and a minor subject. The entire curriculum was divided into four groups as follows: Group I: English, ethics, French, German, Greek, Italian, journalism, Latin, philosophy; Group II: economics, education, history, political science, sociology; Group III: accounting, business law, finance, insurance; Group IV: biology, chemistry, mathematics, physics. The major had to be selected from one group and the minor from one of the remaining three.[9]

Perhaps one of the greatest factors which sustained La Salle during the dark years of depression was the size of the student body. When Brother Anselm took office in 1932, there were 218 men in the college. Since the financial structure of the college corporation included the high school and Benilde Academy, we mention their population here also; that is, 272 in the high school, 37 in Benilde Academy. Total enrollment increased through 1935, when the college, in just five years, had doubled its enrollment. To meet this increase over the five-year span, the faculty was increased from twenty-one members in 1930 to forty-one in 1935. Throughout

Brother Anselm's term, the enrollment continued to swell, so that during his last two years in office there were 408 men in the college department in 1939 and 411 in 1940. Total enrollment went over 1,000, with 592 in the high school, plus an additional seventy secondary students at 1240. Benilde Academy, because of lack of space, had ceased to function in 1939. However, the success story of La Salle students was not found only in numbers at this time. Brother Anselm reported to the Board that every premed student of the class of 1934 had been accepted by Jefferson Medical School before June 1. The following year he reported all premed students accepted by Philadelphia medical schools. Surveying the student body at La Salle in 1934, *The Collegian* reported great scholastic progress at the College. Dwelling on the new professors and extensive changes in the curriculum, the student writer could see only impressive academic accomplishments for the future. He was quite satisfied with the academic posture of the College. "The ratings achieved by the student body in examinations this year show that La Salle rates high among the colleges of the country, while the record of the Senior Premedical Group is an outstanding accomplishment in the college history."

Perhaps one of the most distasteful incidents concerning La Salle students came to Brother Anselm's attention in 1938. A graduate of West Catholic High School, Philadelphia, was apparently refused admission to La Salle because of his race. Brother Anselm insisted the matter be discussed by the Community Council. The President felt the case important and a policy should be established. He warned the Brothers' Council members that should such a situation be called to the attention of the Cardinal, the College would be in jeopardy. Further, it was stated that the Inter-Racial College Association was then soliciting the aid of Catholic colleges in behalf of the Catholic Negro. Brother Anselm wondered how La Salle College could take any other position than that of admitting Catholic Negroes once they fulfilled the requirements. Apparently, nothing was said about non-Catholic Negroes. The Council agreed, and the policy of admitting Catholic Negroes was established. Whether or not the "Catholic" qualification for Negroes was ever enforced, it is difficult to say. All evidence points to the contrary.[10] Another very distressing problem concerning students troubled Brother Anselm just a few months before his term ended. Aware of the threatened expansion of war into a worldwide conflict, the President sought advice on the possible means of deferring college students. However, this problem was passed to his successor.

Many of the organizations still active at La Salle today were founded during the Anselm era. There is no doubt that athletics hit the new campus with a tremendous impact. In reading a variety of literature written by La Salle students from Filbert Street, 1240, and 20th and Olney, one senses a deep student enthusiasm and loyalty for everything that was La Salle. Therefore, when the new campus was opened with its expanded athletic facilities, the pent-up enthusiasm of years past seemed to literally explode on the campus. As a result, there were many athletic activities at La Salle during the thirties. Thus, we mention only the highlights, and those only briefly. La Salle fielded intercollegiate teams in football, basketball, track, and crew. The first football team started its regular schedule in October, 1932. Marty Brill and Tom Conley were the first football coaches. Football remained at La Salle until World War II, when the student population fell so low that the sport had to be dropped. Nationally, and even more so locally, La Salle made a great name for itself in football. Much care was taken that the team represented the College well. For example, regulations handed the football team prior to their departure for a game at Niagara Falls in 1940 read as follows: "All members of the squad should remember they represent La Salle College and should act as gentlemen at all times. Dress properly for all meals: both on the train and in the hotel. Do not wear sweaters." Interestingly enough, on a trip to Providence, the team went by train to New York and then over night by boat to Providence. Frequently, the entire resident body, twenty-five strong, would accompany the team on away-trips.

Basketball proved very popular in the thirties and was able to survive the war period. Under the leadership of such men as James

Henry, Thomas Conley, Leonard Tanseer, "Obie" O'Brien, and Joseph Meehan, a deep-rooted tradition of basketball excellence was fostered at La Salle. Some of the top-scorers of this period such as Mort Gratz, Clem Meehan, Charles Mosicant, Frank Hoerst, Charles McGlone, and Bob Walters are still familiar names in Philadelphia sports circles.

In the meantime, many new activities appeared on the La Salle campus. J. Vincent Taggart, of the faculty and coaching staff, organized the Law Club in 1933. Its purpose was to give prelaw students a wider background and provide contacts in the field of law. Meetings consisted mainly of papers and discussions. At about the same time, the Premedical Society was organized. Its purpose was to provide a forum for those interested in the medical profession; discussion of present and future problems in the study of medicine; observation of methodology in local medical schools; discussion of a doctor's life and his problems; and "a deeper understanding into medicine and surgery with an effort to remove the veil of error and fancy at present found in the minds of many students." Brother Alphonsus, assistant professor of biology, was appointed first moderator. Debating was still a popular activity at La Salle. The Board was informed that the College team had won the Philadelphia Intercollegiate Debating League championship in 1934. Victories were scored over Penn, Villanova, Temple, St. Joseph's, American Institute of Banking — all members of the men's division. Rosemont, women's division champion, was then defeated. The debaters continued their championship ways and began to win national attention. In 1936, teams from Yale, Harvard, Lehigh, Penn, and John Hopkins were defeated, an accomplishment both faculty and students were proud of as noted in the minutes of the Board of Managers.

In 1935, the first fraternity at La Salle was founded: Sigma Phi Lambda. The organizers were John Guischard, Theodore Berry, C. Francis Sullivan, John J. Kelly, and Lawrence Truitt. Brother Leonard was moderator of the fraternity, whose aims were to support all La Salle's social, cultural, and academic activities. In 1943, the war forced the group to abandon its activities. In 1960, Dr. John Guischard, one of the founders of Sigma Phi Lambda, asked COE, a group formed in 1959 with the intention of alleviating student apathy, to consider reactivating Sig Phi. The proposal was accepted, and Sig Phi fraternity today conducts all spirit functions on campus, sponsors the Hospitality Committee for visiting athletic teams, and helps in the orientation program for entering freshmen.

In 1936, the Honor Society of La Salle College, founded in 1932, was reorganized and formed the Alpha Chapter of the Honor Society of Alpha Epsilon. This society was composed of men who were excellent students and who were outstanding in their loyalty to the College. That same year, El Circolo Italiano reached its final stages of organization with the election of officers and the adoption of a constitution. The Italian Club, a movement started by Archangelo Salomone, currently Woodrow Wilson professor of history at the University of Rochester, and Michael Raione, was devoted to social and cultural activities calculated to spread an interest in and understanding of the Italian language. Ugo Donini, assistant professor of history, was the club's first moderator. Professor Donini likewise founded the History Club in 1936. The program of the club called for research on obscure but interesting events and people in history; research on the origin and developmnt of "current customs and mannerisms"; instructions in the methods of research; and presentation of methodology of history in the secondary school.

As the result of a senior class meeting held in December, 1939, La Salle College was to have another publication: *The Explorer,* the college yearbook. Instrumental in bringing the yearbook to reality were *Collegian* news editor, Charles Guerin, and John McMenamin, president of the class of 1940. Financial aid for the yearbook had been promised by Brother Anselm, the Masque, the college dramatic society, and the Mothers' Club. Each senior was charged five dollars, while the underclassmen paid two or three dollars for a less expensively bound book. Surprisingly enough, *The Explorer* managed to appear throughout the war years.

Many religious activities introduced by Brother Alfred were

retained. In addition, a full-time college chaplain was obtained in the person of Father Higgins. Every Thursday, the chaplain delivered a lecture to the entire college student body. Father Higgins must have been quite popular with the students, since favorable comments appeared often in *The Collegian*.

As America moved through its dark years of misery and depression, factions, right and left wing groups, hate and smear groups, crusaders and watchers permeated the American society. Then, as now, there was much talk of involvement. In one outstanding instance, La Salle students became "involved." In 1935, goaded by Brother Anselm, the students organized a petition asking President Roosevelt to condemn the policy of the Mexican government, demanding "that it cease denying fundamental and inalienable rights to the residents of that country regardless of religious affiliation." They also asked for the recall of Ambassador Josephus Daniels, "who has by his conduct, given moral support to the present government, to the shame of American Catholics."[11] La Salle students also became involved with the administration of the College. In 1937, the administration invited student representatives to sit on the Faculty Committee on Extra-Curricular Activities. Presidents of the senior, junior, and sophomore classes became ex-officio members. This was a first in the college history.

Brother Anselm directed his energies and attention toward the alumni also. In 1936, a reorganization meeting of the alumni was held in City Hall, just across the street from the spot where the first meeting of the alumni had taken place in 1871. In his opening remarks, the alumni president called for a closer bond between graduates and students. It was decided, therefore, to hold an annual alumni dinner to honor athletes at the College. Edwin Feeny headed a committee to study the by-laws of the association, while Dr. Francis Braceland was appointed Chairman of a Committee on College Affairs, whose purpose was to find means to link the various clubs and organizations of the College with the alumni. Likewise a thorough revision of the alumni list was called for. In 1937, the first Homecoming Day was planned for Founder's Day, May 15.

Religious services, addresses from prominent alumni, athletic events, and a dinner were scheduled. The general purpose was to introduce the young and old graduates. On October 29, 1941, the Grotto of Our Lady of Lourdes, a gift of the high school alumni, was dedicated. Situated on the southeast corner of the quadrangle, its purpose was to ask the help and protection of the Most Blessed Virgin on all La Salle men in military service.

The year 1941 saw the end of the Anselm era at La Salle College. Brother Anselm had guided the College through trying and vexing times, especially through the circumstances of the impending war. Although destined to lead the College through the valley of fiscal despair, he never allowed its social, intellectual, or religious atmosphere to be enveloped in the haze of purely financial considerations. Deep in debt the College was; but it was a living, active, effective institution of higher learning. And ultimately, he provided the solution for La Salle's financial difficulties. His weapons were an abiding trust in God and a knack for negotiations laced with cajolery. To speculate on the "if's" had the war not developed is useless. The war came, Brother Anselm left to become principal of West Catholic High School, and his successor took the reins of La Salle College. He too was destined to lead the College through a valley — the valley of America at war.

The United States was deeply committed both by principle and action to the anti-Axis powers in the already active European theatre of war by August, 1941, when Brother Emilian took office as President of La Salle College. On the surface, our diplomatic relations with Japan seemed smooth, but today we know that active preparations for war were hidden behind a sinister tranquility. Before 1941 passed into history, the United States was involved in a two-sphere war that would reach to the very fibre of the nation and subject it to a test it had not experienced since the Civil War. No institution would go unscathed; no family, no home, no citizen could pretend the War was not there. It was obvious to Brother Emilian and his colleagues when he took office that the times ahead would be dangerous for the nation and for La Salle College. Brother

Emilian, having served in several administrative positions during the presidency of Brother Anselm, knew first-hand the tremendous struggle that had taken place to put La Salle College in a viable state during the thirties; he knew further the delicate balance that had to be maintained in order to keep the College viable financially and academically. To maintain this delicate balance during a national emergency, an emergency which undermined the very fabric of the College — its student body, was Brother Emilian's challenge. It was a challenge he did not try to bypass. An extremely intelligent and talented individual, Brother Emilian brought to his task a long experience in educational problems, an extremely high quality of professionalism, together with an energetic, demanding, and vivid personality. In a word, leadership was Brother Emilian's outstanding characteristic, and it was recognized by faculty, students, and administration alike.

Just seven days after the Japanese attack on Pearl Harbor, December 7, 1941, Brother Emilian made his first report to the Board of Managers in which he indicated a marked decrease in the college enrollment. It had dropped from 411 to 300. This decrease was attributed to the prospects of serving the armed forces which faced all young men. As the nation reacted to the Pearl Harbor attack and mobilization proceeded apace, the number of students withdrawing from the College for military service grew. Between December 1941 and June 1942, the College population further dropped from 390 to 356. However, despite the war, one of the largest freshman classes in the history of La Salle enrolled in September 1942: 145 strong. But by December, 1942, nineteen had withdrawn for military service. Of the 350 students at La Salle in 1942, at least 127 were members of the reserves of the Army, Navy, and Marines. This meant, in effect, that they could be called at any time. What everyone expected happened in March, 1943. About eighty-four reservists were sent to the camps on March 10. Students who were following premed, predental, and pure sciences were not touched at this time and were told to stay in school until further notice. On July 1, 1943, sixty more reservists were ordered to other college and university campuses which were under the direct supervision of the Navy Department. By December, 1943, the total population of the College had dropped from 356 to 121.

The lack of mess and dormitory facilities might have proved an obstacle in having the armed forces temporarily utilize the La Salle Campus. Although this would have proved a stopgap solution for deterioration of the college population, Brother Emilian stoutly opposed any such plan and did not allow the College to apply for military occupancy. As will be seen below, Brother Emilian had his own plan. Further, he publicly announced his determination to keep La Salle open "even if it were reduced to one student." Fortunately, the College was never to reach that minimal an enrollment. However, by December, 1944, Brother Emilian reported that only 116 students enrolled in the fall. Nineteen were drafted, leaving a total student body of ninety-seven. In this student body, moreover, there were five veterans who, having completed their service, had returned to school and were sponsored by the Veterans Administration.

By December, 1944, the tide of war for the United States had turned, and all were confident of victory. In view of these circumstances, Brother Emilian's plan to keep the College open seemed assured as early as December, 1944. Still, things remained bleak at the College. Spring enrollment for 1945 dropped to ninety students, while the first and second summer terms in 1945 had only sixty-five and fifty students respectively. But when, on August 14, 1945, President Truman announced the surrender of Japan, La Salle was still open and very much alive. In the fall of 1945, 140 men enrolled, of whom twenty-seven were veterans.

Brother Emilian's concern over the college population was alleviated to a degree by an increase in the population of the high school department. Throughout the war emergency, the high school enrolled slightly over 1,000 students each year. Facilities vacated by the dwindling college population were available for the high school department. Of course, 1240 was still in use, housing about

125 high school students. Since the high school was an integral
part of the college corporation, the increased revenue from the high
school enabled the College to maintain at least a respectable fiscal
stability. In spite of this, financial considerations remained a cause
for grave concern throughout the War period. Naturally, both the
President and Board hesitated to tamper with the delicate fiscal
structure of the College. As long as the debt service could be maintained, the College could go on. Hence, Brother Emilian was chary
about involving the College in a military occupancy plan. Another
plan had to be found.

In explaining his position to the Board of Managers in 1942,
Brother Emilian stated that several colleges, fearing financial ruin
without government aid, had asked the armed forces to occupy
their facilities. He expressed the College's desire of cooperating
fully with the government, but declined to follow the lead of colleges asking for occupancy. "At La Salle we are convinced that
we can weather the storm with our regular students." Further, he
explained that if the College became a training center, both high
school and college students would have to be dismissed. The problems of starting over again after the emergency would, he felt, be
much greater than those involved in riding out the war. The policy
was put into operation, and after a year of trial Brother Emilian
had to defend his decision before the Board. He readily admitted
the College had suffered a decline in population, but contended
that he had expected this. He felt that those institutions which had
become training centers would "probably not reopen for years after
the cessation of hostilities." Actually, this proved incorrect. Moreover, he stated the College could remain open with men who were
under the draft age and those rejected for some physical defect.
"The number of the latter is surprisingly large." Brother Emilian
then discussed trends in the government which indicate that federal funds would be provided for veterans who wanted to attend
college. Since these funds would be usable at any college, Brother
Emilian stated he had every reason to believe that La Salle students
and others serving in the armed forces would select La Salle Col-

lege for completion of their education. Concluding his defense, Brother Emilian argued, "It is our judgment that the college should remain a civilian college because the presence of an army, navy, or marine unit on the campus would sound the death knell to the high school in toto and to the civilian college."[12] From this statement, it became obvious that high school tuition was playing an important role in financing the college during the emergency. Further, when studying Brother Emilian's defense of his policy in perspective, it is quite evident that he was an able predictor of the future of La Salle College. He had made an astute projection of the college vis-à-vis the emergency.

Brother Emilian's announced intention to keep the college open was strengthened when John McShain, La Salle Board Member and well-known builder, cancelled a $7,000 note he held against the College. In addition, Mr. McShain graciously donated materials and labor for the rearrangement of classrooms and laboratories necessitated by the transfer of the overflow high school population to College Hall.[13] With Mr. McShain's magnanimity, and a large high school enrollment, La Salle was able to move through the war period with relatively little financial distress. It was not until the fall of 1944 that the financial status of the College was called into question. The Real Estate Trust Company, then holding the $700,000 mortgage on La Salle, called in the President and Secretary of the College for examination of La Salle's fiscal health. In reporting the results of this meeting, Brother Emilian stated that "after examining the academic and financial status of La Salle, the bankers expressed confidence in the Brothers' ability to weather this wartime storm and to satisfy their financial obligation." Again, Brother Emilian's stay-open, stay-civilian policy proved sound under the most objective scrutiny.[14]

As was to be expected, wartime academic operations had to be adjusted, but these changes were made in line with the basic college policy of keeping La Salle open for the duration. In the summer of 1942, an optional third semester was added to the regular program. This enabled students to complete as much of their education as possible before being called to military service. As a result, the College was in session twelve months a year, with a week of recess at Christmas and a half week at Easter. Because of the accelerated program, two and sometimes three graduations were held each year. The first special commencement took place on January 31, 1943, in College Hall auditorium; thirty-five men were graduated. The students seemed to take the summer semester in stride. *The Explorer* stated, "The added semester was unusual in that, despite weather more suitable for romancing, dips in the ocean, and the like, students did accomplish much, and scholastic grades suffered little." However, the faculty reaction was understandably mixed. Twelve months' teaching caused an apparent strain on the faculty. As a result, arrangements were made to have half the faculty teach eight summer weeks, while the remaining half vacationed and vice versa.

That many students took advantage of the accelerated programs is quite evident. Two more commencements were held in 1943, sixteen men graduated in May and twenty-four received degrees on September 26, 1943. Four of the latter had already entered the service and were represented at the exercises by their parents. This was the only year in which three commencements were held. Six men graduated on January 30, 1944, while ten diplomas were conferred on May 28, 1944. At the former commencement, Brother Felician Patrick, an outstanding professor of English who was celebrating his 50th anniversary in religion, gave the commencement address. In 1945, there were only seven graduates, an accurate indication of the effect the war had on La Salle.

During the war, a special program of studies leading to the Bachelor of Science degree in business and management was established for men who were required by their draft status to work. The program included courses in business English, mathematics for managers, survey of physical science, industrial management, and psychology of adjustment. Also, industrial psychology, labor problems, personnel administration, labor legislation, propaganda and censorship, postwar political reconstruction, the writing of business and military reports, and economic problems were offered. In order to take care of shift workers, identical lectures were offered between eleven a.m. and three p.m. and again from seven p.m. to ten p.m. In September, 1943, twelve men began their studies; others joined as the war situation extended.[15] Two courses were added to the regular curriculum in order to help students fulfill their wartime duties. Science students in the junior year were offered thermodynamics and meteorology. In 1943, a pre-induction course, suggested by the armed forces, was offered for those who wished to enter special forces or Officers Candidate School. Students who successfully completed the program were given college credits for their work.

Because of the nature of the war emergency, regulations requiring a thesis for graduation were dropped and comprehensive examinations substituted. To meet the requirements for a degree, the candidate had to achieve passing grades in comprehensive examinations in his major subject and two minor subjects. The major was defined as thirty semester hours credit in one subject, or twenty-four hours in one and twelve hours in closely related subjects. In addition to the comprehensives, the seniors had to take general examinations in all subjects save the major. Comprehensives were given in mid-January.[16]

In the fall of 1944, when American hopes were rising with the tide of anticipated victory in Europe and the Pacific, the College laid plans for the future of the students and the institution. *The Collegian* for October 25, 1944, carried detailed instructions from the new Dean of the College, Brother Gregorian Paul, for those La Salle men in service who were interested in sustaining their academic interests while in service. These men were encouraged to take advantage of ASTP and Navy V-12 programs and, where that was not feasible, to follow courses sponsored by the USAFI. All men were encouraged to write to La Salle to help formulate their plans. At the annual meeting of the Board of Managers in December, 1944, Brother Emilian noted that it was the opinion of the faculty that La Salle should continue to emphasize and strengthen the liberal arts rather than follow the more popular courses in such newly discovered techniques as radar, television, and the like. Finally, the administration felt that men returning from two or three years' absence in the service would find it quite difficult to resume their education. As a result, La Salle invited all former students returning from the service to matriculate for one semester as auditors, free of charge. It is quite evident that, despite the dark days of the war, the College had managed to preserve its spirit of intense interest in student welfare and academic progress.

With the onset of war conditions, several faculty changes took place. Men who were teaching parttime were called either to the service or essential industries. When the Brothers closed St. Thomas College in Scranton, Brother D. Luke, Brother Augustine, Ph.D., and Brother Timothy were assigned to La Salle. The last took Mr. Donini's place when he transferred to Drexel. John Guischard, an alumnus, joined the staff in 1942. As noted above, the faculty members who remained at the College had very demanding schedules. As a result, Brother Emilian announced to the Board of Managers in 1944 that "acceleration will be discontinued as soon as possible because of the baneful effects on the faculty and because of the doubtful educational results achieved by the students." At the same time, it was noted that several Brothers had been assigned to teach in the high school department because of its increased size. However, once these Brothers were assigned, it was established that the number of teachers required by the accrediting agencies was not met. Therefore, laymen were hired to correct this situation.

Finally, in May of 1944, some administrative changes affecting the college were announced. Brother Felix, Ph.D., Vice-President, was named Secretary General of the College. The vice-presidential office was filled by Brother George Lewis, who vacated the office of Dean of the College. Brother Gregorian Paul, Ph.D., destined to lead La Salle in a vast postwar expansion, was named Dean. Brother Paul had come to La Salle in 1933 as instructor in chemistry. Following graduate studies in Washington, D. C., he returned to La Salle in 1941 as teacher, member of the Roster Committee, and faculty advisor to the Alumni Association until his appointment as Dean.

In time of national emergency, institutions usually have to trim some areas of operation or find that conditions force certain interests into the background. Such was the case with activities at La Salle. The fluctuating size of the student body played havoc with the activities schedules. Naturally, intercollegiate athletics were hard hit. In 1942, La Salle dropped intercollegiate football because of the draft situation. And football did not make a comeback after the war. At the same time, a compulsory course in physical fitness was introduced. Three hours a week were devoted to gymnastics, obstacle races, and sports. All students were required to take the course. Further, once or twice a week, the entire student body hiked through the local neighborhood and parks. *The Explorer* for 1943 reported that there were only two seniors athletically active, "Masterson and McCarthy"; and they captained the basketball team, which, incidentally, managed to survive the war. Swimming almost made it through the war; but in 1944, it, along with ice hockey, was dropped. However, track was the only other sport to remain throughout the duration. But the college newspapers of the period indicate that basketball and track received the same enthusiastic support of the dwindling student body as they did before the war.

A few other activities managed to survive. Surprisingly enough, in February, 1942, another literary magazine, *La Salle Colophon,* appeared. However, shortage of essential materials forced its early demise. In January, 1943, the Beta Chapter of the Theta Beta National Honor Biology Society was formed at La Salle under the leadership of Brother Alphonsus, professor of anatomy and embryology and chairman of the biology department. The purposes of the society were to promote and foster interest in biological research; to develop the science and ethics of biology in all branches correlated with scholastic philosophy and based on Christian principles. The establishment of a Theta Beta group on campus was a national honor and commendation for La Salle College. More active student interest in campus affairs was achieved in December, 1944, when the student body elected the first Student Activities Committee in the college history. The committee was composed of fifteen men whose major function was to sponsor all social activities during the spring term and to organize and advance all extra-curricular activities on campus. When one considers the curtailed enrollment and the forced inactivity of many athletic groups, the La Salle student demonstrated an indomitable spirit and enthusiasm in his cocurricular life despite, in most cases, rather grim prospects of having to fight a war upon graduating.

With a majority of its graduates in the service or in essential industries and with wartime conditions affecting both the civilian and military population, the alumni of the College were also rather inactive. However, in 1942, the alumni instituted the Signum Fidei Medal, which was to be bestowed annually on the person who had best displayed Christian principles during the year. In 1943, the medal was bestowed posthumously upon Karl Rodgers, founder of the Narberth Society. As the war grew in intensity, so did the gold stars on the Alumni Service flag. By December, 1943, six men had been killed in action; in Decemebr, 1944, the number rose to fifteen, with the final number reaching thirty-one.

With the advent of spring and summer, 1945, the United States saw the bastions of war crumble. The surrender of the Third Reich in May, the creation of the atomic bomb, lifted America out of the valley of war. Laced with the heady wine of victory, life in the United States seemed to surge toward the new age with a new rest-lessness. As La Salle College emerged from the war, it too would enter a new age, an age that would carry it to an unbelievable physical and intellectual development. La Salle, thanks to Brother Emilian's courage and foresight, did not have to wait long to swing into the new age. The structure had been preserved. However, Brother Emilian, having led La Salle out of the valley of war, was not to take it to the promised land of intellectual maturity. Rather, Brother Emilian was called, in the summer of 1945, to serve as Provincial Superior of the Brothers of the Baltimore Province. Upon public announcement of Brother Emilian's resignation as President, *The Collegian* fittingly paid the following tribute: "Through his ability, alertness, and courage, La Salle has weathered the storm. He made good his promise to keep the college open if it were reduced to only one student."

When La Salle College reopened in the fall of 1945, the students found a new President and a new challenge. The challenge was phrased by Brother Luke, the new President. Brother called the student body the "Post War La Salle College." The term was packed with meaning which Brother Luke explained as follows: "With you rests the glorious tradition of service to American youth of which La Salle rightly boasts, together with the hope and dream of a forward-looking La Salle, willing and eager to do its best for every student who enters its halls." Perhaps Brother Luke saw La Salle's future all too clearly. Realizing the vast influx of students that would swell the College to unbelievable proportions, he set the La Salle tradition of personal interest in its students in its proper perspective.

Brother Luke first came to La Salle College in 1942 as professor of English, a post he had previously held for nine years at the University of Scranton. While at La Salle, his kind and personal interest in his students and their activities, along with his sparkling lectures, won him deep respect, admiration, and affection. Thus, the student body was quite pleased with their new President. Strangely and ironically enough, however, his presidency lasted only a few months. Since Brother Luke never presided over a meeting of the Board of Managers, it is difficult to record his presidency. One change in organizational structure did take place, however. Brother Stanislaus, Ph.D., returned to La Salle after several years of graduate study. He was named Dean of Men and took charge of all veterans' affairs and extracurricular activities. On November 20, 1945, the Men of La Salle gave a testimonial dinner at the Benjamin Franklin Hotel, honoring Brother Luke's appointment as President. There were over six hundred guests, including church, state, and civic officials. In these circumstances, Brother Emilian, then Provincial Superior, had to announce that Brother Luke would be unable to continue as President because of ill health. He further stated that Brother Gregorian Paul, Dean of the College, had been named acting president. When Brother Luke was called upon to speak, he thanked those who had helped him and praised the gathering for their loyalty to La Salle.[17] Needless to say, the announcement of Brother Luke's resignation stunned the crowd. Many could not believe it; the entire situation proved a mysterious page in the history of the College. Shortly thereafter, Brother Luke left La Salle and went to Calvert Hall College, Baltimore, where he taught English in seemingly good health. Brother eventually became President of St. John's College in Washington, D. C., where his great kindness, coupled with leadership and a sense for business, convinced the friends of St. John's they should build a new school, today one of Washington's most outstanding schools. At his untimely death in 1965, he was principal of Central Catholic High School, Canton, Ohio. No one will ever know just how great a loss La Salle College suffered in the untimely "resignation" of Brother Luke.

7. Postwar Expansion

For a few months after the end of World War
II on August 14, 1945, the United States was caught
up in unbounded exultation and joy over the great victory achieved
and the end to a searing and devastating holocaust. As the first
tide of happy excitement ebbed and reason returned to the serious
business of national living, new fears developed among the people
despite victory. The United States had joined the United Nations
to achieve world peace. But the people soon found their nation
engaged in many strange and alien relationships and, finally, the
new hostilities of the "cold war." The actions and words of Stalin
even raised fears of a third world war, more devastating than the
war just ended; the nuclear age had arrived. Perhaps the most
personal of all fears was that the United States, in gearing down
from a wartime to peacetime economy, would be hurled back
into the dark jaws of depression. On the other hand, though, a
tremendous backlog of purchasing power, built up during the war,
threatened a runaway inflation. President Truman attempted to
impose federal controls but was opposed by Congress. Tremendous
pressure groups and movements built up in the country, seeking
special privileges. Moreover, the demand for demobilization, much
to the delight of Russia, thundered throughout the nation. Congress

insisted the troops be swiftly reduced from eleven million to two million. Despite this swift demobilization, the labor market was not weakened. This was due, in part, to the G.I. Bill of Rights, whereby the federal government financed veterans' education, set them up in small businesses, or gave them farm loans. The program, administered by the Veterans Administration, was highly successful. Veterans literally swamped the colleges. Many performed well and opened the doors to mass higher education, although crowded conditions immediately after the war broke down academic standards to some extent. La Salle College found itself engulfed in this stampede of veterans into higher education.

In the fall of 1945, the student population at La Salle showed a very definite increase, even though the war had been over for only a few months. Nonetheless, the College was strained to provide for the increase. This was especially true as regards the faculty. It was difficult to narrow, in a short time, the vastly expanded high school program. Therefore, many of the college faculty had to carry a rather heavy schedule to take up the slack. Brother Gregorian Paul, Dean of the College, taught a full schedule. It was while teaching a lab section that Brother Paul was called out of class on November 8, 1945, and told he was to be named President of La Salle in a few days. The decision to terminate Brother Luke's presidency had been made then, although public announcement was withheld until November 20, 1945. Brother Paul, admittedly shaken by his surprise appointment, accepted the situation at first with aplomb, then with determination to meet the challenge presented. His colleagues generally accepted him and admired his common sense, objectivity, keen insight and intelligence, sense of fair play, willingness to entertain the opinions of others, inexhaustible energy, and air of self-sufficiency. With these qualities, he provided the necessary leadership to see La Salle College through many grave and complex problems of the postwar era, the least of which proved to be the population and space problems.

As President Truman beat a hasty retreat before the demands of Congress and the American public to bring the boys back home, the number of veterans in the United States by Christmas, 1945, was well over eight million. Moreover, the tide of veterans flowed uninterrupted through the spring of 1946. As a result, that spring La Salle College experienced a one hundred per cent increase in students over the fall term. Over 280 men completed registration. Hastily made wartime alterations were torn down. Space was at a premium at the college. However, the worst was yet to come. In the summer of 1946, over 435 students enrolled. Since the high school had been dismissed for the summer, space was readily available. But in the fall of 1946, even though the numbers in the high school had been intentionally cut back, the college was hard put to accommodate the 1,215 men who enrolled. By class, there were forty-five seniors, eighty-five juniors, 202 sophomores, and 882 freshmen. A total of seventy-nine percent of all students matriculating at the college were veterans. And tuition, fees, books and supplies expenses were paid by the federal government for all veterans. By December, 1946, La Salle had accepted eighty men for the spring term and was processing 250 applications. As a result, by the spring of 1947, the enrollment jumped to 1,385. The following summer, over 900 men continued their studies. Many of these men took courses missed while in the service. Others who first matriculated in the spring term followed fall-term courses during the summer. Student population continued to climb at La Salle through 1948. In the fall of 1947, about 1,700 men matriculated; 76.4 percent were veterans. The following year, however, veterans made up only 65 percent of La Salle students while the total number enrolled rose to 1,995. It became obvious by December, 1949, the postwar boom had reached its peak. Each year the percentage of veterans enrolled dropped. In 1949, the fall term saw only 1,970 matriculating at La Salle, a decrease from the previous year of twenty-five. Brother Paul, in his *Annual Report* for 1949, warned that "unless new sources of students are sought, there will be a gradual decline during the next several years."[1]

In June, 1950, the population was further reduced at La Salle when nearly 500 seniors were graduated. This was the largest graduating class up to that time in La Salle's history. As a result, the ceremonies were held on Wednesday, June 14, in McCarthy Stadium with a capacity crowd looking on. Further pressure was removed, as Brother Paul had predicted, by a decline in registrations. For the scholastic year 1950-51, student enrollment leveled off at 1,700; while the following year, it dropped to 1,320 students in the fall term with a total of 310 freshmen, or about 100 less than those graduated in June, 1951. By December, 1951, only nineteen percent of the day students were veterans. By the end of Brother Paul's term as president, the regular college population had leveled off and nearly returned to postwar normalcy. However, in reviewing the postwar boom in students, it must be kept in mind that La Salle College established an Evening program which, by 1950, enrolled over 800 students, and, in 1951, over 1,100 students. Of these latter, sixty-six percent were veterans.[2] We will treat the Evening story at La Salle in greater length below. The overall picture of student expansion at La Salle is relatively simple in terms of numbers. But the vast and complex problems La Salle encountered as a result of the student boom are of more interest. From the outset, Brother Paul realized that some changes in administrative procedure would have to be made.

He lost no time in making these necessary administrative changes. The operation of the complete plant was divided into five distinct areas: Administration, Facilities, College, High School, and Community, the latter referring to the operations of the community of Brothers who constituted part of both college and high school faculty. The new Administration Division consisted of the President's Office, the Business Office, the Public Relations Office, and the Service Supplies Office. The Facilities Division included the supervision of buildings and grounds. Both the Administration and Facilities Division functioned in direct relation to the other three divisions, college, high school, and community. On July 1, 1946, a new accounting system was introduced throughout the college. All areas were budgeted, and periodic statements on budgetary expenditures were published. With this division of labor and responsibility, along with previously unheard-of delegation of authority, Brother Paul was able to prevent the college situation from becoming hopelessly muddled, while at the same time, he provided a sturdy framework for the advancement of the learning process under the most trying circumstances.

One vexing problem of administrative organization which grew in intensity as the college expanded was that of the members of the Board of Managers; specifically, the by-law calling for the Bishop of Philadelphia to be Honorary President of the Board. For twenty-six years, Cardinal Dougherty held this position. Throughout his long association, he was intensely and seriously devoted to the interests of La Salle. Still, he was not above pushing his own ideas, and it was difficult to oppose him. Further, his busy schedule forced the Board to wait on him; it would appear that he set the date for the annual meeting. Typical of the Cardinal were his remarks to the Board on December 7, 1945. "They (The Christian Brothers) have gone through a great many trials . . . God bless their work. We want to encourage them to keep it up, and may they continue in a businesslike way to stick to the last; to educate and leave out anything irrelevant, so that this is an educational institution and nothing more." Thus, in one statement he congratulated the Brothers while at the same time obviously expressing his displeasure over Brother Alfred's Labor School, which he had already suppressed. He nailed shut the coffin of Brother Alfred's public career and issued fair warning to anyone else who might have liberal tendencies.

This rather delicate situation was eased in June, 1951, with the death of Cardinal Dougherty. When his successor, Archbishop John O'Hara, was appointed, Brother Paul sought an interview with the new Archbishop. Much to the relief of Brother Paul, he discovered that the Archbishop was opposed to the notion of serving as Honorary President of the Board. He wished the College well, but declined to accept the position. As a result, the problem was settled, although arrangements for changing the By-Laws were made by Brother Paul's immediate successor. The same month that Cardinal Dougherty died, Brother Stanislaus, Dean of the College, was sent to Rome for a year of study. He was replaced by Brother Christopher, Ph.D., who assumed his duties on June 15 with the opening of the Summer Sessions. Little did the La Salle administrators, above all Brother Paul, realize that upon Brother Stanislaus' return, he would be appointed President of La Salle College.

With the administrative changes effected immediately after the war, La Salle seemed better able to handle the complex problems of expansion and growth. One important area of growth was that of the faculty. In order to keep pace with the increasing student body, more faculty were sought. However, the Province of Baltimore could not spare the number of Brothers needed. As a result, many laymen were hired. From 1946 to the present, laymen on the faculty have outnumbered the Brothers, and their relative proportions in the faculty has probably become a permanent characteristic of the College. The *Annual Report* for 1946 notes the addition of fourteen faculty members: one Brother and thirteen laymen. Of the latter, Joseph M. Carrio, Robert J. Courtney, Ph.D., and Frank J. Guerin are presently members of the La Salle faculty. From 1946 on, the faculty continued to grow. In the spring of 1947, four fulltime and six parttime instructors were added. By December, 1947, the combined Day and Evening faculty totaled seventy. Of these, twenty-two were Brothers and forty-seven laymen. One diocesan priest completed the staff. In the fall of 1948, eleven men were added to the faculty; five were appointed to the English department, three in philosophy, one in Spanish, and two in the area of mathematics and chemistry. Of the eleven, three were graduates of La Salle; and of three, Dennis J. McCarthy remains on the staff today. With the advancing number of laymen on the faculty, the administration was justifiably concerned over the economic security of the faculty. Accordingly, in the fall of 1948, Brother Paul announced salary increases, along with a retirement-insurance plan. In this new plan, the College paid half of the premium, the faculty the remaining half.

By the scholastic year 1951-52, the La Salle College faculty totaled 120 fulltime professors. With this comparatively large gathering of talent, it was fitting that the faculty, as a body, should contribute in a very special way to the cultural heritage of the academic community in general. This contribution appeared in tangible form on November 15, 1951, when the first copies of *Four Quarters* appeared. This worthy and erudite publication, a product of faculty initiative, was established to give focus to the "appreciation and the practice of good writing in the Catholic tradition and to produce an outlet for students, alumni, etc." *Four Quarters* has enjoyed tremendous success, and today merits international subscription. This publication proved to be the mark of the college faculty during the period of great expansion, a growth that, in so many instances, militated against the development of the proper cultural and intellectual atmosphere so necessary to any institution of higher learning. The faculty of La Salle had achieved a solid contribution both to their own students and others throughout the English-speaking world; and this was accomplished under the most adverse conditions. *Four Quarters* today continues to enrich the lives of students and faculty alike at La Salle, while at the same time, it stands as a symbol of intellectual and cultural commitment as a worthwhile objective for the faculty.

It would seem, then, that postwar La Salle had gathered a good faculty. A more difficult problem was to furnish the faculty with the proper instructional, recreational, and cultural facilities to complement and supplement their devoted service to the students. The students, likewise, had to be provided with adequate instructional, recreational, and cultural areas. In plain language, La Salle College needed more buildings. The federal government was fully aware of the crowded conditions caused by returning veterans in the colleges and universities throughout the United States. In order to alleviate the situation to some extent, Congress enacted Public Law 697 in 1946. The purpose of the law was to supply educational facilities to assist colleges in providing for veteran students through the Federal Works Agency. Once the law was passed,

Brother Paul swung into action in order to get much-needed facilities for La Salle College. By December, 1946, La Salle had received approval for three temporary buildings. One of them was to serve as the temporary Student Union. Mr. John McShain, Board member and benefactor, did much to expedite federal approval of La Salle's request, and before the end of 1946, the material for the Student Union building began arriving. The only expense the College incurred in erection of buildings under Public Law 697 was that of preparing the site. Once erected, the buildings became property of the College. Early in 1947, the Student Union building was completed and included brick facing to match the original college buildings. It was named Leonard Hall in honor of a former teacher at the College. The two remaining buildings consisted of Quonset huts and were erected adjacent to McCarthy Stadium facing the playing field, serving as athletic dressing rooms. Further acquisitions were made in 1947 under Public Law 697, when building materials from a former Army administration building were allotted the College. These were used for the construction of a classroom building which included nine lecture rooms, a student reading room, six faculty offices, and rest room facilities. This building was due for completion in September, 1948, and proved a welcome relief to a college with an enrollment of 1,385 men and only nineteen available classrooms, five science laboratories, and six faculty offices. On September 19, 1948, Benilde Hall, as the new building was called, was dedicated by Rt. Rev. Monsignor Francis J. Furey. On the same day, graduation ceremonies were held for the 86th graduating class composed of the last accelerated group at La Salle. Brother Charles Henry, President of De La Salle College, Washington, D. C., gave the commencement address.[3]

As the campus expanded, arrangements were made for increased maintenance. Late in 1947, an engineer was hired to superintend the buildings and grounds. He was placed at the head of a newly-hired staff of skilled workmen. As a result, Brother Paul was able to report, in 1948, the realization of great savings in construction and repair costs. The new maintenance department was further enhanced in 1948 when a metal building with a floor area of 2,400 square feet was donated by the Federal Works Agency. The maintenance department constructed the building, and it served as storage and work shops. At the same time, in order to provide easier access to the new Benilde classroom building, a new entrance was constructed at the east end, rear of College Hall. The work was done completely by the College engineering staff. In the meantime, while buildings were being erected at the Belfield campus, 1240 was put on the realty block. In May, 1947, the Laundry Workers International Union, Local 10, Health and Welfare Trust agreed to buy 1240 for $105,000. However, the sale was not completed, and the College claimed a rather sizeable deposit. Further efforts at sale culminated in a final agreement with C. Harry Johnson, Inc., representative of Bury Motor Company. Settlement was made for $75,000 and signed on March 4, 1948. The sale price more than covered the remaining mortgage.[4] The Bouvier Mansion, South Wing, and Carlisle Hall have all since been razed. When one sees the conditions of some of 1240's brownstone friends, today, perhaps the wrecker's medicine ball was the best treatment for the 1240 campus.

In a supplement to the *Annual Report* of 1948, the first hint of one of the most important building projects on campus was given. Under the leadership of Mr. Joseph Schmitz, Jr., a small group of men interested in La Salle and higher education had pledged $350,000 for the construction of a library. Brother Paul pointed out that the generous donation would solve two pressing problems at La Salle: "It will provide a new and enlarged space for our library and release the library area for administrative areas." The following year, this group of generous men, incorporated as the La Salle Endowment Foundation, sought and received permission from Cardinal Dougherty to solicit funds through a private campaign among the alumni and friends of the Foundation and La Salle College. Besides financing the construction of a new library, the Foundation was looking to "other long-range plans for future expansion."[5] In the spring of 1950, the "long-range plans" were revealed. Brother Paul announced a $4,500,000 expansion program. This plan included a new library, dormitories, cafeteria and dining hall, a student chapel, and a field house. Each building was desperately needed at the time; however, the first project started was the library. Brother Paul planned to break ground for the library in the spring of 1951. By December, 1951, Brother Paul reported to the Board that the library was approximately sixty percent complete. Moreover, the estimated cost, on November 30, 1951, was $338,980. La Salle, by December, 1951, had already paid $300,949 on the library construction; surely, this was the harbinger of a new era at La Salle. Unfortunately, before the new library commenced full operations, Brother Paul had vacated the office of President.

In the meantime, the search for available space went on. In 1950, construction was started under the west stands of McCarthy Stadium. Six classrooms and a music practice room were built. With a major portion of the work being done by the La Salle staff, the total cost of the "McCarthy Hall" construction was $37,533. That same year, Brother Paul told the Board he thought the next area of expansion should be the dormitories. He pointed out that over 200 students from other cities lived in the neighborhood with private families, while others commuted from places like Chester, Wilmington, and Trenton. Brother Paul felt the College could exercise better supervision if these men were housed in campus dorms. He likewise stressed the academic advantages lost by commuters and those boarding in private homes. Incidentally, as the College developed, this latter reason for the construction of dormitories took on an even greater significance. The Board was convinced by Brother Paul's arguments and authorized him to proceed with plans for two dormitory buildings.[6] At the same time, and by and large at the suggestion of Monsignor Fitzpatrick, Board member, La Salle purchased a five-acre tract of land bounded by Olney Avenue, Twentieth Street, Chew Avenue, and a line west of Twenty-first Street. The total cost of the land was $112,500, and it proved to be an ideal spot for the location of the projected building.[7] Finally, during the seven years of Brother Paul's postwar administration, La Salle College added one classroom building, a Student Union building, and three general facilities buildings. All of these structures were intended as temporary buildings, but all stand today and are very much in use. Further, a classroom facility was developed under McCarthy Stadium. This also is in use today. Under Brother Paul, the library was started as well as the first two dormitories.

One of the most difficult problems of the postwar period at La Salle College was the crowded academic calendar. It was Brother Paul's intention to shorten its duration as soon after the war as possible. Immediately upon taking office he cut short the scholastic year by eight weeks. The sixteen-week summer term was dropped to eight weeks in the hope of promoting faculty welfare while at the same time continuing to provide educational opportunity to returning veterans. In this way, the faculty had time for rest and research, while veterans could start their education during the summer half-term. However, the decision to cut back the school year proved to be a hasty one. In 1946, Brother Paul reported to the Board that the administration had yielded to the majority opinion of the veteran population of the College and, hence, "the accelerated program consisting of three terms per year remains in force and will continue until June of 1948." He stated further that, although the process of deceleration had begun, La Salle would not completely return to the traditional four-year program until September, 1948. While the accelerated program remained in effect, however, arrangements were made so that no member of the faculty would be called upon to teach sixteen weeks during the summer.[8]

In December, 1947, Brother Paul again stated his determination to bring the traditional calendar back to La Salle. He admitted that it would be necessary to provide courses for some students during the summer of 1948, and that would absolutely be the end of the accelerated program. Other academic regulations were necessitated by the unique situations of some veterans. In May, 1947, the Committee on Academic Standing announced a new

policy for graduation. "Veterans whose course of study at La Salle
had been interrupted because of military service between June 1942
and September 1945 are eligible for a degree after seven semesters, provided that these semesters were spent in residence at La
Salle College, and provided that the veteran earned . . . one hundred and twenty-eight credits (excluding credits in religion) which
are required for graduation."[9] With the end of the accelerated
program and a return to academic normalcy, requirements for
honors were raised in 1950. Based on a 4.0 quality-point system,
students prior to 1950 had to achieve an average of 3.0 for the
previous semester to be named to the Dean's List. The new regulation required a student to gain an average of 3.4, computed on a
cumulative basis rather than on the grades of the previous semester.
In announcing the new rule, Brother Stanislaus, Dean, stated, "The
requirements now are consistent with the minimum necessary to
graduate *cum laude,* the lowest commencement honor."

While the expanding College was resolving student academic
problems, Brother Paul urged the faculty to make a thorough study
of the curriculum. As a result, a new curriculum appeared in 1945.
Courses of study were divided into two parts: lower division and
upper division. Also, five areas of instruction were offered: business
administration; history and social science; literature, natural science
and mathematics; philosophy and religion. The basic requirements
for the lower division, designed to provide a general education, were
as follows: one course in social science; one course in natural science
and mathematics; six hours of English composition; six hours of
English and American literature; eight hours of intermediate and
advanced foreign languages; and formal and applied logic, and
religion instruction. Electives were also required so that the student
would earn a total of sixty-four credit hours in lower division
courses. Based on a 3.0 system, he had to have sixty-four quality
points. At the end of his fourth semester, a student chose an area
of concentration. However, he was required to have at least a "C"
grade in lower division courses in his area. In the upper division,
half of the student's work, thirty-two credit hours, had to be in his

area of concentration. The remaining thirty-two upper division hours were to be taken in philosophy and subjects "more or less" related to his field. Actually, eighteen hours of philosophy were required including three hours of metaphysics, three hours of natural philosophy, six hours of social and moral philosophy, and six hours of theodicy.[10] Of all the curricula initiated at La Salle College, this proved the most traditional to that date. Much of the framework of the 1945 curriculum remains in effect today.

In 1948 a new system of course numbering was introduced which effectively maintained the distinction between upper and lower division courses. Courses numbered in the one- and two-hundreds were lower division, while those designated three- and four-hundreds constituted upper division offerings. Moreover, all lower division courses were offered each scholastic year, whereas, upper division courses were given only according to student demand. At the same time, programs of concentration were tightened in the lower division. All men who majored in a particular subject were then required to follow identical courses in the lower division. When the two-division concept had been introduced, a student could select lower division courses within a required area; in 1948, he had to follow required courses in his major area.

In December, 1949, the area of Business Administration expanded its offerings. New courses in industrial management, industrial relations, marketing, and psychology were added. In 1951, the teacher training program was enhanced with the addition of Dr. Edwin Adams to the staff. Dr. Adams had been Associate Superintendent of Schools in the Philadelphia Public School System and president of the Philadelphia Teachers College.

A new segment of the curriculum was developed at La Salle College with the establishment of the Army Reserve Officers' Training Corps in the fall of 1950. A field artillery unit was assigned to La Salle. Some veterans and all freshmen were eligible to apply for the R.O.T.C. program on a voluntary basis. In 1951, the R.O.T.C. program became mandatory for all freshmen and sophomores. Basic courses in the program were spread over the first two years. Men who wanted to qualify for the advanced program, leading to a reserve commission upon graduation, had to complete successfully the basic program.

For the second time in its history, graduate study was introduced at La Salle in 1950. In order to commemorate the tercentenary of the birth of St. John Baptist de La Salle, founder of the Brothers of the Christian Schools and a great innovator in the field of education, La Salle College inaugurated a graduate program in theology designed to meet the growing needs of collegiate and secondary school teachers of religion. At the outset, the program was generally restricted to the Christian Brothers. The Baltimore Province had established a house of studies in Elkins Park for its young men in training, and the graduate program was tailored to meet their needs. Brothers from communities throughout the Philadelphia area also followed the program in late afternoon, Saturday, and summer courses. A few laymen availed themselves of the opportunity to study theology on the graduate level. The first group to complete the required thirty credit hours of study were awarded Master of Arts degrees in June, 1953. Beginning in 1960, candidates for the M.A. were required to take comprehensive examinations in addition to the thirty credit hours' work. Likewise, a candidate could submit a thesis and only twenty-four credit hours plus comprehensives. In 1964, discussions were carried on with the Archdiocese of Philadelphia to open the graduate theology program to priests, Brothers, Sisters, and laymen and to rearrange the program in order to orient it more toward the area of religious education and make it kerigmatic in content and method. As a result, the original program was phased out, and the newly-orientated scheme was inaugurated in the summer of 1965. Again we see the recurring influence of programs initiated during Brother Paul's administration on the College today.

Before Brother Paul assumed the office of President and before the hostilities of the war had come to an end, some La Salle students, thinking victory for the United States was assured, were eagerly looking forward to the expansion of student activities in the postwar College. As early as December, 1944, a *Collegian* editorial urged all students to cooperate in the reorganization of the swimming team. Further, La Salle men were reminded that plans for other future activities were not out of place in view of the general feeling that the end of the war was approaching. As a result, a plethora of activities, new and reorganized, marked the development of postwar La Salle. In 1947, the Gamma Chapter of Sigma Beta Kappa fraternity was founded at La Salle through the instrumentality of Glen Robertson. Father Robertson, now a priest in the diocese of Camden, is currently principal of Holy Spirit High School, Absecon, New Jersey. Sigma Beta Kappa is a national Catholic social fraternity with each chapter limited to sixty members. The fraternity colors of green and white fittingly symbolize the work carried on by S.B.K. at La Salle. Each day of the scholastic year, two S.B.K. brothers go to St. John's Orphanage in West Philadelphia and conduct recreational activities for the children living there. In a real sense, they bring a ray of hope to these neglected children. In 1947 also the Newtonian Society was organized. Membership was opened to all students who were interested in any branch of the sciences. Each week public seminars were held during which a member would lecture on some subject pertinent to his field of science. In January, 1949, the Equestrian Society was formed. It was mainly social and sought members who were particularly interested in riding. The La Salle campus had, and still has, nearby a variety of fine stables and well-protected trails to choose from. Unfortunately, the Equestrian Society surrendered to the motorized age which spread so rapidly in the fifties and sixties. That same year, the Out-of-Towners Club was founded by Brother Stanislaus. Open to men who attended La Salle from distant places, its purpose was mainly social. In its first year, the club had fifty-five members. However, with the development of residence and recreational facilities on campus in the fifties, the club lost its usefulness and disbanded.

In his *Annual Report* to the Board of Managers in 1949, Brother Paul mentioned certain student activities that were of significance for the individual student, while contributing to the realization of the College objectives. Several La Salle students, under the sponsorship of the rector of St. Elizabeth's Church, a local Negro parish, had formed the Inter-Racial Club. Their main activity was the organization and running of an adult education program for the members of St. Elizabeth's Parish. The program proved quite effective and the students' contribution to the people substantial. Meanwhile, on campus, representatives of La Salle in the National Federation of Catholic College Students carried through a highly successful European relief drive. Many La Salle men had witnessed the distressing conditions caused by war in Europe and were generous in their response. Under the direction of the Rev. Charles F. Gorman, College Chaplain, the Adoration Society was formed. Each day members would spend a specified time in the chapel before the Most Blessed Sacrament, praying for the conversion of Russia. Another group of students organized themselves to study ways and means for securing a new student chapel. The matter was passed on to the Student Council, and the Council resolved to go on record as approving a plan to build a separate chapel building. It was to be constructed on lines of the architecture of College Hall and seat 500 students, and was estimated to cost $200,000. President John Ryan, in presenting the resolution to Brother Paul, suggested a variety of means for securing funds both from students and alumni.[11] Unfortunately, these plans never got off the ground.

The Student Council at La Salle after the war was, nonetheless, a very influential body. The Council acted as an official representative of the College with other institutions and associations and with the public in general. The Council consisted of elected representatives of each class. Members voted on all matters brought before the Council while, at the same time, receiving the help of the leaders of campus organizations who acted as an advisory body. In the case of the student chapel, for instance, it was obvious that the Council spoke for the majority of the 1,900 students who wanted a new chapel, in lieu of the seventy-seat faculty-student chapel then available. Rounding out the new activities on campus was the Glee

Club and Choir, organized during the 1949-50 scholastic year. This new organization, certainly not strange to the earlier traditions of La Salle, met with notable success in its first year.

Intercollegiate athletics also blossomed in the postwar era. Much to the chagrin of students and alumni, football did not return after the war. However, basketball, which had managed to survive throughout the war, was taken up with vigor. It became the most popular and publicized sport on campus. In 1947, competitive rowing was organized at La Salle. Three years later, an organization known as the La Salle Rowing Association, under the direction of Jack Bratton and Glen Robertson, Sr., purchased facilities of the Crescent Boat Club, which housed three boat rooms, four large social rooms, and locker and shower facilities for over 100 men. For many years, both the college and high school rowing teams enjoyed the use of these facilities on the Schuylkill River. During the scholastic year 1949-50, the La Salle College swimming team merited national attention. Four members of the team were named to the All-Intercollegiate Swimming Squad as selected by the College Coaches Swimming Association. The four All-Americans were Joe Verdeur, Bob Fitzgerald, breaststroker; Bob Regan, freestyler; and William Dorsch, backstroke. Naturally, there were many other outstanding athletic accomplishments; but they are too many to mention here. Both intercollegiate and intramural athletic activities made a rapid and strong comeback after the ravages of the war years.

Perhaps the most significant alumni activity of the immediate postwar era took place on Sunday, November 24, 1946. A bronze plaque, a memorial to the thirty-one La Salle College men who paid the supreme price of liberty with their lives in World War II, was unveiled and dedicated. The plaque was erected at the base of the Sacred Heart Shrine in the center of the College quadrangle. Assisted by Brother Paul, President, Thomas Cunningham, four-year-old son of Ensign James J. Cunningham, the first La Salle man to give his life in the war, unveiled the plaque. Today the plaque stands as a vivid reminder of a La Salle heritage, one that administrators, faculty, and students alike can be justly proud of, and one that gives deeper reason to everything that evolves in the history of the College.

One aspect of postwar La Salle which lightened the burden of the administration in struggling with a galloping student population was the bright fiscal picture that developed with the college expansion. Just a few days after Brother Paul was thrust into office without warning, the Real Estate Trust Company and its affiliates asked for a meeting with the College financial officers. Brother Paul, who had very little time to study the College financial condition, was accompanied to the meeting by Brother Edward John, who, for many years, had served as Secretary of the Corporation. From the outset of the meeting, it was obvious that the bankers wanted to increase the interest rates on the mortgage. After many arguments were advanced by the bankers for raising the rates, Brother Paul was asked to reply. He informed the bankers that he could not prevent them from raising the interest on the mortgage; at the same time, he would not return to La Salle and ask the Brothers, who represented the College endowment, to extend themselves further, since he had already asked them to do more than was humanly called for. With that, John Sullivan, Esq., proposed that the interest rates be unchanged. He withdrew from the meeting; taking his example, the other bankers followed suit.[11] The College was carried one more year by the banks and that was sufficient. The surging tide of postwar students, the majority financed by the G.I. Bill, helped to ease the fiscal pressure at La Salle. In a special letter to the Board of Managers, written on April 30, 1947, Brother Paul informed the members that he had paid $100,000 "in reduction of the mortgages held by the Real Estate Trust Company and the Board of City Trusts on the Olney Avenue and Broad Street properties respectively." By December, 1947, the College still owed $616,000 to creditors, while at the same time, the balance for the fiscal year was well over $150,000. This was indeed indicative of expansion, but it was only the beginning.

In December, 1948, the situation was further improved. In his

Annual Report, Brother Paul stated that "during the past two years, we have made payments on these mortgages amounting to $295,000." However, $100,000 was still owed the banks, while $221,000 was due the Province. Despite the debt of $321,000 in 1948, the College offered limited student aid in the form of campus employment and outright grants. The Faculty Committee on Scholarship Grants based its decision on scholastic qualifications and/or individual needs. A year later, the amount owed the banks was cut to $50,000, while the figure due the Province did not change. Moreover, the income available to the College during the 1949 fiscal year was well over $1,500,000. Out of this, the College was able to realize a balance of approximately $310,000. By December, 1950, the College corporation was free of all encumbrances, both to local bankers and the Province. Moreover, the College was able to realize a balance of over $322,000 at the end of fiscal year 1950. Of course, proper credit must be given to local bankers who patiently waited for their investment in La Salle College. In the long run, and in view of the deflated and inflated conditions of the economy between 1928 and 1950, the bankers, in all probability, fared well.[12]

While the College was out of the financial woods and its credit was well established, it was not long before expansion plans necessitated the borrowing of more money. In September, 1951, the College borrowed $350,000 from The Pennsylvania Company for Banking and Trusts for general expenditures. One month later, $400,000 was borrowed from the United States government for the construction of two dormitory buildings. With such evidence of readily-available credit, it is obvious that the College, after eighty years of almost constant fiscal distress, had at last come into its own. Perhaps one of the factors contributing to the financial success of the College during Brother Paul's administration was the institution of the increased use of available facilities. This was especially true at La Salle when the Evening Division, as it is now called, was inaugurated on a permanent basis.

Several attempts to hold evening classes at La Salle had been made prior to the establishment of the current Evening Division in

1946. Brother Noah, President 1873-1875, informed the Board of Managers in 1874 that the College would conduct night classes beginning October 1, 1874. After receiving many requests for such courses and in view of the possible financial advantages, it was decided to offer an evening program during the months of October, November, December, and January. Arrangements were made for 100 students. The night school proved a success, but it was operated for one season only because "it was found very fatiguing to the teachers who had also to teach day school."[13]

Not until 1915 did the College again offer night courses. Then special courses were taught in English and mathematics. "Here the primary object is to give the students who have failed in these branches a chance to redeem themselves." In 1915, Brother Edward, President, expressed hopes of extending the evening program, since many students had applied. In fact, the numbers were so great the College was unable to accommodate them. However, World War I seemed to put an end to any plans for a permanent evening program. Again in 1940, proposals were advanced for opening a "night school" at La Salle. It was suggested that such a school should be staffed chiefly by laymen. Its projected purpose was to help students who were not able to complete regular courses and to enable others to "make up" courses failed in previous years. In January, 1941, the whole idea was dropped. Brother Anselm, President, stated the proposed night school was impractical for several reasons. Further, the Assistant Superior General was not favorably inclined toward the project. Actually, the latter objection was probably the greatest obstacle for several years to the establishment of a night program.[14] As was seen above, a night program was established at La Salle during the war in February, 1942. Its aim was to help men who were anxious to complete college while employed in essential industry. This program was dropped after the scholastic year 1943-1944.

The establishment of what is today a permanent and very significant branch of La Salle College, the Evening Division, occurred in the fall of 1946. Since every possible facility at La Salle

had been expanded for the admission of returning veterans, Brother
Paul announced that the College "couldn't possibly discharge its
moral obligations to the veterans who fought for the American
ideal unless every possible effort was made to educate them, some-
how, someway." Thus, evening classes were begun. At first, the
decision to offer classes at night having been made so near to the
opening date, the response was poor. Dr. Joseph J. Sprissler, who
was named the first Director, relates that he turned on all lights
in empty classrooms in College Hall just to let the public know that
La Salle had begun an evening school. Still, only thirty-six students
matriculated in the evening division the first year. The following
year, however, 228 men were in attendance. The evening school
continued to grow beyond the greatest expectations. In 1949, 675
men were in attendance, while by 1952 over 1,000 had matriculated.
After a decade of operation in 1956, over 1,600 men were enrolled
in the Evening Division. Dr. Sprissler had held the position of
Director until a fulltime Dean was appointed in 1953. The first
Dean was Brother Gregorian Paul, who had resigned as President
in June, 1952. Commenting on Dr. Sprissler's efforts with the Evening School, *The Collegian,* noting the tenth anniversary of the
Evening Division, stated: "The phenomenal growth of the Evening
Division during its first ten years is due in no small measure to the
insight, enthusiasm, and hard work of the one who conceived the
idea, nurtured it, and developed it into the well-organized establishment that it is today. His fundamental concern for the success of
the students, and his untiring efforts to provide them with the very
best advantages, has implanted an esprit de corps in both faculty
and student body which is significantly characteristic of the Evening Division . . . without the inspiration and leadership of Dr.
Joseph Sprissler, a beginning might never have been made." Today,
Dr. Sprissler, currently serving La Salle as Vice-President for Business Affairs, is generally acknowledged to be the founder of the
Evening Division.

When established in 1946, the Evening Division curriculum
was quite restricted. Courses were given only in the area of Business

Administration. Also, students at first worked only for Certificates of Proficiency; no degree program was available. However, in 1947, the curriculum was developed to such an extent that men could earn the B.S. degree in five years. But the degree was granted only in the area of Business Administration. Beginning in 1953, students in the Evening Division could work for B.S. degrees in chemistry and electronic physics besides business administration. In 1958, further curriculum changes were made in the chemistry department. A five-year program in chemistry, leading to the Certificate of Proficiency, was inaugurated. The curriculum was so designed that students wishing to study further for the B.S. degree could do so without loss of time or credit. At the same time, the electronic physics program was revised to incorporate developments in transistors and transistor circuitry. Further, several new courses were added to the curriculum: corporate and other taxes; integrated and electronic data processing; problems of moral philosophy; and marriage and the family.[15]

With the appointment of Brother Gregorian Paul as fulltime Dean of the Evening Division, the parttime school began a period of organizational consolidation. At the same time, the student body continued to grow. Moreover, it became quite evident that La Salle's Evening Division was having a tremendous impact on Delaware Valley industries. In 1954, over 350 different business and industrial concerns were represented in the Evening Division student body, which numbered about 1,300 men. About twenty-nine percent of the 1954 Evening Division student body worked for companies which offered financial assistance to their employees for educational purposes. Also, twenty-eight different companies had employees on the Evening Division faculty.[16] The Evening Division population continued to grow through the spring of 1961, when Brother Paul gave up his duties as Dean and returned to teaching. By the spring of 1956, over 1,500 men followed Evening classes. In his *Annual Report* to the Board of Managers in 1957, Brother Stanislaus, then President, called specific attention to the Evening Division. Noting the continued growth of the Evening school during its first decade of operation, the President proudly announced that eighty-three percent of the student body at night was enrolled in degree programs. This was an indication of the seriousness of the Evening student as well as a comparatively high average for any similar program in other colleges and universities. "The character of the student body unquestionably makes the Evening Division of La Salle College distinctive in the Philadelphia area." Brother Paul, Dean, voiced the opinion that the Evening Division student proved to be the best recruiter for that school. Many students suggested that their fellow employees and friends apply for admission. Further, many transfer students repeatedly spoke of the good teaching and personal attention they received in the Evening Division. Brother Paul added: "I am convinced that the whole operation of the Evening Division is an achievement of distinction. We have led other institutions in the establishment of well-organized curricula of study . . . morale among the staff and students is high."[17] Evidence of the Evening student's success at La Salle was seen at the 1950 commencement at which the B.S. in business administration was conferred on 102 Evening men, while two received the B.S. in chemistry and fifteen the B.S. in electronic physics. Also, twenty Certificates of Proficiency were awarded. The good word about La Salle's Evening Division continued to spread, and by the fall of 1959, over 2,000 men were enrolled. Of these, eighty-four percent were degree candidates; about two percent were certificate candidates; and slightly over thirteen percent were special or non-matriculated students. At that time, the faculty totaled 129. Of these, twenty-seven taught fulltime in the Day Division, while the remaining 102 were classified as parttime instructors. Of these, some seventeen held the Ph.D. degree; sixty-five had the M.A., while thirty-five possessed the B.A. In addition, five held law degrees and seven were licensed C.P.A.'s.[18]

Once the Evening Division at La Salle was well established, both administration and students worked together in attempting to provide both atmosphere and opportunities comparable to the Day Division, in so far as that was possible under parttime operations.

Despite the obvious drawbacks imposed on student activity under Evening program conditions, the La Salle night men were enthusiastic in developing an activities program. In the spring of 1949, the Evening Division students voted for the election of student officers. They further indicated that they favored participation in regular college activities rather than limited activities of their own. In view of the student interest and enthusiasm, Dr. Sprissler announced that a program of activities would begin in the fall of 1949. However, as activities were initiated for the Evening students, it became obvious that, due to their limited time spent on campus, few students actively participated in extracurricular activities except in the case of socials. Some organizations did manage to develop, but not on the same scale as the Day Division activities. In 1951, the Accounting Association was organized successfully. Its purpose was "to bring prominent men in the accounting field to lecture on this subject." Another very successful organization in the Evening Division was student government. Brother Paul, Dean, asserted in 1957 that the high quality of student government in the La Salle night school was unique among Evening Colleges in the country. As the years passed, Evening student activities grew in dimension. For example, in 1958, the Evening Division chapter of the Society for the Advancement of Management won a national first-place award. Finally, although many of the Day Division activities, mostly social and athletic, were open to Evening Division students, participation in Day school activities was never realized to the extent advocated by night school students in 1948. Nonetheless, the extracurricular activities of the Evening Division provided a good parallel program to the curriculum program. By the time Brother Paul's term as Dean ended, the Evening Division, originated while he was President of the College, was a solidly-established and integral part of La Salle College.

In reviewing Brother Paul's administration of La Salle College, it is difficult to say which of his innovations was most important. Being too close to his time perhaps we cannot view his work with proper perspective. That will be for future historians to decide.

However, it is obvious that he accomplished much in a short time. Despite the complexities of a rapidly-expanding institution and hampered by the lack of both physical and academic facilities, Brother Paul saw the College through the postwar chaos, while at the same time providing a blueprint for the future La Salle. Despite many contributions he made to La Salle's progress, after seven years as President, he felt he had exhausted the possibilities at his command to further the interests of the College. As a result, he resigned as President in June, 1952. The following scholastic year, he taught chemistry at Calvert Hall College, Baltimore, Maryland. In June, 1953, he was appointed Dean of the La Salle College Evening Division, and, after nearly a decade of service in that capacity, he became professor of chemistry at La Salle, a post he still holds today. La Salle in 1952, like the nation, readjusted to another administration.

8. Consolidation

As the world moved into the fifties, the great American postwar dream lay shattered. The Korean War with the United States deeply involved was in full swing. For the first time in the twentieth century, forceful aggression had been met with aggression. Although most people in the United States agreed with President Truman's resolution against the expansion of Communism, they soon began to weary of the exasperating circumstances involved in the Korean conflict. Moreover, the appearance on the domestic scene of dubious activities on the part of men in high positions initiated an age of doubt and fear. Senator Joseph McCarthy, in his communist witch-hunt, did not help matters by labeling the Roosevelt and Truman administrations "twenty years of treason." The Kefauver exposures of organized crime in the United States, along with scandals in official Washington over the "five percenters," the mink coats, and deep freezers, convinced the people that a change in political control was in order. Thus, with President Truman out of the race by his own wish, the swing toward the personable war hero, Dwight Eisenhower, mounted. All of this, however, did not seem to affect the nation's prosperity. Many had regarded the upsurge in the national postwar economy as a dangerous bubble. But, as time went on, with the help of some built-in stabilizers, the economy entered one of the most lengthy periods of prosperity in its history. This upsurge, despite the Korean War, proved helpful to the nation's colleges and universities, which were in the process of stabilization after the stormy expansion of the postwar veteran invasion.

In June, 1952, while the nation became deeply involved with the problem of changing administrations, La Salle College, in a rather sudden move, changed presidents. Shortly after Brother Paul's resignation was formalized, Brother Stanislaus, Ph.D., assumed the office of President. Brother Stanislaus had already served in an administrative capacity at La Salle as Dean of Men and then Dean of the College. With this experience, he took office as President with a profound understanding of La Salle's problems as an institution of higher learning and with some ability in guiding corporate operations. In carrying out the obligations of his office in an intelligent and zealous manner, however, Brother Stanislaus had at times the unhappy knack of taking his closest advisors and key faculty members for granted. Despite this drawback, he was able to bring about changes necessary at La Salle after its breathtaking experience of rapid postwar expansion. He first turned to some points of administrative reorganization started by his predecessor. As was seen above, Archbishop O'Hara, successor to Cardinal Dougherty, declined the position of Honorary President of the La Salle College Board of Managers. Therefore, at the annual Board meeting in December, 1952, some constitutional changes were resolved. Article III was changed to read: "The Board of Managers shall be limited to twelve members, seven of whom shall be chosen from among the Brothers of the Christian Schools." A change in Article V provided that the Brother Provincial of the Baltimore Province would be Honorary President of the Board, whereas Article VI was changed so that the President of the Board of Managers would be a Christian Brother who was appointed President of the College by the "lawful superiors of the Baltimore Province of the Institute." At the same Board meeting, Brother Stanislaus, President, announced several organizational changes. The office of Vice-President was reactivated and was made responsible especially for public relations. A Director of Public Relations was appointed and was responsible for coordinating the activities of the publicity office, placement services, and alumni activities. Further, the Publicity Director was responsible for the recruitment program of the College. The Vice-President was likewise held responsible for the general services of the College. At the same time, the office of Director of Student Personnel was created. All activities of the Guidance Center, Health Service, Dean of Men, the College Chaplain, and the Dean of Freshmen came under the direct supervision of the Director of Student Personnel. The Business Office, under the direct, personal control of the Comptroller, assumed responsibility for the supervision of maintenance of buildings and grounds. Finally, the announcement of the appointment of a fulltime Dean for the Evening Division was made at this time.[1] This division of areas was an indication of the extent of La Salle in growth. Although many positions were newly created, some were not filled immediately. For example, Brother Daniel Bernian was not appointed Dean of Men until the following year.

At a special meeting of the Board of Managers held March 26, 1953, the members resolved to institute legal proceedings to change the college charter. Section One of the Charter which dealt with deeds, title, transfer, and the seal was amended by the addition of the following: "and to confer such honors, degrees, diplomas, in the Arts, Letters, Education, Sciences, Religion, Philosophy, and Commerce, as are usually granted by other colleges and universities in this Commonwealth, and the right and authority . . . to grant Bachelor degrees as aforesaid, and the degree of Master of Arts in Religious Education, in course, which it has heretofore conferred, be and is hereby specifically confirmed, and the right and authority . . . to grant honorary degrees . . . subject to the general policy of the State Council of Education. . . ." Section Two of the Charter which dealt with the purpose of the corporation was changed so as to read "that the object and design of the said corporation shall be the establishment of a college in the city of Philadelphia and the vicinity thereof. . . ." Further changes were made in the part of Section Two which dealt with subjects to be taught. It was changed to read "in which are to be taught the elementary branches of education, together with the Arts, Letters, Sciences, Modern and Ancient Languages, Religion, Philosophy, and Commerce, and such other subjects related thereto as are usually taught in other colleges and universities in the United States, in the manner that it may be determined from time to time by the proper officers of the said corporation."[2] With these changes effected, a proper and legal framework was developed to provide for future consolidation of the college's interests.

Following a visit by the Middle States Association of Colleges and Secondary Schools to La Salle College in 1953, further organizational changes were contemplated. Since the Middle States evaluators were dissatisfied with some administrative arrangements, a management and consultant firm was hired to "conduct a close study of the organization, methods, and procedures in use at the college with a view of bringing them up to the level required of a college of our present size." Despite the disgruntled protest of faculty and administration, who felt they had been passed over, the study was carried through. As a result, in 1954, the Office of Dean of Men was reorganized as the Office of Vice-President of Student Affairs. In effect, the offices of Dean and Vice-President divided duties formerly assumed by the Dean alone. Brother Bernian, the first Vice-President for Student Affairs, was responsible for guidance, counseling, health services, athletics, campus employment, and student aid. At the same time, a new office, that of Director of Properties, was established. The duties of the latter office were to regulate purchasing procedures, supervise maintenance and physical properties.[3]

Again in 1955, the Middle States Association recommended further organizational development at La Salle, especially in the academic area and in the area of business management. Likewise, the Middle States Inspection Committee was concerned with the question of greater participation by the Board of Managers in the management of the College. Finally, the Middle States indicated its dissatisfaction with the lack of coordination between the Day and Evening schools in several areas: requirements for admission and degrees; course listings in the Bulletins; and organization and coordination of student activities. In view of this, several changes in organization were made. The College was divided into a School of Arts and Sciences; a School of Business Administration; and an Evening College. Brother Vincent, Ph.D., was appointed Dean of Arts and Sciences, while Brother David headed the School of Business Administration, and Brother Paul remained as Dean of the Evening College. Brother John, Ph.D., was named Dean of the College, with responsibility for coordinating both schools of the Day Division. Brother Bernian, Ph.D., remained as Vice-President for Student Affairs, with all student personnel services placed under his office. Brother Christopher, Ph.D., headed the newly-created position of Dean of Admissions, while Mr. John McCloskey was named assistant to the President. Finally, the By-Laws were revised to provide for a fuller and more active participation of the Board of Managers in the management of the affairs of the College.

In 1958, Brother Stanislaus proposed the formation of an Associate Board of Managers. It was to be composed of civic leaders, professional men, corporation officers, and industrialists. Their function would be to advise the College in matters of curricula and activities; to serve as a public relations arm for the College; to effect stronger liaison between the College, business, and industry; to explore ways and means by which the development program of the College was to be promoted; and to give the development program public endorsement. Membership of the Associate Board was to be limited to fifty representatives. Unfortunately, this group was never realized. In general, reorganization of the College proved adequate during the short six-year presidency of Brother Stanislaus. New world conditions and a new president would make further changes. In the meantime, however, Brother Stanislaus looked to the physical expansion of the College.

At a special meeting of the Board of Managers held on November 20, 1952, La Salle College, by accepting title to the Christian Brothers' Scholasticate for the consideration of one dollar, acquired a fifty-two acre campus in Elkins Park, Pennsylvania. The title was accompanied with the usual financial responsibilities which, at the time, were quite formidable. In January, 1950, the Baltimore Province of Christian Brothers had purchased slightly over forty-six acres of land, formerly owned by Mrs. Eleanor Widener Dixon, for $275,000. Eleven months later an additional six and a fraction acres were purchased at $26,000. The property is located in Cheltenham Township, Montgomery County, approximately half a mile north of the Philadelphia city line, and thus subject to the township tax structures. The estate is used as a house of studies for young men of the Province. However, the township claimed taxes on the property due to the nature of its use. A long, involved, and expensive court battle developed. In its early stages, the decisions went against the Brothers. As a result, they were advised to incorporate with La Salle College in order to attain a tax-exempt status. This explains the action of the Board in accepting title. The mansion on the property was built in 1923 and is an exact reproduction of Compton Wyngate Manor, England. The fireproof building contains fifty-two rooms and thirty baths. All windows are finished in fine leaded glass and all main rooms paneled in oak imported from England. Many fireplaces date back to the seventeenth century, and one came from the hunting lodge of George III of England. The mansion was renamed Anselm Hall after Brother Anselm, President Emeritus, and it continues to be used for dining and dormitory facilities as well as study rooms. Another rather large residence on the property serves as a dormitory, while the butler's house is used as Provincial headquarters. Bathhouses, swimming pool, badminton court, handball courts, and greenhouses were also on the property. Today the Elkins Park campus has facilities for over one hundred student Brothers. It likewise provides private recreational facilities for college organizations, special summer programs, and faculty gatherings.

One of the greatest events in the history of La Salle College in the twentieth century was the completion of the new $700,000 library in the fall of 1952. Of course, today we measure the capability of an institution of higher learning by many norms, but most agree that the library is of prime importance in any such measurement. Where all other sources of knowledge run dry, both students and faculty alike turn to the library as the wellspring of knowledge during their academic preparation and an abiding friend throughout their careers.

As we record this most important event in La Salle's history, it might be well to establish its significance by reviewing the rather checkered history of La Salle's library. From the earliest days of the College, it is evident that there was deep concern for the quality of the library. In the *Annual Report* for 1873-74, Brother Noah, President, stated: "We have not been unmindful of the promise made in our last *Report*, to increase our library as soon as possible." He noted that nearly three thousand volumes were added during the year. Also, several "extensive library cases" were purchased to hold newly-ordered "serial works" such as *Notes and Queries; Dublin Review; Brownson Review; Edinburgh Review*, and several "popular and scientific reviews." *The Catholic World, Philosophical Transactions*, and the *Intellectual Observer* were likewise added. As an afterthought he added, "the historical and literary portion of the library has also been increased by about one thousand volumes." There is little evidence to indicate that much was done to improve the library at this pace after Brother Noah left La Salle in 1875. We know, in fact, that the space allotted the library after the move to 1240 was miniscule. When Brother Edward took office as President in 1911, he was appalled at the condition of the library. As noted above, he took immediate steps to remedy the situation and he kept abreast with improvement of the library until the end of his term in 1917.

When the College moved to its present location, the library was housed in the first floor of College Hall. Compared to 1240, the new library seemed quite large, but actually this was not the case. Likewise, many Brothers who witnessed the transfer from 1240 to Belfield feel that much was lost in the haphazard removal. It is significant that the first major contribution to the new college library in 1931 came from Brother Edward, President Emeritus, who, at the time, was President of St. Thomas College, Scranton. He gave La Salle over two hundred German books. Other efforts were made to improve the library collection. Since the library budget was extremely modest, the College depended, to a large extent, on contributions. For example, in 1936, J. Burrwood Daly contributed a complete set of bound volumes of the *Congressional Record* of the first session of the seventy-fourth Congress. That same year, the library acquired additional space. What constituted the original library in College Hall was used exclusively for a reading room, and what had constituted the sophomore lounge was turned into a stack area. In November, 1936, 1,600 volumes were acquired from the *Public Ledger* reference library. However, many of these books proved of little worth. This addition, however, brought the total collection to 18,000 volumes by the end of 1936. Again in 1941, several large acquisitions were made by the library. Dr. Ralph J. Schoettle contributed his collection of art books which numbered nearly 600. The Feeny family and Mr. Joseph Schmitz, Jr., contributed an additional two hundred volumes. Further, the private library of Joseph A. Finnegan, numbering over 1,500 volumes, was added to La Salle's collection. *The Collegian* noted, "There are in this latest addition . . . many excellent biographies and books on history, art, literature, and travel." In 1943, 600 selected volumes from the library of Joseph Jackson, noted Philadelphia artist, bibliophile, authority on colonial history and architecture, were acquired by La Salle.

The library continued to grow, albeit slowly. Its progress certainly did not reflect the growth and postwar expansion of the College. By April, 1950, there were only 30,876 volumes in the library. Likewise, the amount of space available in College Hall was a limiting factor. Thus, when the new library was opened in the fall of 1952, La Salle had every hope that the three-story, modern, well-equipped structure would signal a new age for the College library. Conditions in the library during the early fifties from a physical point of view were excellent. However, only three percent of the college budget was allotted for the purchase of books. This unfortunate condition was not remedied until Brother Bernian assumed control of the College. Although the library building, opened in 1952, could house holdings of over 150,000 volumes, by September, 1958, when Brother Stanislaus resigned, there were fewer than 50,000 volumes in the library. When one considers that there had been over 30,800 volumes in 1950, the growth of the library, despite its excellent facilities was undeniably minimal. Despite the availability of local libraries, many of which are excellent, there is no doubt that one of the prime considerations in the sixties for improving the educative milieu at La Salle College is library development.

At the same time that Brother Stanislaus announced the completion of the library, he also reported two other important building projects: two resident halls were under construction at a cost of $500,000, while a new cafeteria was installed in Leonard Hall for approximately $40,000. Despite the positive side of the *Annual Report,* Brother Stanislaus stated that some facilities at the College were "woefully inadequate." Required laboratory facilities for increased enrollment in physical and biological sciences were unavailable. Moreover, programs in industrial management and accounting were hampered by the lack of space. Finally, a student chapel was needed, along with additional outdoor recreational facilities. Therefore, Brother Stanislaus expressed the opinion that the postponement of the separation of the high school and college was unthinkable. Most Board members agreed with Brother Stanislaus, but the financial problems alone involved in such a move proved a tremendous obstacle. Nonetheless, the idea had been planted and would eventually bear fruit.

With the opening of the academic year 1953, double dedications took place at La Salle on September 28. Ceremonies started in the Church of the Holy Child with the Mass of the Holy Ghost. Shortly thereafter, Archbishop John O'Hara blessed and dedicated the library, while at the same time, the Right Reverend Thomas F. McNally, Board member, blessed and dedicated two new dormitories. With the opening of the latter, it soon became evident that the new dorms did not provide the number of spaces required. As a result, the Board, on December 2, 1954, resolved to borrow $500,000 from the federal government through the Housing and Home Finance Agency for two additional dormitories to house 126 students and twelve faculty.[5] As the resident population of the College grew, Brother Stanislaus and his colleagues became painfully aware of a lack of a recreational and social center for the students. As a result, Brother Stanislaus' suggestion that the college construct a one million dollar Student Union with borrowed funds involved the Board of Managers in a rather lengthy discussion. Monsignor McNally suggested faith in God's Providence, whereas Brother Anselm hoped such indebtedness would be undertaken cautiously. Mr. McShain noted that his business frequently called for courage and investments beyond his grasp. Mr. Kelly felt conservatism in a time of expansion was a luxury, and that private education should meet the demands made on it. Brother Daniel Bernian stated that the residence halls would lose their attractiveness without facilities a Student Union would provide. Finally, a vote was taken, and with three members abstaining, the Board resolved to borrow one million dollars to build the student center. The following May, ground was broken for the Student Union, and construction began in the early summer. However, the building was not completed until after Brother Stanislaus left office. At the same meeting, during which the Student Union loan was approved, the Board further authorized the President to purchase land south of Olney Avenue and North of Cottage Lane, between 20th Street, Elkins Avenue, and the Philadelphia Electric Company's property bordering Wister Street. In all, there were three tracts of land totaling about eight acres, which shortly thereafter were purchased for approximately $25,000 an acre.

Included in the President's *Annual Report* to the Board was a rather formidable building projection for the College, the estimated cost of which was ten million dollars. It included the above-mentioned one million dollar Student Union, removal of the high school to another site at an estimated cost of $1,750,000, a Science Building at $1,750,000, a Business Administration building priced at $1,250,000, a Field House to cost $1,500,000, and a student chapel for which no estimates were available.[6] However, the projection, after ten years, has still not been accomplished; the Field House, Business Administration building, and separate student chapel are still in the offing. In lieu of the last building, a temporary student chapel was completed in the summer of 1965 at a cost of $65,000. It is located in what was formerly College Hall auditorium. In September, 1956, the third and fourth residence halls were completed, while the areas immediately adjacent to the dorms were paved for parking at a cost of $20,000. Finally, in 1957, a committee of the Board was appointed to examine the question of acquisition of the remainder of the Belfield Estate adjacent to the campus. The following year the Committee suggested that the College await the action of the Mayor's Committee on Higher Education before proceeding further with attempts to acquire the land. When some Board members objected to the delay, the President stated quite frankly that the owners did not feel inclined to sell at the time. Therefore, the entire matter was dropped. In reviewing La Salle's expansion under Brother Stanislaus, one must admit that he was far from the conservative in his plans for the College. In retrospect, the five buildings constructed and land acquired during his administration provided a basis for further expansion in the sputnik age. Besides physical facilities, moreover, the academic program received some attention in Brother Stanislaus' pre-sputnik administration.

As the nation began to deactivate military units with the advent of the Korean cease-fire, many veterans, including some who had interrupted their college work to go to war, returned to La Salle. Because many were ready to matriculate at the beginning of the spring term, a freshman class was formed in February, 1954. Approximately fifty men enrolled in the first group; most were veterans. They followed the regular first semester core courses, and in June, began the second semester core. By September, 1954, most were able to merge with the class which had first matriculated in September 1953. This rather rugged program carried through the early sixties when it was discontinued due to faulty student academic achievement. A uniform policy on admissions was established early in 1955. All applicants for admission to the Day Division were required to present credentials from the College Entrance Examination Board. At the same time, an intensive Reading Program was offered at La Salle. The five-week course was held several times a year and repeated in the Summer Sessions. In 1956, the School of Arts and Sciences prescribed new regulations on student progress. To qualify for admission to the upper division, a student had to complete a minimum of sixty-eight semester credit hours with a scholastic index of 2.00 based on a 4.00 system. Likewise, a "C" grade was required in courses listed as prerequisities for advanced work in the student's chosen field of concentration. Once in the upper division, sixty-four semester credit hours were required in courses designated as upper division courses for the particular curriculum the student followed. In general, upper division requirements were thirty-two hours in the area of concentration; twelve hours of philosophy; four hours of theology; and electives. The following year special requirements were established for non-Catholic students. In addition to eighteen required hours of philosophy, courses in basic philosophy, philosophy of religion, and Old and New Testament were added. These courses proved a substitute for the theology courses required of all Catholics.[7] Thus, during the consolidation administration there were actually very few curriculum innovations. Those initiated during the postwar expansion were allowed to mature.

Meanwhile, a maturation process was evident among the faculty in the early fifties. The summer of 1953 proved active for some faculty men: one visited and lectured at Brothers' colleges in England; another took a summer fellowship at Case Institute of Economics; three Brothers pursued postdoctoral work at a midwestern university. These and many other activities were good indications of professional growth which accompanied numerical growth. In the fall of 1954, five Brothers, four laymen, and one priest were added to the Faculty, whereas four laymen and one Brother separated from the College. The following year six laymen and one priest were added. The fall of 1955 saw eleven laymen and one priest added, bringing the total faculty and administrative staff to 129 laymen, thirty-two Brothers, and five priests. Of the laymen, seventy were fulltime faculty and fifty-nine parttime. By the fall of 1956, the total fulltime faculty jumped to 111. At the same time, many fulltime men were allowed to teach parttime in the Evening Division. Finally, by 1957, the Day Division faculty consisted of sixty-four fulltime laymen; twenty-eight fulltime Brothers; and four priests. These were assisted by twenty-seven parttime lay instructors.[8]

With the college growth and a basic change in the makeup of its faculty, new policy had to be formulated for the major portion of the faculty, the laymen, who had fully committed themselves to the interests of the College. Therefore, in 1954, the Board of Managers voted to establish a new salary scale. The old scale had four levels for each of the usual ranks. For example, an assistant professor would earn $2,810 on the first level and could advance to $3,950; a full professor received $4,470 on the first level and $5,920 on the fourth level. The latter was the top salary prior to 1954. According to the new scale, an assistant could earn between $3,400 and $4,200, whereas a professor could start at $4,800 and advance to $6,300. At the same time, the President was authorized by the Board to appoint a committee to draw up a tenure policy for lay members of the faculty. Another motion favoring the lay faculty was passed; La Salle agreed to relinquish its right to the contribution which it made to the annual premium paid on the retirement policy of those faculty who participated; the contribution was to be given to the policy holder.[9] A few months later the College received a Ford Foundation grant of $214,000 to help increase faculty salaries. In accepting the grant, La Salle was expected to match the amount received before executing the fund. By 1956, therefore, the President was able to announce a substantial increase in faculty salaries. With this new increase, La Salle's salaries compared with all other colleges and universities in the state of Pennsylvania, ranked seventeenth for professors, twenty-second for associate professors, nineteenth for assistant professors, and twenty-third for instructors. Likewise, by 1956, the Committee on Tenure reported to the Board, and their recommendations were accepted; tenure was granted several lay faculty members. In 1957, La Salle compared its faculty salaries with those of forty-two colleges of the Foundation of Independent Colleges. The comparison resulted as follows: La Salle professors $6,430; Foundation $6,094; La Salle associates $5,400, Foundation associates $5,255; La Salle assistants $4,910, Foundation assistants $4,601.[10] Obviously, then, faculty salaries at La Salle were not the worst in the nation; neither were they among the best. However, it must be admitted that during the fifties the College took giant strides in advancing its salary policy. Of course, maturation of faculty policy was accompanied by heretofore unknown occupational hazards. One Professor Kelleher brought suit against the College over contractual negotiations. Although the case could have been avoided by a bit more caution on the part of the President, the legal involvement was an indication that faculty policy at La Salle had come of age.

In the area of student population, La Salle paralleled the national trend of increased enrollment in both Day and Evening schools. At the same time, a shifting population in Philadelphia furthered the development of the Northeastern section of the city, which is relatively convenient to the La Salle campus, and many students attended La Salle from that area. Between 1952 and 1956, the student population of La Salle's Day Division jumped from 1,250 to 1,683; while at the same time, the Evening Division grew from 1,029 to 1,457 for a total population of 3,410 in 1955. The following year the total enrolled was 3,528 with 1,853 Day and 1,675 Evening students. For the scholastic year 1954-55, 953 men applied to La Salle; the following year, 1,252 applied. Again, Brother Stanislaus, like every one of his predecessors, was confronted with the space problem. With the college already involved in several building projects worth millions of dollars, the construction of more classrooms was impossible. The immediate solution was to extend the day schedule till 5:30 p.m. Despite the heavy enrollment, however, every effort was made to maintain small classes and encourage academic excellence.[11]

The success of the College's interest in academic achievement was evidenced in 1953, when twenty-seven premed students were admitted to medical schools. Also, sixteen other men were awarded fellowships and assistantships to several local graduate schools. Another aspect of student interest which developed in the fifties was student aid. In 1954, over $100,000 in scholarships and student employment had been given La Salle students. It is significant that in 1954, $100,000 was "considerably" more than the amount of contributed services rendered by the Brothers on the faculty that year. The following year, La Salle initiated a pre-registration policy. Surprisingly, the student body vehemently objected to the innovation. The administration replied that the maintenance of the "small college" atmosphere necessitated the change. With pre-registration, more individual attention could be given to the student. The explanation was accepted and the crisis passed; pre-registration became a permanent feature of student life at La Salle, bringing benefits to students, faculty, and administrators. Finally, a new tradition was inaugurated at La Salle in October, 1957: the Honors Convocation. These academic meetings are held to give recognition to the academic achievement of the students. Mr. Walter Kerr, noted Catholic artist, critic, lecturer, and teacher, was the speaker at the first Honors Convocation. Academically, the college was slowly moving toward maturity. The realization by the administration, faculty, and students, as well as those whose criticism was sought, that La Salle could be a better school, spurred men in responsible places to even greater efforts. It was fortunate that the College, prodded by the Middle State Association, was not allowed to flirt with complacency after accomplishing so much in so short a time.[12]

Paralleling academic opportunities for La Salle students was the rather well-developed activities program. Some activities enabled students in certain cases to acquire greater depth of knowledge in their fields of endeavor while, on the other hand, they provided students with experience in expressing and developing their own ideas. Likewise, many activities helped in the development of the young man's religious perspective. Finally, physical recreation was well provided for.

In December, 1953, the Student Council sponsored La Salle's first Open House. Over 1,500 friends and parents took advantage of the opportunity to see La Salle in action. Further, in 1953, a new cultural arts program was initiated under the direction of Mr. Claude Koch. Eight different exhibitions of contemporary artists appeared throughout the year. At the same time, a series of evening film classics was introduced, along with an Italian Music Festival. That same year, the Mathematics Department established a chapter of the National Mathematics Honor Society, the third national honor society to appear on campus. In January, 1952, the College was fortunate in obtaining the services of the Order of Preachers as fulltime resident chaplains and teachers. Father Mark Heath, O.P., Ph.D., LL.D., was the first member of his order to take up residence. As a result, religious activities at the College were vastly expanded as is evidenced by the *Annual Report* of the President dated October, 1956. Each school day, two masses were said and confessions were heard twice daily. Every Thursday evening, devotions in honor of Mary were held, while Rosary devotions were conducted several times a week in May and October. During Lent, the Stations of the Cross were said on Tuesday evenings for the resident students. Each year a Novena of Masses and Communions was held in preparation for Mother's Day. The Sophomore class, Senior class, the Masque, S.B.K., and the Evening Division all held Communion breakfasts. In addition, a weekend closed retreat was given for resident students, and an open retreat for Day students was held during the first three days of Holy Week. A series of lectures was presented for those students who were preparing for marriage. For married students, the Mr. and Mrs. Club was formed by the chaplain. The club organized discussions, sponsored socials, and held an annual Day of Recollection. Finally, the Ph.T. ceremony was inaugurated. Honoring primarily the wives of the married men, the "putting him through" exercises consisted of conferral of the Ph.T. certificates and a religious ceremony at the Lourdes Grotto during which the couples renewed their marriage vows. Every possible means was taken to give La Salle men opportunities to complement the development of their intellects through a spiritual revitalization of the soul. This ever available, knowledgeable, but intangible unity of Christian higher education was, and still is, basic to the La Sallian tradition. If one must be found, this is the explanation for the existence of the Catholic college, the Christian Brothers' college.[13]

La Salle, in the fifties, had a plethora of sports activities. It was during this period that La Salle went "big" in basketball. Two successive years in the N.C.A.A. finals helped tag the school as a basketball college. Moreover, today many still refer, for the most part nostalgically, to the "Tom Gola" era. There is no doubt that Tom Gola, everybody's All-American, brought much notoriety and acclaim to La Salle. And today many alumni talk of reviving the "Tom Gola" era. However, what many seem to have missed concerning Tom Gola are his personal qualities. No one questions his basketball ability; on the other hand, one should not forget that he was a gentleman, a good student, and the highest type of character. The "Tom Gola" era included another once-in-a-lifetime gentleman in the person of Kenny Loeffler, La Salle's outstanding coach through the fifties. There were other people involved in the Gola era, but to bring two men like Gola and Loeffler together again might be too much to hope for in the lifetime of any institution. Of course, other sports took secondary roles to basketball, but the track team and the swimming team carved a respectable niche for themselves in the Middle Atlantic Conference, while the crew team swept aside all Dad Vail competitors for several seasons.

As the chaotic conditions brought on by World War II and the Korean War started to fade, the La Salle Alumni Association began more concerted efforts on behalf of the College. In 1952, a new program of alumni contribution was organized under the title of the Annual Giving Campaign. In view of the tremendous physical expansion planned for the College, it was felt that the Alumni could be of great service to the College in carrying through part of its expansion program, while at the same time, the alumni would develop a sense of participation in the education process of the College. At first, the plan moved slowly. One of the major problems of implementation was communication with the alumni. Following the war, many graduates had changed addresses, and the increased mobility of the population in the postwar economy made it difficult to contact many alumni. Progress was made, however, for in 1955 an increase of sixty-four percent over the preceding year participated in Annual Giving. The following year, the number contributing was ninety-five percent higher, which constituted an increase of over 6,200 individual replies from graduates. In 1957, further efforts to consolidate the Alumni Association were made by the establishment of regional chapters in Washington, D. C., Levittown, Pennsylvania, Wilmington, Delaware, and New York City.

That same year an Alumni Medical Society was organized; a constitution was approved and the following officers elected: Dr. James Lehman, President; Dr. Herb Sussman, Vice-President; Dr. Edward Coverdale, Treasurer; and Dr. Charles Tribit, Secretary. The Society promoted the interests of young La Salle men interested in the study of medicine, while at the same time making substantial contributions to the development of the College.[14]

At this time, a new consideration had to be entertained relative to the development of the alumni. Many men were going directly to graduate or professional schools immediately upon graduation. Of the 346 graduates in 1954, over eighty went directly to graduate or professional schools. Once settled in their new schools, many of these men understandably did not have the time or resources to become active in the La Salle Alumni Association. The main problem was to keep the lines of communication open until these men were ready for active alumni participation. This was accomplished at a later date through various programs of the Association.

In the wake of postwar expansion and in the attempts of the
College to readjust itself to new dimensions, a totally new approach
was developed in fiscal matters. Shortly before Brother Paul gave
way to Brother Stanislaus as President, Mr. William T. Connor,
Esq., Board member, spoke appreciation of the Board of Managers
for the financial status of the College. He asserted that "great credit
should be given Brother Paul for his administrative ability as evidenced by the financial statement." Just a few months later, Brother
Stanislaus, in his first *Annual Report,* stated, "the college has
reached the point where it is unable to meet operating costs from
tuition cost alone." At first glance, this would seem to be both a
contradiction of Mr. Connor's statement and an indication of impending financial disaster. It was neither. True, in December,
1952, La Salle was $800,000 in debt; but as long as its debt service
could be met, there was no pressing need for a balanced account.
The ability to carry the debt service, then, became the yardstick of
the financial condition of the College. Likewise, rather than spend
interest-bearing net revenues to remove the debt, a long-term financing proved much more beneficial. As noted above, several building
projects were started under Brother Stanislaus. This would not
have been possible without the new College fiscal policy. The credit
of the College was good, and this made all necessary funds readily
available.

Naturally, since tuition alone could not pay for college costs,
other sources of income were sought. By 1954, the La Salle Endowment Foundation proved a source of fiscal help to "satisfying proportions." That year the College received about $23,300 in direct
contributions. Of this, $15,000 came from the Foundation. Likewise,
economy of operations was stressed. Before 1954, expenditures of
previous years were used to forecast expenditures for ensuing years.
In 1954, all departments of the College, high school, and community were budgeted according to estimated need; each section had
to operate within the budget. The new system proved reliable except in a few cases. Nonetheless, the overall financial picture was
good as the College moved through the middle fifties. In March,

1956, the President reported that "La Salle College has arrived at a steady financial operation enabling reliable forecasts to be made. It appears that the college now operates at an annual gain of $300,000. This fund must serve as the source of capital improvements." Because of plans for further expansion in 1957, the College called in an accounting firm to make a thorough search into La Salle's financial status. The results showed La Salle in 1957 as having total assets of $6,029,410, while current liabilities were $578,103. The accumulated funds of the College were $5,541,306, or ten times the amount of the liabilities. However, seventy-seven percent of the net worth represented plant and equipment. In view of this report, the Board of Managers, at its meeting on October 15, 1957, approved measures of expansion involving four million dollars. These actions included the issue and sale of $500,000 dormitory bonds and acceptance of the applicable indenture; taking a loan from the United States Government of $1,075,000 for construction of the Student Union; and taking a $2,500,000 loan from the Northwestern Mutual Life for construction of the Science building and relocation of the high school. Despite these considerable debts, the fiscal condition of the College was sound and evidenced a great future for La Salle College, a future Brother Stanislaus was not destined to share.

As the College prepared to move into the 1958-59 scholastic year, Brother Stanislaus suddenly resigned and withdrew from the College. For the fourth straight time since Brother Anselm's term of office ended in 1941, La Salle College had lost its President with little advance warning. Just how much harm this has caused, it is difficult to estimate. One would suspect, however, that such a circumstance is not in the best interests of any institution and something to be avoided in the future for the sake of administration, faculty, and students alike. Brother Daniel Bernian, Ph.D., was appointed to succeed Brother Stanislaus on September 10, 1958. He still fills the office of President today.

9. *Alma Mater*

WITH THE LAUNCHING OF SPUTNIK I ON OCTOBER 4, 1957, American education initiated some rather profound changes. Perhaps the first and most evident was a change of mood. The new mood was one of seriousness and determination. The new goals were deeper substance and better quality in educational programs — for more students. The new acceleration and higher goals came in a period of rapid expansion in American higher education generally: enrollment in colleges and universities jumped from 1.5 million in 1940 to 5.3 million in 1964.

Initially the race to keep abreast of Russia had much to do with the new stage of development in colleges and universities. Increasingly, however, higher learning is considered a necessity by a major segment of the American populace. Rising qualifications for jobs, the development of an economically sound middle class, the emphasis on education by the modern businessman — all have contributed to the development of a culture of mass higher education. This was, and still is, the challenge to institutions of higher learning today. Education for the masses could not be achieved by private institutions alone; thus, local, state, and federal funds were provided in unbelievable sums. This, in part, helped to relieve crowded physical facilities. Eventually, these funds filtered through to the learning process. Money was provided for a variety of specialized and experimental courses. Libraries were improved. Deserving students were helped through college with grants, loans, and subsidized jobs. Faculty salaries were subsidized, along with faculty research. All in all, the very nature and concept of the American college and university were and are changing at a very rapid pace. We are too near these fast-changing times to make an effective evaluation of the results of the "new" education. But the new age in higher education has arrived. It demands flexibility in policy along with an intense development of academic innovation. This, in turn, demands new leadership, viable, alert, flexible, humane, and understanding. This La Salle College found in its twenty-fourth president, Brother Daniel Bernian, Ph.D.

Brother Bernian began his academic training at The Catholic University of America, where he received the Bachelor of Arts degree. Shortly thereafter, he began his teaching career at West Catholic High School in Philadelphia. While there, he also coached the track and cross-country teams and directed the dramatic and language clubs. In 1943, he received his Master of Arts in French and Spanish from the University of Pennsylvania. Later he taught at College St. Patrice, Quebec, Canada, La Salle College High School, The Catholic University, Washington, D. C., and Colegio Buonanova in Spain. In 1952, he was awarded the Doctor of Philosophy degree by Laval University, Quebec, Canada. Likewise, honorary degrees have been conferred on Brother Bernian by Villanova University, St. Joseph's College, and Temple University. In 1951, Brother Bernian was appointed Assistant Professor of French at La Salle College. Two years later he was appointed Director of Housing. From 1954 to 1958, he held the offices of Dean of Students and Vice-President of the College. In view of Brother Bernian's background and experience, La Salle was fortunate to have a man of his achievements available to take charge upon the sudden resignation of Brother Stanislaus in September, 1958. Seven years later, the College yearbook, *The Explorer,* was dedicated to Brother Bernian with the following appropriate words: "His profound understanding of the purpose of a college and his foresight in planning for the future of La Salle are well known to the students, alumni, and friends of the college. During his tenure as President, Brother Bernian has consistently advocated an enlarged role in education for the college and has warned of the necessity of future expansion. His leadership and determination have been decisive factors in the realization of primary objectives." Hindered by the lack of perspective so necessary to any historical essay, we now examine the details of an apparently successful era in the history of La Salle College.

As teacher and administrator at La Salle under two Presidents, Brother Bernian was able to observe closely the operations of the College. He was convinced that much talent available to the College was wasted due to the organizational structure of the institution. In order to attain "maximum effectiveness" in operations, Brother Bernian attempted to bring all available resources of the College into play. As a result, the College administration was decentralized, while at the same time, greater delegation of authority and responsibility was given to several administrators. Brother Bernian established what he called "education's four estates." In the area of academic responsibility, the Dean of the College was replaced by a Vice-President for Academic Affairs. The academic Vice-President was responsible for coordination of the academic divisions; the administration of all academic activities cutting across these divisions; and the development of long-range academic planning. At the same time, a new set of College statutes conferred more responsibility on Deans of Schools. The Dean became the administrative head of his school and was responsible for the general efficiency of the instructional program of his school. Further, the Dean of a school was now involved with Department Chairmen in hiring teachers and assigning teaching schedules. Additional changes occurred in the academic organization. The office of Assistant to the Dean of the College was abolished; the incumbent was transferred to Chairman of the Roster Committee. Also, the authority of Department Chairmen was increased. Such problems as the recruiting and employment of staff, promotions, pre-registration, and supervision of majors were made the responsibility of the Chairmen. Moreover, Brother Bernian established a policy of definite terms for Department Chairmen to be implemented during the academic year 1960-61. "It is felt that such a policy will provide stimulus to the Chairmen as well as to members of the Department, and will afford the Administration and the Chairmen an easier avenue for replacing temporarily those who may desire such a change."

La Salle's first Academic Vice-President was Brother John, Ph.D., who had been Dean of the College. In 1960, Brother John was appointed Provincial of the Baltimore Province. Brother Fidelian, Ph.D., then became Academic Vice-President. Brothers David and Robert were Deans of the School of Business Administration and the School of Arts and Sciences respectively. All of these men fill the same positions today. Brother Paul, who was Dean of the Evening Division, remained in office till 1961, when he was replaced by Brother Emery, Ph.D.

The second "estate" comprised the area of student personnel programs. The new office of Vice-President for Student Affairs was created and filled by Brother Gavin Paul, Ph.D. Brother Paul still holds this vital position today. The Student Affairs Vice-President is responsible for the following areas: Chaplain's office, the Counseling Center, the Reading Development program, on-campus and off-campus housing, the athletic program, the health program, the Student Union program, and all student clubs, fraternities, and organizations on campus. More will be said below about some of these areas.

The third and fourth "estates" round out the organizational structure. Two new vice-presidential areas were established: Public Relations and Business Affairs. The former was first organized in 1948, when a Public Relations officer was appointed to control publicity, special functions, and placement. Placement proved to be a rather sizeable job in itself and so did publicity. By 1954, three men were handling the work of the original Public Relations officer.

Therefore, when Mr. John McCloskey was appointed Vice-President for Public Relations in June, 1959, he was assisted by several directors and was responsible for the areas of publicity, alumni, placement, and development. The La Salle News Bureau, staffed by two men, handles publicity. Directors were appointed for the Alumni and Placement Bureaus. All these men are responsible to the Public Relations Vice-President. Mr. McCloskey, former Assistant to the President, handles the development program directly with the help of an assistant Director of Development.

Dr. Joseph Sprissler, founder of the Evening Division and former Comptroller, assumed the duties of Vice-President for Business Affairs. In establishing the fourth "estate" Brother Bernian spoke of "the task of handling enormous financial affairs and physical properties" as creating the necessity for the new office. As a result, the Superintendent of Buildings, Grounds, and Maintenance, and the Bursar are directly responsible to the Business Affairs Vice-President. Further, matters involving payroll, tuition, loans, grants, student aid, scholarships, purchasing, construction, food services, bookstore, security, and many others pass over the desk of the one Vice-President who has no executive assistants.

One month after Brother Bernian assumed the Presidency, expansion plans were formulated which seemed to be a sign of Brother Bernian's determination to develop La Salle. Although negotiations had been started under his predecessor, Brother Bernian was informed by the Finance Committee of the Board of Managers of its approval to purchase seventy-six acres of ground known as the Clarence M. Brown estate. This beautiful property, located in Springfield Township, Montgomery County, was purchased for $330,000 for the purpose of relocating La Salle College High School. As soon as the purchase was completed, plans were developed for a high school building and faculty house in hopes of achieving occupancy by September, 1960. Construction of the $2,500,000 plant began on July 6, 1959. In the meantime, an additional purchase of 9.77 acres, contiguous to the new property, was approved by the Board, especially since an exchange of land was involved, that proved quite favorable to the College corporation.[1] Moreover, construction of the high school plant proceeded on schedule, and classes were begun in the new buildings on September 12, 1960. Although this rather significant separation in the College history was not unique, from all appearances it will remain effective at least for the sixties. In view of the amazing expansion of the College in the fifties and sixties, this writer would not preclude the possibility that college and high school might meet again, next time perhaps on the Montgomery County campus.

In his first *Annual Report* to the Board in October, 1958, Brother Bernian noted that the Student Union building was under construction and that plans were formulated to occupy the building the following September. Likewise, contracts for a Science building were ready for bids. After one year in office, Brother Bernian announced "the launching of a modern expansion program equal in area and cost to three times the total area acquired and cost expended during the College's ninety-six year history." Included in this expansion was the above-mentioned high school plant; the Student Union building, which was occupied in September, 1959 and whose total cost was $2,050,000; and the Science building, whose construction began on February 1, 1959. By October, 1959, the Science building was eighty-two percent complete. Overall cost of the project, including furnishings, was $1,800,000. The interior contains 85,000 square feet of floor space and, when first opened, housed twenty-one laboratories, five special laboratories, seventeen office and project laboratories, three amphitheatre-type lecture rooms, three recitation-lecture rooms, seminar rooms, library, greenhouse, animal room, and a variety of utility rooms.

Several other changes were made on campus to fit the expansion pattern. Leonard Hall was converted from Student Union to classrooms and offices. The heating and electrical plants were rebuilt, while an incinerator building was constructed. The College internal communications system was completely modernized. Finally, Brother Bernian reported an expansion of the southern boundary of the campus due to the passage of the Finley Ordinance which struck

Somerville Avenue from Ogontz Avenue to Twentieth Street from the city map.

In 1960 Brother Bernian informed the Board that the Residence Halls were filled to capacity and applications for campus housing were mounting. In response, therefore, the Board resolved to arrange for a $500,000 loan from the Federal Housing and Home Finance Agency in order to build two new dormitories. The buildings, located between Cottage Lane and the boundary of the Philadelphia Electric Company and Elkins Avenue property lines, accommodate 150 students. The *Annual Report* likewise noted major changes in every building on campus, save the new Science building, Student Union, and dorm buildings. The third floor of College Hall was completely renovated; major alterations were made to relocate several administrative offices on the first floor; and the Counseling Center took over the first floor of McShain Hall. Wister Hall, formerly occupied by the high school, was converted to administrative and faculty offices, lecture rooms, and athletic facilities. Further, property on Cottage Lane was leased from Mrs. Daniel Blain, life-tenant and trustee of the estate of Sarah Logan Wister Starr. A house on the property was converted into a residence hall and was known as "The Mansion."[2]

Thus, after only a few years of Brother Bernian's tenure, the College had accomplished a much-needed and worthwhile expansion. By 1961, La Salle College contained all the basic facilities customary in the modern college. It no longer had to assume an apologetic position when compared to similar institutions of higher learning. In the decade between 1951 and 1961, the value of La Salle's campus grew from $2,060,000 to $11,816,000. College equipment, valued at $306,000 in 1951, was worth over $1,340,000 by 1961. But complacency was not to characterize the college administration after such accomplishments. Brother Bernian, in looking to the future, reminded the Board of Managers that "growth will require expansions to our basic facilities, such as ground, additional classrooms, larger and more modern athletic facilities, a student chapel, additional dormitories, and perhaps an administration building." Of course, an initial step had already been taken in construction of two additional dorms which were forty percent complete by October, 1961.

However, even as new buildings sprang up on La Salle's campus, the lack of space continued to become painfully evident. In view of this, John McShain, Board member, moved that an investigation of the possibility of acquiring the Belfield Estate or at least getting an option on the property be undertaken without delay. This rather desirable property, adjacent to the campus, could prove helpful in settling the space problem at La Salle. However, only in the Fall of 1965 was there progress in securing an option on one section of the property. This section will be the key to the one drawback in the next stage of expansion program of the present era. In 1962, when plans were laid for the construction of a $600,000 student chapel, the lack of campus space blocked the project. Originally, the chapel was to be built on ground now occupied by McShain, Leonard, and Benilde Halls. Mr. McShain generously indicated he would bear the expense of moving McShain Hall to another location if feasible. However, because of tight classroom space, it was impossible to demolish the temporary classrooms of Benilde and Leonard Halls. As a result, plans for a permanent student chapel were shelved, and a beautiful, contemporary, but still temporary chapel in the basement of College Hall was substituted. This latter chapel opened in July, 1965.

Additional residence facilities were acquired by the College in March, 1963. The Olney Garden Apartments, located on the northeast corner of Wister Street and Chew Avenue, were purchased for $250,000. The building was converted into a residence hall to accommodate 110 students. Complete apartment facilities were made available to students over twenty-one years of age. The following October, the Board of Managers, aware of an urgent need for additional classroom facilities at the college, authorized Brother Bernian to "move in whatever direction was best suited to the interests of the College" in order to borrow $2,500,000 to construct a classroom building. Despite the approval, the new classroom building is still not off the drawing boards. The lack of a desirable area on campus on which to build such a unit has been the partial cause of the delay. Another facility urgently needed by the College is a physical recreation building. With over 600 students living on campus or in off-campus housing, available facilities for strenuous recreation are woefully inadequate and strained beyond capacity, As a result, in March, 1964, the Board resolved that the President "devise and carry out a plan for the acquisition of all property bounded by Cottage Lane, Wister Street, Clarkson Avenue, and the Belfield Estate." This area comprises about four acres and contains thirteen private residences. The estimated purchase price was between $160,000 and $180,000.

Due to the generosity of an alumnus, Dr. Blake Hayman, who gave the College $150,000, the resolution was implemented in a short time. By September, 1965, several residences had been purchased and were immediately drawn into service. Two buildings, Shaw Manor and Windsor Hall, were converted into residence halls. Another was taken over by the Music Department, while the fourth was used by the Art Department. In the future, all are to be demolished to make way for the physical recreation building, plans for which are not yet on the drawing boards. At the same time, the Board authorized the College to enter into an agreement with the Wissahickon Watershed Association whereby the College could erect a small building for research on the property of the Association.[3] The building, subsidized by several foundation grants, will cost about $30,000. Finally, in the spring of 1965, La Salle secured a million dollar loan from the Federal Home and Housing Agency in order to build a $1,300,000 dormitory complex. The project, now under construction, when completed in August, 1966, will include additional residence facilities for 250 students, four student lounges, a post office, and a separate infirmary.

In retrospect, the amount of expansion at La Salle under Brother Bernian has been impressive, both in buildings completed, lands purchased, and plans fulfilled. Having provided sufficient facilities for the basic needs of an institution of higher learning, the administration still has the problem of keeping pace with a controlled expansion, both as to facilities needed for academic consolidation of the College and accommodating the increasing number of men desiring to matriculate at La Salle. That the present administration is aware of future needs was clearly demonstrated when plans for a ten-year twenty-five million dollar expansion program were released to the faculty in the fall of 1965. The plan is twofold: to gradually increase the student population to 10,000, with some 3,400 fulltime students, while at the same time to provide adequate physical, cultural, religious, and instructional facilities for the best possible liberal arts education. Since it is not the historian's task to predict the future, we happily leave evaluation of the projection to another generation and turn to academic development during Brother Bernian's administration.

Under the organization established by Brother Bernian in 1959, the area of curriculum development properly fell to the initiative of the Academic Vice-President, Brother Fidelian. The College *Bulletin* for 1960-61, 1961-62, the first of the series of *Bulletins* covering two scholastic years, noted some changes in academic regulations. Requirements to advance to the upper division were as follows: a 1.75 scholastic index based on a 4.0 scale after completion of sixty-eight semester credit hours; a "C" grade in prerequisites for the student's major; and the successful completion of a two-hour examination in expository writing. To graduate, sixty-four hours of work were required in upper division courses; of these, twelve hours of philosophy and eight hours of theology were required. It was likewise announced that La Salle participates in the Advanced Placement Program of the College Entrance Board. Thus, students who performed satisfactorily in college-level courses taken in high school and in the advanced placement examinations could receive credit and advanced placement at La Salle. At the same time, a new program called "La Salle in Europe" was opened to men who had completed their first four semesters at La Salle and wanted an opportunity to study and travel in Europe. Arrangements were made for students to spend their fifth and sixth semesters at the

University of Fribourg, Switzerland, and receive full credit at La
Salle for course work taken there. Since the financial arrangements
of this plan are quite favorable to the student, many have taken
advantage of study abroad. On the other hand, some problems in
course content and curriculum adjustment have been encountered
by those returning from European study. Necessary adjustments
are currently under study.

As the nation moved into the sixties, one of the main characteristics of colleges and universities across the nation was the ques-
tioning of curricula structure. As a result, at La Salle, the Curriculum Committee was revitalized and chaired by Brother Fidelian.
The objective of the committee was to study La Salle's curriculum
in the light of changing conditions and concepts in higher education.
Prior to fundamental change, the committee proposed a mild revamping of the core curriculum. "The principal suggestions are
for a tightening of the theology and philosophy programs, a reduction of the social science requirement, a strengthening of science and
math courses, and a fine arts requirement." In view of the direction
taken by the Curriculum Committee, most departments took a long
and serious look at their course offerings, departmental requirements, and general effectiveness of their programs. The results of
these studies and re-evaluations appeared in the College *Bulletin*
for 1962-64. "The School of Arts and Sciences requires a core curriculum of courses in theology, philosophy, English, modern languages, science, and the social sciences." In effect, the revised
curriculum substantially strengthened the tradition of the liberal
arts and sciences in the College. In detail, the plan provided for
a reduction of overlapping in theology and philosophy and a total
revamping of curricula in both these departments, a reduction of
social science requirements, and the addition of a requirement in
fine arts and psychology. Moreover, business students were required
to take mathematics or science and additional requirements in either
humanities or social science.[4] At the same time, the history, English,
mathematics, physics, geology, biology, and philosophy departments
introduced new courses. In the School of Business Administration,

courses in Management Simulation and Business Communications were inaugurated.

The Curriculum Committee remained active; and just two years after the new core program was implemented in 1962, further revisions were suggested. As the College engaged in a self-study in preparation for evaluation by the Middle States Association of Colleges and Universities in the spring of 1966, a pre-evaluation team was invited to inspect the College. One of its suggestions concerning the curriculum involved the number of hours required in contrast to the lack of elective hours available to the student. The general suggestion was to reduce the overall number of semester hours required for graduation, tighten the core, and increase opportunities for free electives. Every possible line of communication to both faculty and students has been opened in order to get a consensus. This involved, complex, and sometimes emotional issue is still under debate. Curriculum at La Salle in the sixties has been and still is a vital and lively issue. This, we think, is a good omen of future academic revitalization for the College.

When Brother Fidelian assumed responsibility for curriculum policy, he was intent on establishing a much-needed Honors Program for gifted students. With little fiscal elasticity, he was at first able to introduce some special courses, dubbed "independent study" honors courses. By 1962, however, the program showed signs of expanding. Honors sections were established in required courses for first and second year students, while, at the same time, independent study courses, taught, in many instances, by visiting professors, were arranged for Dean's List students in their third and fourth years. One of the major drawbacks of the program was the inability of the College to acquire a fulltime Director for the program.[5] In 1963, a definite program for screening candidates for the Honors Program was established. Freshmen applying for Honors status spent their first year on a probationary basis for consideration for fulltime participation. Quality of the Honors courses continued to improve, but the program still lacked a fulltime Director.[5] Finally, in 1964, Brother Patrick Ellis, Ph.D., was appointed Director of the Honors Program. He brought to his task all the energy, imagination, and insight he had so ably demonstrated in putting La Salle High School, Miami, Florida, on a sound operational basis. In a short time, his vigorous administration of the Honors Program has made an impact on the academic life of the College. An adequate Honors Center has been established, along with a Colloquium Program which includes student, faculty, and guest discussions on a high intellectual level. Noted scholars and professionals such as E. Digby Baltzell, Margaret Plass, Richardson Dilworth, Hilary Kelly, F.S.C., and Frank Ewing have established the Colloquium on a solid foundation. One could only describe the condition of the Honors Program at La Salle today as a healthy, vigorous, scholarly, forward-looking organization, one that makes a great contribution to the academic milieu of the College.

Another important area of academic interest that received the calm, quiet, unassuming, but persistent attention of Brother Fidelian was the Library. To Brother Fidelian's mind, La Salle had all the prerequisites for a good library: an astute and knowledgeable librarian in the person of Brother Edmund Joseph and, of course, a sizeable library building. Through the efforts of both Brothers Fidelian and Joseph, the missing element, money, has been extracted from the college budget in larger and larger appropriations. In June, 1959, the Library contained over 54,000 volumes, of which 5,000 volumes had been added that year. Continuing a policy of strong cooperation with area libraries, La Salle's holdings were listed with the Philadelphia Union Catalogue and with the National Union Catalogue at the Library of Congress. At the same time, Brother Joseph, Librarian, and Georgette Most, Reference Librarian, co-authored the *1959 Directory of Services and Supplies for Catholic Colleges.* In the following years, the Library acquired between four and five thousand volumes a year. By 1962, the holdings numbered over 64,000 volumes.

However, this yearly increase was not sufficient; and a crash program, dubbed Project 74, after the library expansion program under the presidency of Brother Noah in 1874, was inaugurated in

1963. The aim of Project 74 was to double the library holdings in three years. The undergraduate listings from the University of Michigan were acquired and used together with Harvard's Lamont List as a prototype for the acquisition of essential volumes for an undergraduate library. Further, each department of the College submitted what it considered minimal holdings in its area of instruction. As a result, by the fall of 1965, the Library listed holdings of over 103,000 volumes. The crash project will continue through the fall of 1966, when it seems certain it will achieve its goal.[6] In addition, certain physical changes have been made in the Library building. All classrooms and non-library offices have been removed, providing additional stack and reading areas. Likewise, the Library will be completely air-conditioned by summer, 1966. At long last, La Salle has achieved a reasonably good undergraduate library. This writer believes that soon the College will be faced with the happy problem of insufficient space for all its holdings; and perhaps, by 1974, a new library will celebrate the crash program of 1874.

With the academic outlook of the Day Division thus rather promising, Brother Fidelian turned his attention to the Evening Division. Brother Bernian, in his *Annual Report,* noted that the Academic Vice-President had made recommendations for the appointment of a new Evening Division Dean as stipulated by *College Handbook.* Further, he suggested a clarification of the Evening Division's place in the general structure of academic administration. The new Dean was Brother Francis Emery, Ph.D.; this energetic, young, intelligent man took the reins of the Evening Division in September, 1961. This branch of the College had built an impressive tradition and accomplished a number of firsts among evening colleges: first in Pennsylvania to offer a formal evening program leading to a bachelor's degree; first college or university in Philadelphia to have its evening division fully accredited by the Middle States Association; first in Philadelphia to appoint a full-time Dean; and first college or university in the area to confer B.S. degrees on its evening graduates at its regular commencement exercises. Brother Emery accepted the challenge of carrying forward and improving the program of his school.

Since plans for 1961-62 had been established before Brother Emery took office, Brother Emery spent his first year in office devising several innovations for the Evening program. In 1962, he established a Liberal Arts Program which provided for concentration in education, physical sciences, mathematics, history, and social sciences. Because of the extent of the program, classes were offered for the first time on Saturday mornings. At the same time, in order to provide more direct contact and personal interest in the Evening Division student's welfare, several departmental chairmen were assigned to regular counseling duties. In addition, the Dean planned to interview each student by the end of the scholastic year.[7] This proved to be a formidable task as the after-dark enrollment was 2,273, largest in the Evening Division's seventeen-year history.

The story of the Evening Division continues to be one of growth and expansion. By the fall of 1964, over 2,500 students were enrolled in over 175 courses leading to bachelor's degrees in mathematics, English, history, chemistry, electronic physics, prelaw, accounting, general business, industrial management, industrial relations, marketing, economics, insurance, and finance. In addition, Certificates of Proficiency programs were available in business administration and chemistry. This rather extensive Evening program involves over 160 faculty and administrators. Every available classroom space is utilized by the Evening Division. Moreover, Brother Emery obtained an option to use the facilities of adjacent Central High School should the need arise. Brother Emery, then, provided the answer to Brother Fidelian's question of the Evening Division's place in the College's academic structure. It is, in effect, a fully academic complement to the College, operated under parttime conditions, a school which contributes to the excellence of academic opportunity at La Salle. Finally, the Evening Division today is a vastly different institution from the one described by Dr. Sprissler in 1946: "Our catalogue consisted of five mimeographed sheets, the tuition charge was $9 per credit hour; my office contained a war surplus desk, a straight back chair, a wooden file cabinet — minus one side — all in a space about ten feet square, illuminated by one naked bulb."[8] From this inauspicious beginning, La Salle's Evening Division has developed into one of the most outstanding and effective parttime institutions of higher learning in the Middle Atlantic States.

Today, La Salle College has another effective parttime instructional branch, the Summer Sessions. Started under Brother John, Dean of the College in 1955, the Summer Sessions as we know them today were expanded during Brother Bernian's and Brother Fidelian's tenures. However, the history of summer study at La Salle goes back to 1931. That year, Dr. Emil Doernenburg was appointed "Director of the Summer School of Languages." Both upper and lower division courses in English, Spanish, French, and Latin were offered. The school enrolled only about seventeen students and was dropped the following year.[9] As noted above, during the national emergency created by World War II, full summer sessions, consisting of two eight-week semesters, were held from 1942 through the summer of 1945. Moreover, shorter sessions were held in the summers of 1946 through 1948 in order to accommodate returning veterans. In March, 1951 *The Collegian* announced "Proposed summer sessions" of two six-week semesters. "The proposed summer school would allow students to carry lighter rosters during the regular terms; to make up deficiencies; or to complete their courses of study before being drafted." However, the plan was shelved for a few months due to lack of student interest and technicalities involving the nation's draft law. When the latter changed favorably, a decision was made to reactivate the plans, and two six-week sessions evolved. At the same time, a nine-week evening session was started. This was designed to "enable veterans to initiate or reenter college before the G.I. Bill deadline on July 25, 1951." Summer sessions were offered through 1955, with Brother Cyril, Ph.D., Assistant to the Dean, in charge. Only La Salle students were permitted to attend, and the offerings were quite limited. Students who entered as freshmen in February were required to follow summer courses in order to catch up with their class by the following September.

The Summer Sessions, as we know them today at La Salle College, were inaugurated in 1959, when Brother John, Ph.D., Dean of the College, appointed Dr. E. Russell Naughton as Director of Summer Sessions. Dr. Naughton was charged with responsibility "for planning, establishment, supervision, and development of the La Salle Summer program." For the first time, a *Summer Bulletin* was published; courses were open to students from other institutions, and course offerings were increased. During the summer of 1959, 370 students enrolled in fifty courses in the La Salle Summer Sessions.[10] In 1961, Brother Francis Emery, Ph.D., succeeded Dr. Naughton as Director of Summer Sessions. Brother Emery reactivated Evening summer sessions, and, in general, the summer sessions made "remarkable progress" that year. In addition to an increase in La Salle students, over 100 men from other colleges and universities enrolled. Likewise, many students appeared to be following summer courses for enrichment purposes. Before the 1961 summer sessions were completed, Brother Emery was appointed Dean of the Evening Division. The following November, Brother Lewis, Ph.D., was appointed Director of Summer Sessions. The La Salle summer school continued to grow both in courses offered and student enrollment. By 1962, over 900 men matriculated in the summer program; this figure jumped to nearly 1,400 students by 1964. After 1964, the Summer Sessions administration was split; and Evening Summer sessions became an integral part of the Evening Division.

In the meantime, special programs were added to the summer sessions. In 1963, a Workshop in Teaching Elementary School Science was opened to Sisters of the Archdiocese of Philadelphia. At the same time, the Biology Department, supported by the National Science Foundation, offered special training for gifted high school students. In 1965, a B.S.C.S. — Yellow Version for high school biology teachers and a Vocational Counseling Workshop for Brothers were added to the other special programs. In this writer's opinion, future summer sessions at La Salle will outgrow all expectations and form an integral part of the educative process of the College.

In returning to the story of the fulltime operations of the College under Brother Bernian's direction, we note that there was a corresponding increase of student population with physical expansion. In October, 1958, one month after Brother Bernian became President, more than 3,900 men were enrolled at La Salle in both Day and Evening divisions. By 1961, frosh matriculation in the Day school was up thirty percent over 1960, while the total enrollment for the fall semester was 4,204. The following year, the one hundredth anniversary of the granting of La Salle's charter, the total enrollment went above 5000. By 1965, 6000 men were matriculating at La Salle.[11] Another parallel development was that of student aid. By 1965, scholarships and grants to students amounted to $370,000. This included aid amounting to $90,000 given to Brothers Scholastics of the Baltimore Province. In addition, about 230 students participated in the National Defense Student Loan Program with loans amounting to over $180,000.

In view of the vast increase in enrollment and the La Sallian tradition of concern for the individual interest in the student, the college administration developed a more effective counseling program. Counseling services were not new at La Salle in the late fifties. In 1948, a "guidance Clinic" had been established for the improvement of admission procedures, student orientation, selection of courses, and to help students find employment after graduation. However, the Clinic was severely hampered by the lack of office space, and as a result, the staff directed its attention principally to the freshmen and seniors. In 1949, the Clinic expanded its services, while at the same time inaugurating a new testing program for all incoming students. Also, orientation courses were developed: lectures on study habits, note-taking, as well as lectures designed to acquaint the student more fully with the aims and ideals of the College. By 1954, the "counseling program" was made compulsory for all new students. By this time, the Guidance Clinic took the name of Counseling Center, which it bears today.

The number of student contacts with the Center increased rapidly; meanwhile expanded services were offered. In 1956, 875 students were interviewed; of these, 612 were tested. Services available the same year included aptitude testing, interest inventory, individual counseling, improvement in reading and study habits, information on graduate fellowships and scholarships, and occupational information. By 1958, over eighty percent of the student contacts in the Counseling Center were self-referrals. Moreover, the Center was placed on the approved list of the American Board of Professional Standards in Professional Counseling.[12] Through 1963, La Salle was the only college in the Philadelphia area to achieve this approval. That same year, arrangements were made to bring the number of counselors to four. Today this group is headed by Dr. Thomas McCarthy, who serves as half-time counselor during the academic year and fulltime during the summer. Finally, the Counseling Center extends its services to the alumni, children of faculty and staff, and the Philadelphia community, the latter done on a limited basis only. In addition to counseling, the Center carries out studies of student characteristics and makes recommendations relative to policy and procedure for student development.

An additional student service developed at La Salle during Brother Bernian's term was placement. The concern of the College for the welfare of its graduates dates back to 1873. The *Annual Report* for that year noted: "Our friends might greatly encourage the Commercial Department of the College, by sending to us for clerks or assistant bookkeepers. Young men who can present a certificate of good conduct and proficiency from us may be relied upon, as we will recommend none with whom we are not perfectly satisfied." As noted above, the first official placement officer in the College was the Public Relations Director appointed in 1948. Under the college reorganization in 1959, however, a fulltime Director of Placement was appointed. At the same time, the primary objectives of Placement Service at La Salle were outlined "to aid seniors and alumni in efforts to find their proper vocation and to seek career opportunities commensurate with their interest, abilities, and college preparation; to assist employers in contacting qualified men trained at La Salle College." Moreover, the Placement Bureau works in close conjunction with the Counseling Center to provide information service, vocational guidance service, and interview service. Today over 100 companies send representatives to the campus for job interviews with the seniors. Likewise, the Placement Bureau handles student placement for campus employment and the Work Study Program. It is obvious, then, that every possible opportunity for vocational objective and achievement is provided for La Salle students through the Counseling Center and the Placement Bureau. With student guidance assured, we turn now to the instructional service of the College vis-à-vis the faculty.

One of the most gratifying trends at La Salle during its post-sputnik expansion was the development of the general quality of the faculty. Using their formal training as a yardstick, Brother Bernian, in his *Annual Report* for 1959, noted the general improvement. Excluding military personnel, forty-six percent of the full-time faculty held the Ph.D. degree; fifty percent the M.A.; and four percent the B.A. National Education Association statistics for 1955 for all types of degree-granting institutions indicated the following percentages: Ph.D., 40.5; M.A., 49.1; and less than the Master's degree, 10.4. Thus, the La Salle faculty norm was and still is better than the national norm in this regard. On another matter, after just two years as President, Brother Bernian indicated painful awareness of a faculty problem that has plagued La Salle since its opening: the few Brothers on the staff. He reported that out of a total faculty of over 300, only twenty-two Brothers taught fulltime. Six others taught parttime while carrying out administrative duties. No Brothers taught in the Evening Division, and no Brothers taught in the School of Business Administration. Thus, Brother Bernian restated his objective of 1959: to have Brothers compose fifty percent of the faculty by 1964.[13] This goal, of course, was not to be realized.

The year 1961 saw a vast improvement in the economic posture of the faculty at La Salle. In order to secure solid teaching talent and to hold faculty already engaged, the College introduced a new salary scale. Moreover, a Lindback Foundation grant enabled the College to present two $1000 awards for excellence in teaching; Roland Holroyd, Biology, and Joseph Flubacher, Economics, were the first recipients. Further, the La Salle Endowment Foundation made available several grants for short-term departmental research grants, while, at the same time, the College initiated a research leave policy. In addition, the faculty was occupied in increasing professional activities: radio and TV discussions; publication of reviews, articles, and books. Likewise, faculty members were called upon by industry and educational groups for consultation and services. Many faculty members actively participated in developing closer relations with secondary school systems: meetings with counselors and principals explored problems common to both the high school and college; advanced courses were offered in certain high schools; debate tournaments brought high school students on campus in an intellectual rather than social atmosphere.[14]

In the meantime, many additions to the faculty were made to keep pace with growing student population. In 1962, fifteen additional faculty were appointed in the School of Arts and Sciences, while four were appointed to the School of Business Administration. Of the nineteen newly appointed, only four were Brothers, thirteen were laymen and two priests. These additions brought the fulltime faculty to 115; thirty-six men were parttime instructors; eight administrators taught parttime; and ten other administrators and librarians had faculty status. That same year, a resolution was passed by the Board of Managers approving a salary scale increase. "No point of business received more sympathetic interest and attention by the Board."[15]

When the College reached the one hundredth anniversary of the reception of its charter, 1963, faculty status provided an excel-

lent indication of college growth and future expansion. In the Day
Division, in 1963, there were 127 fulltime teachers and thirty-one
parttime teachers. Moreover, there were over 100 additional parttime teachers in the Evening Division. In the Day school, a threefold increase in faculty remuneration evolved: teaching hours were
reduced to twelve; a new salary scale became effective; increased
insurance benefits were provided; and the number of teaching
awards was expanded to three per year. At the same time, a chapter
of the American Association of University Professors was founded
at La Salle in November, 1962. This was only the third chapter
founded at a Catholic college in the state of Pennsylvania.[16] Dr.
E. R. Naughton served as first president. This is not an exclusive
organization for lay faculty; Brother Mark, Ph.D., Chairman,
Physics, currently serves as president. Indeed, faculty and administration alike had attained in many ways the maturity expected of
institutions of higher learning.

Despite the myriad problems of development and expansion,
La Salle paused in 1962-63 to commemorate the anniversary of its
founding. On September 27, 1962, twin ceremonies inaugurated
the Centennial year. Governor David L. Lawrence officiated at a
Centennial flag-raising ceremony. Immediately after this, a solemn
Mass of the Holy Spirit was celebrated in Wister Hall gymnasium.
Father Francis B. Schulte, Assistant Archdiocesan Superintendent
of Schools, preached the sermon. He noted that La Salle faced its
second century as the Church assembled in council for the "age-old
task of renewal and rebirth." La Salle, he suggested, should take
stock and strive to become a microcosm of renewal and rebirth in
a world of contradiction. "The College must make this contribution
in its own way — by renewed dedication to its proper object: truth
in all forms."

Special efforts were made during the Centennial year to enhance
the annual Concert and Lecture series. Such representative people
as Senator Eugene McCarthy, Dr. Mortimer Adler, Frank J. Sheed,
Judith Anderson, Katherine Anne Porter, Susanne Starr, and many
others fitttingly complemented the work of the College by their

active appearance on campus. In addition, famous scholars were invited to La Salle to receive Centennial medals. Each month, certain departments would select an individual who, in his field, had made a vital contribution to Christian education. Under the theme "the Christian and the Economy," the departments of Economics, Accounting, Finance, Marketing, and General Business joined to confer a Centennial medal on Dr. Karl R. Bopp, President of the Federal Reserve Bank of Philadelphia. In April, 1963, the Psychology Department, in observing the theme "The Christian and the Individual," made an award to George Christian Anderson, Director of the Academy of Religion and Mental Health. Carrying through this same idea, twelve prominent members of the alumni who represented in a distinguished way the monthly themes of the Centennial medal program were awarded medals for outstanding work in their respective fields.

Centennial year celebrations climaxed during Charter Week, March 17 through 24, 1963. The week officially opened with a civic dinner at the Bellevue-Stratford Hotel with over 800 church, state, and local dignitaries, alumni, faculty, students, and friends in attendance. Archbishop John J. Krol, D.D., extended greetings from Pope John XXIII. The principal address was given by Brother Bernian, who spoke of the future of La Salle with its changing and complex problems and the solutions to be found in the traditions of the College: trust in God and courage and zeal to live up to the challenges of our age.

On Wednesday, March 23, La Salle commemorated its one hundredth Charter Day with a special academic convocation. The Honorable William W. Scranton, Governor of Pennsylvania, received an honorary doctor of laws degree and delivered the principal address. The Most Reverend Gerald V. McDevitt, D.D., Auxiliary Bishop of Philadelphia, was also awarded an LL.D. degree and presided at the convocation. Other honorary degrees were bestowed on the Mayor of Philadelphia, James H. J. Tate; Charles E. Beck, President of Philco Corporation; United States Treasurer, Kathryn Granahan; Joseph T. Kelley, Secretary-Treasurer of Philadelphia AFL-CIO; and Dr. Stephen Kuttner, canon lawyer of The Catholic University of America, all of whom received the degree of doctor of laws. Sir Hugh Taylor, President of the Woodrow Wilson Foundation, received a doctor of science degree. Dr. Roland Holroyd, senior faculty member, spoke "for the College." In reminiscing of the 1920's Dr. Holroyd said, "We could not at that time afford expensive research equipment; consequently we had to specialize in teaching." He continued that "the art of teaching consists in making a student want to learn."

On Sunday, March 24, a Pontifical Mass of Thanksgiving was celebrated by Archbishop John J. Krol, D.D., in the Cathedral of Saints Peter and Paul. The sermon was preached by the Most Reverend Gerald V. McDevitt, who praised the College as a "source of pride to priests, religious, and laity." In concluding, Bishop McDevitt stated that as long as La Salle continues to thrive, faithful to its beliefs and purposes, "there is still hope for society." Over 300 Christian Brothers attended the Mass and received communion from the Archbishop. That same day, the Alumni Association installed a commemorative tablet at St. Michael's Parish marking the original site of the College. It is fitting that the last official act of the Centennial year took place on December 29, 1963, at the Sheraton Hotel during the annual meeting of the American Historical Association. The history department conferred a Centennial medal on the late Aaron Abel, noted historian from the University of Notre Dame.

Aside from the normal academic experience of lecture hall, laboratory, informal counseling, and discussions, every college and university of necessity provides a variety of social, cultural, religious, and athletic activities. It is obvious that as La Salle moved into the sixties, these same advantages were offered its students. It is uncalled for, then, to devote much space here to a litany of the usual and already-mentioned activities. However, some activities did develop as the College approached its centenary which deserve attention. Of these, one of the most important, stimulating, and universal is the Concert and Lecture series, sponsored annually by the Academic Vice-President. Started as a "Lecture Program", during the scholastic year 1957-58 with such lecturers as R. S. Black, Dr. Gottfried Land, Russell Kirk, Hanson W. Baldwin, and Rocco E. Porrecco, the Concert and Lecture series today brings to the La Salle campus world-renowned actors, playwrights, novelists, musicians, politicians, church and state leaders; each in his own way helps to further the education of the La Salle student.

In addition to this general college series, various departments and clubs continued to present their own programs. One of the most successful student-faculty activities during this period was the "You and Marriage" lecture series organized by Father Heath, O.P., and the late Brother Augustine, Ph.D. Good topics, excellent speakers, and an intelligent student committee contributed toward making this annual event well worthwhile. In 1960, an important change took place in student government. The Student Organization Commission was formed as a standing committee of the Student Council. The Commission is composed of thirty-seven officially recognized student organizations. At the same time, Phi Sigma Epsilon and the St. Thomas More Society, a prelaw group, were given official recognition. Finally, in 1961, the Reserve Officers Training Corps Drill Team, an organization of great reputation in the Philadelphia area, adopted the title of "President's Guard." Today, these and a host of other traditional student activities at La Salle provide a varied complement to an education in the liberal arts tradition.

Just as Brother Bernian was convinced, upon becoming President, of the inevitable nature and necessity of La Salle's expansion, he was as equally convinced that this expansion could not be achieved without the enthusiastic interest of the alumni. Therefore, John McCloskey, Assistant to the President, was charged with furthering the organization of the alumni. Additional regional chapters were founded in Schuylkill County, Berks County; Harrisburg, York, Lancaster area; Trenton; Hammonton and Vineland, New Jersey. At the same time, the "Century Club," an honorary group of Alumni who contribute one hundred dollars or more to the annual Giving Fund, was organized. In 1959, *La Salle,* the official alumni magazine, was first published; it appears quarterly. The Alumni Hall of Athletes, located on the second floor of the Student Union, was dedicated in 1962. Four of the five charter members were present for the ceremonies: Frank Loughney, '42; Al Cantello and Tom Gola, '55; and Ira Davis, '58. Joe Verdeur, '50 was not present. That same year, the "Gradu-Eights," an organization of alumni crewmen, was formed to promote the sport at the College and promote social functions for alumni members. Brother Christopher, Ph.D., Director of Admissions, and Roland Holroyd, professor of Biology, reactivated the Alumni Medical Society in 1962. In February of the same year, the Continuing Education lecture series was started again after an absence of nearly ninety years. Outstanding academicians from La Salle and other colleges and universities gave ten lectures on topics ranging from family life to international relations. In October, 1963, the Alumni Admissions Association was formed. Its purpose is to assist the Director of Admissions in attracting better students to La Salle. The alumnus makes follow-up contacts in his home area on men who have applied and been accepted but have not completed matriculation. Started on a small scale, this program today has grown into one of the most important and significant contributions of the Alumni to La Salle. At present, the Alumni Association, under the fulltime direction of Mr. James McDonald, is a growing, vibrant group in which the College has anchored many of its hopes for the future.[17]

When one considers the wobbly fiscal structure of La Salle's past, a legitimate concern could be voiced over the financial structure of the College. However, from the outset of Brother Bernian's administration, the financial foundation proved sound. For the fiscal year ending June 30, 1959, total income at La Salle amounted to $2,437,000 compared to $2,359,000 in 1958, while total expenditures equaled $1,946,400 compared to $1,938,700 the previous year. Thus, the net surplus for 1959 was over $490,000. This sum was sufficient to carry the annual debt service, provide some modest funds to be used as endowments, and barely fund some capital improvement. By 1960, this net surplus jumped to over $500,000. Today, the fiscal picture of the College is still sound, though compared to other institutions wholly or partially endowed or receiving state aid, it is modest indeed. La Salle College today is a twenty-million dollar corporation with current income of approximately 5.5 million dollars and expenditures of five million. This is in sharp contrast to 1945, when the net worth of the College was a minus quantity. On the debit side, however, is a debt of some seven million in building loans and mortgages. However, the College has some fiscal protection should an emergency arise which would upset the fiscal stability of the nation or institution, since funds used as endowments are in excess of several years of debt service. As the College continues to expand, fiscal responsibility will likewise grow. To date, Brother Bernian has managed a calm fiscal course. From this writer's vantage point, the picture looks good. But we shall all have to wait for tomorrow's recorder for a reasonable evaluation of current fiscal policy.

Tomorrow's recorder will have to evaluate more than just the financial aspects of the Bernian years. La Salle's future will test the soundness of the expansion program: physical, intellectual, cultural, and fiscal. What about the structural reorganization of the entire College? If this writer may be allowed one violation of the rules of the historian, he suggests that tomorrow's recorder will point to the delegation of authority in the Bernian years as the key to the new, the unparalleled, La Salle of the future.

Epilogue

WHAT HAS BEEN SET DOWN HERE IN RICH DETAIL is the chronicle of an institution. We have seen traced the beginnings and the development of La Salle College — its various sites, the progress of its curricula, its prosperity and financial strain, its service to the community. We have seen, too, the growth of a tradition. What is central to this tradition, and what could only be suggested here, is the daily work of quiet men — Brothers, laymen, and priests — performing in classroom and office the essential tasks of a Christian college: teaching, seeking in scholarship whatever is relevant and significant, taking a personal interest in students, devoting themselves to a common effort. What is also central is the ordinary work of students in the classroom, in activities, in the gift of friendship to one another and of loyalty to the College's ideals. What we have not been able to read about at all, but what we must, after this account, have a deeper sense of, is how the finger of God has traced in the lives of men on both sides of the desk His own meaning, and how He has used La Salle College in the last hundred years for His own glorious and more ultimate purposes.

The recent Self-Study of the College (1962-64) has suggested the difficulty of capturing in words the uniqueness of its character.

The larger structure is clear enough in its outlines: in 1965 La Salle is a complex entity — a Catholic college, a Christian Brothers' college, a city college, a liberal arts college, a preprofessional school — with day, evening, and summer sessions, a graduate program in theology, and a variety of workshops and institutes. But the ethos of the institution, in the interaction of its parts, is more difficult to describe. The essential fabric of its century-old tradition, however, must, as Brother Donaghy's account emphasizes here, include a consistent stress on educational essentials, especially good teaching; a friendliness and community spirit that have in some measure survived recent expansion; a "common-sense" approach to the whole educational enterprise; a strong spirit of self-criticism; and what can only be described as a certain liveliness and dynamism.

In 1965, La Salle has a number of definite ideas about its present status and the directions it wants to take for the future. Several decisions are basic to what the College is projecting for its future: the decision to maintain the large variety of programs which the College presently has; the decision, however, not to expand graduate work further than the present theology program, and now to concentrate all resources at the undergraduate level; the decision, after rapid expansion in the Day Division for more than a decade, to shift emphasis to expansion in the Evening Division and summer sessions; the decision to remain an area college, with primary responsibility to the Philadelphia area and, in its residence program, to the northeast section of the country, where forty-six percent of American Catholics are concentrated. Within the framework of these decisions, the College intends to channel its energies to improving the fundamentals of teaching and learning. The academic qualifications of students will continue to improve. It is foreseen that in the next few years, the large majority of entering freshmen will be first quintile students with College Board scores over 500. With faculty development programs, it is hoped that the proportion of teachers with doctoral preparation will continue, as at the present, well above national norms and hopefully reach the fifty to sixty percent range; that more faculty will be engaged in higher level professional activity in addition to their teaching; that their teaching will be supported by improved classrooms and office space and by enlarged library resources; and that their economic status will continue to improve along lines recently proposed by a faculty committee.

The various areas of the College have presented recently a survey of present resources and a projection of how programs and services in student affairs, public relations and development, and business affairs can extend and support this central effort. We take now much satisfaction in the progress described in this history, great pride in the patient toil and self-sacrifice of the men who went before us, great confidence that, with the Lord as builder and preserver of the work, the College has a magnificent destiny before it.

— BROTHER FIDELIAN, *Academic Vice-President*

FOOTNOTES

CHAPTER I:

[1] Francis X. Talbot, S.J., *Jesuit Education in Philadelphia, St. Joseph's College,* 1851-1926, Philadelphia, 1927, 67.

[2] Brother Clementius, F.S.C., "History of the District of Baltimore," Mimeographed, 1948, 25-26; W. J. Battersby, *History of the Institute of the Brothers of the Christian Schools in the Nineteenth Century, 1850-1900,* II, London, Waldegrave Ltd., 1962, 103.

[3] Minutes of the Meeting of the Board of Managers, La Salle College, Philadelphia, 18 May 1863, 25 May 1863, 20 May 1869; hereinafter cited as MOB.

[4] "Historic Account of La Salle College or St. Mary's Community," La Salle College. Archives.

[5] "The Brothers in Philadelphia in 1863," Brothers of the Christian Schools, District of New York. Archives. Misc. MSS.

[6] Talbot, 6.

[7] *Ibid.,* 7.

CHAPTER II:

[1] "Historic Account," 3.

[2] MOB, 20 Mar. 1873.

[3] Francis Donohue, "A History of La Salle College," unpublished MSS, La Salle College. Archives.

[4] "Historic Account," 4-5.

[5] Brothers of the Christian Schools, District of New York. Archives. Scrapbook F-14.

[6] "Historic Account," 6.

[7] Brothers of the Christian Schools, District of New York. Archives. Scrapbook G-27.

[8] Donohue, 18.

[9] MOB, 20 Mar. 1873.

[10] La Salle College, *Annual Report* (Printed), 1873-1874.

[11] *Ibid.*

[12] MOB, 21 Sep. 1874.

[13] MOB, 20 Mar. 1873.

[14] MOB, 18 Sep. 1873.

[15] MOB, 12 Oct. 1885.

[16] Brother Casimir Gabriel, F.S.C., *The Tree Bore Fruit, Manhattan College,* 1853-1953, New York, 1953, 24-25.

[17] Mary Lou Adams, "Report on La Salle College," 1942, La Salle College. Archives.

[18] MOB, 18 Sep. 1873.

[19] La Salle College. Archives. Misc. MSS.

[20] Minutes of Meeting of La Salle Debating Society, La Salle College, 29 Jan., 6 Oct., and 13 Nov. 1885; hereinafter cited as MLDBS.

[21] Brothers of the Christian Schools, District of New York. Archives. Misc.

[22] MOB, 17 Sep. 1869.

[23] MOB, 18 Sep. 1879 and 16 Sep. 1880.

24 *Quaint Corners in Philadelphia,* John Wanamaker, Philadelphia, 1922, 249-250.
25 Minutes of a Special Meeting of the Board of Managers, La Salle College, Philadelphia, 14 Dec. 1882; hereinafter cited as SMOB.
26 La Salle College, Archives. Misc. MSS; MOB, 20 Sep. 1883.
27 SMOB, 18 Dec. 1885.

CHAPTER III:
1 SMOB, 14 Jun. 1887.
2 *The Collegian,* 13 May 1931, 3.
3 MOB, 6 Oct. 1897.
4 *The Evening Bulletin* (Philadelphia), 12 Mar. 1909, 1.
5 MOB, 26 Sep. 1889.
6 MOB, 12 Oct. 1885.
7 La Salle College, *Bulletin,* 1886, 9-12, 16; hereinafter cited as LSC *Bulletin.*
8 *Ibid.,* 10-11.
9 "Historic Account," 19; MOB, 26 Nov. 1900.
10 MOB, 8 Nov. 1909.
11 LSC *Bulletin,* 1902-03, passim.
12 MOB, 28 Oct. 1908.
13 Donohue, 87-88.
14 SMOB, 8 Nov. 1897.
15 *The Catholic Standard and Times* (Philadelphia), 6 Jan. 1894, 2; hereinafter cited as *Catholic Standard.*
16 MOB, 12 Oct. 1905.
17 MOB, 9 Oct. 1895.

CHAPTER IV:
1 MOB, 10 Oct. 1912.
2 La Salle College. Archives. Misc. MSS.
3 MOB, 10 Oct. 1912.
4 LSC *Bulletin,* 1912-13, passim.
5 *Ibid.,* 1914-15, 35; MOB, 4 Feb. 1915.
6 La Salle College, *Annual Report* (Printed), 1915, 7, 10.
7 MOB, 23 Oct. 1917.
8 *Ibid.*
9 MOB, 19 Dec. 1918.
10 Minutes of the Meeting of the Community Council, La Salle College, Philadelphia, Dec. 1918, 2-3; hereinafter cited as MCC.
11 MOB, 17 Dec. 1919; 20 Dec. 1921; 20 Nov. 1926; Donohue, 316.
12 La Salle College. Archives. Misc. MSS.
13 MOB, 18 Dec. 1920.
14 La Salle College. Archives. Misc. MSS.
15 LSC *Bulletin,* 1927, 13; passim.
16 La Salle College. Archives. Misc. MSS.
17 LSC *Bulletin* (Supplement), 1922-23, passim.
18 La Salle College. Archives. Misc. MSS.
19 Clementius, 139; MOB, 15 Dec. 1925.

CHAPTER V:

[1] Charles Coleman Sellers, *Charles Willson Peale: Later Life, 1790-1827*, Philadelphia, The American Philosophical Society, 1947, 220-221.

[2] *Papers Read Before Site and Record Society of Germantown*, Germantown, The Site and Record Society, 1910, 180.

[3] MOB, 20 Nov. 1926.

[4] La Salle College. Archives. Portfolio, "Belfield Property."

[5] SMOB, 26 Mar. 1928; La Salle College. Archives. Portfolio, "Belfield Property."

[6] La Salle College. Archives. Misc. MSS.

[7] "La Salliana." Private collection of Brother David, F.S.C., Dean, School of Business Administration, La Salle College; La Salle College. Archives. Misc. MSS.

[8] La Salle College. Archives. Portfolio, "Belfield Property"; Clementius, 142-143.

[9] Clementius, 141.

[10] Brothers of the Christian Schools, District of Baltimore. Archives. Misc. MSS; MOB, 29 Dec. 1930.

[11] LSC, *Bulletin*, 1929, 9, 21.

[12] *Ibid.*, 1931-32, 21-23.

CHAPTER VI:

[1] MOB, 29 Nov. 1932.

[2] Letter from John McShain to Hoffman-Henon Co., 2 Dec. 1932.

[3] MOB, 19 Dec. 1933.

[4] MCC, 20 Jan. 1935.

[5] MOB, 30 Oct. 1937; 15 Dec. 1938.

[6] MOB, 14 Dec. 1939; La Salle College. Archives. Portfolio, "Belfield Property."

[7] LSC *Bulletin*, 1940-41, 7; MOB, 16 Dec. 1940.

[8] LSC *Bulletin*, 1932-33, 17-18, 25-32; 1933-34, 28.

[9] *Ibid.*, 1940-41, 19-20.

[10] MCC, 16 Feb. 1938.

[11] Letter from La Salle College Student Body to President Franklin D. Roosevelt, Feb. 1935.

[12] MOB, 10 Dec. 1943.

[13] *Ibid.*

[14] MOB, 1 Dec. 1944.

[15] Clementius, 145; *The Collegian*, 19 Oct. 1942, 1.

[16] *The Collegian*, 2 Nov. 1942, 1; LSC *Bulletin*, 1942-43, 17; La Salle College, *Student Handbook*, 1943-44, 38.

[17] *The Collegian*, 4 Oct. 1945, 3.

CHAPTER VII:

[1] *The Collegian*, 15 Feb. 1946, 1; La Salle College, Annual Report of the President to the Board of Managers, 7 Dec. 1946; 6 Dec. 1948; 6 Dec. 1949; hereinafter cited as AR.

[2] *The Collegian*, 27 Sep. 1950, 1; 26 Sep. 1951, 1; AR, 5 Dec. 1951.

[3] AR, 7 Dec. 1946; 16 Dec. 1947; *The Collegian*, 1 Oct. 1948, 1.

4 SMOB, 28 May 1947; AR, 6 Dec. 1948.
5 AR, 6 Dec. 1949.
6 MOB, 5 Dec. 1950.
7 *Ibid.;* AR, 5 Dec. 1950.
8 AR, 7 Dec. 1945; 7 Dec. 1946.
9 *The Collegian,* 14 May 1947, 1.
10 AR, 7 Dec. 1945; LSC *Bulletin,* 1945-46, 19-22.
11 AR, 7 Dec. 1945.
12 AR, 16 Dec. 1947; 6 Dec. 1948; 6 Dec. 1949; 5 Dec. 1950; Letter from Market Street National Bank to Brother Paul, President, 1 Nov. 1950.
13 MOB, 21 Sep. 1874; "Historic Account," 9.
14 MCC, 17 Nov. 1940.
15 AR, 16 Oct. 1958.
16 AR, 2 Dec. 1954.
17 AR, 15 Oct. 1957.
18 AR, 21 Oct. 1959.

CHAPTER VIII:
1 MOB, 4 Dec. 1954; AR, 4 Dec. 1952.
2 SMOB, 26 Mar. 1953; La Salle College. Archives. Misc. MSS; Court action to change the College Charter was withdrawn upon sound legal advice. It proved to be totally unnecessary. See Commonwealth of Pennsylvania, *Statistical Report of the Superintendent of Public Instruction, For the School Year Ending July 5, 1954.* Series No. 1. Department of Public Instruction, Harrisburg, 1957, 90.
3 AR, 3 Dec. 1954; *The Collegian,* 29 Sep. 1954, 1.
4 AR, 1955-56; *The Collegian,* 5 Oct. 1955, 1.
5 MOB, 2 Dec. 1954; AR, 2 Dec. 1954.
6 AR, 1955-56.
7 LSC *Bulletin,* 71-82 passim.
8 AR, 1955-56; 15 Oct. 1957.
9 MOB, 2 Dec. 1954; AR, 15 Oct. 1957; 16 Oct. 1956.
10 AR, 3 Dec. 1953; 2 Dec. 1954; 1955-56; 16 Oct. 1956; 15 Oct. 1957
11 AR, 3 Dec. 1953; 2 Dec. 1954; 15 Oct. 1957; *The Collegian,* 9 Nov. 1955, 3.
12 AR, 3 Dec. 1953; 16 Oct. 1956.
13 AR, 15 Oct. 1957.
14 MOB, 15 Oct. 1957.

CHAPTER IX:
1 MOB, 21 Oct. 1959.
2 AR, 11 Oct. 1960.
3 MOB, 18 Mar. 1964.
4 AR, 17 Oct. 1961; 16 Oct. 1962; LSC *Bulletin,* 1962-63, 63-64, **48**.
5 AR, 16 Oct. 1962; 16 Oct. 1963; 21 Oct. 1959.
6 AR, 21 Oct. 1959; 16 Oct. 1962; 16 Oct. 1963.
7 *Ibid.*
8 La Salle College, *La Salle,* Oct. 1964, 2.
9 *The Collegian,* 22 May 1931, 1; "La Salliana."

[10] *La Salle,* Apr. 1959, 7; AR, 21 Oct. 1959.

[11] AR, 16 Oct. 1958; 17 Oct. 1961; 16 Oct. 1963; *The Collegian,* 30 Jan. 1963, 2.

[12] LSC *Bulletin,* 1949-50, 15-16; 1954-55, 19; 1956-57, 55; AR, 3 Dec. 1953; 16 Oct. 1956; 16 Oct. 1958.

[13] AR, 21 Oct. 1959; 11 Oct. 1960.

[14] AR, 17 Oct. 1961; MOB, 17 Oct. 1961.

[15] *The Collegian,* 10 Oct. 1962, 1; AR, 16 Oct. 1962; MOB, 16 Oct. 1962.

[16] AR, 16 Oct. 1963; *La Salle,* Jan. 1963, 6.

[17] AR, 16 Oct. 1958; 21 Oct. 1959; 16 Oct. 1962; 16 Oct. 1963.

BIBLIOGRAPHY

I. Unpublished Materials:

Adams, Mary Lou, Report on La Salle College, Philadelphia, Pennsylvania, 1942. La Salle College. Archives.

"Annual Report of the President to the Board of Managers," La Salle College, Philadelphia, Pa., 1873-1965.

"Belfield Property," La Salle College. Archives.

Clementius, Brother, "History of the District of Baltimore," Compiled 1948. La Salle College. Archives.

Donohue, Francis Xavier, "A History of La Salle College," La Salle College, Philadelphia, Pa., 1963.

"Historic Account of La Salle College or St. Mary's Community." La Salle College. Archives.

"La Salliana." Private collection of Brother David, F.S.C., Dean, School of Business Administration, La Salle College.

Minutes of the Board of Managers, La Salle College, Philadelphia, Pa., 1863-1965.

Minutes of the Community Council, La Salle College, Philadelphia, Pa., 1918-1945.

Minutes of the La Salle Debating Society, La Salle College, Philadelphia, Pa., 1885-1898.

Register for Renovation of Vows of the Christian Brothers, 1872-1921. La Salle College. Archives.

II. Published Works:

Battersby, W. J. *History of the Institute of the Brothers of the Christian Schools in the Nineteenth Century, 1850-1900.* 2 vols. London, Waldegrave Ltd., 1963.

Bouvilliers, Dom Adelard, O.S.B. *Dictionnaire Des Bouvier.* Belmont, Caroline Du-Nord, 1943.

Bouvier, John Vernou, *Our Forebears: From the Earliest Times to the First Half of the Year 1940.* New York, 1940.

Coolidge, Susan. *A Short History of the City Of Philadelphia From Its Foundation to the Present Time.* Boston, Roberts Brothers, 1887.

Chandler, Joseph R. *In Memoriam: Michel Bouvier, Decede a Philadelphia Le 9 Juin, 1874, a L'Age De 82 Ans.* J. B. Lippincott & Co., Philadelphia.

Department of Public Instruction. *Report of the Superintendent of Public Instruction of the Commonwealth of Pennsylvania For the Two-Year Period Ending May 31, 1926.* Harrisburg, 1926.

———. *Report of the Superintendent of Public Instruction of the Commonwealth of Pennsylvania For the Two-Year Period Beginning May 31, 1930.* Harrisburg, 1930.

———. *Statistical Report of the Superintendent of Public Instruction For the School Year Ending July 6, 1952.* Commonwealth of Pennsylvania, Harrisburg, 1954.

———. *Statistical Report of the Superintendent of Public Instruction For the School Year Ending July 5, 1954.* Commonwealth of Pennsylvania, Harrisburg, 1957.

Historical Sketches of the Catholic Churches and Institutions of Philadelphia. Philadelphia, Daniel H. Mahoney, c. 1895.

Gabriel, Brother Angelus, F.S.C. *The Christian Brothers in the United States 1848-1948. A Century of Catholic Education.* New York, Declan X. McMullen Co., 1948.

Gabriel, Brother Casimir, F.S.C. *The Tree Bore Fruit, Manhattan College, 1853-1953.* New York, 1953.

Gabriel-Marie, Brother, F.S.C. *Consequences of the Suppression of the Teaching of Latin.* Instructive and Administrative Circular, No. 101, Paris, 1901.

Gerard, Brother Hubert, F.S.C. (ed) *Mississippi Vista, The Brothers of the Christian Schools in the Mid-West, 1849-1949.* Winona, Minn., St. Mary's College Press, 1949.

La Salle College, *Bulletin.* 1873-1964-65.

"La Salle College: Still Booming at 100." *Greater Philadelphia, The Magazine for Executives.*

La Salle College. *Student Handbook,* 1945-1965.

Laws of the General Assembly of the State of Pennsylvania Passed at the Session of 1863. Harrisburg, Singerly and Myers, 1863.

Oberholtzer, Ellis Paxon. *Philadelphia: A History of the City and Its People.* 3 vols. Philadelphia, S. J. Clarke Publishing Co. n.d.

Our Forebearers: From Earliest Times to the End of the Year 1925. New York, 1925.

Papers Read Before Site and Record Society of Germantown. Germantown, The Site and Record Society, 1910.

Quaint Corners in Philadelphia. Philadelphia, John Wanamaker, 1922.

Sack, Saul. *History of Higher Education in Pennsylvania.* 2 vols. Harrisburg, The Pennsylvania Historical and Museum Commission, 1963.

Sellers, Charles Coleman. *Charles Willson Peale: Later Life, 1790-1827.* Philadelphia, The American Philosophical Society, 1947.

Talbot, Francis X., S.J. *Jesuit Education in Philadelphia, Saint Joseph's College 1851-1926.* Philadelphia, 1927.

Taylor, Frank H. *Philadelphia in the Civil War, 1861-65.* Philadelphia, Dunlap Printing Co., 1922.

INDEX